Whose Town is it Anyway?

The State of Local Democracy in Two Northern Towns

Stuart Wilks-Heeg and Steve Clayton

ISBN–13: 978 1 903196 09 0
ISBN–10: 1 903196 09 4

A CIP catalogue record for this report is available from the British Library.

Cover design by York Publishing Services Ltd

Prepared and printed by:
York Publishing Services Ltd
64 Hallfield Road
Layerthorpe
York YO31 7ZQ
Tel: 01904 431213   Fax: 01904 430868   Website: www.yps-publishing.co.uk

Contents

Foreword   x

Glossary   xiii

1   Whose Democracy? Whose Local?   1
   1.1   Introduction   1
   1.2   Re-conceptualising local democracy   2
   1.3   Whose democracy?   5
   1.4   Whose local?   10
   1.5   The research project   14
   1.6   Structure of the book   16

2   From ABIs to YOTs: Digesting the alphabet soup   19
   2.1   Introduction   19
   2.2   Types and functions of sub-national public bodies   20
   2.3   Scales of operation in local governance and 'closeness' to local residents   22
   2.4   Partnership working: Re-joining policy agendas?   28
   2.5   The expanding role of the voluntary and community sector   30
   2.6   Locality: The changing position and politics of district councils   32
   2.7   Conclusion   36

3   Votes Count, Resources Decide   38
   3.1   Introduction   38
   3.2   Estimating the relative significance of elected and unelected bodies   39
   3.3   Wealth, social capital and democracy   49
   3.4   Conclusion   52

4   Between the Devil and the Deep Blue Sea?: Can there be local democracy without local autonomy?   54
   4.1   Introduction   54
   4.2   Local democracy and the 'target culture'   55
   4.3   Differential autonomy?   62
   4.4   Conclusion   65

5   **Who's in Charge Here?: Representation and accountability**
    in local governance   67
    5.1   Introduction   67
    5.2   Representation: Elections and appointments in local
          agencies   68
    5.3   Accountability, community representation and local
          partnerships   77
    5.4   Conclusion   81

6   **In Defence of Politicians?: The role of elected**
    representatives in local democracy   82
    6.1   Introduction   82
    6.2   The role of elected councillors   83
    6.3   The role of MPs   91
    6.4   The role of parish councillors   96
    6.5   Conclusion   99

7   **The Party's Over?: Local political participation and**
    civic engagement   101
    7.1   Introduction   101
    7.2   Defining political participation and civic engagement   102
    7.3   National trends in political participation and civic
          engagement   103
    7.4   The stratification of citizenship   104
    7.5   Political representation and participation in Burnley and
          Harrogate   106
    7.6   Conclusion   119

8   **Power to the Person?: From participatory democracy to**
    customer responsiveness   121
    8.1   Introduction   121
    8.2   The evolution of citizen/consumer engagement with
          public services   122
    8.3   Does public participation enhance local democracy?   131
    8.4   Citizen involvement with public services in Burnley and
          Harrogate   132
    8.5   Conclusion   148

9 Information's What We Need? 151

   9.1 Introduction 151

   9.2 Opening up public bodies 152

   9.3 Communications strategies, marketing and 'branding' 156

   9.4 The role of the local press 160

   9.5 Conclusion 167

10 Strengthening Local Democracy: Lessons and limitations 170

   10.1 Introduction 170

   10.2 English local democracy in comparative perspective 172

   10.3 Reviving local democracy 181

References 191

Appendix 1: Research Framework 202

Appendix 2: Interviews Conducted 209

Appendix 3: Membership Organisations Contacted 216

Appendix 4: Meetings Attended 218

Figures, Tables and Case Studies

Figures

Figure 1.1: The local democratic mix in Burnley 8

Figure 2.1a: The multi-scalar governance of Burnley 24

Figure 2.1b: The multi-scalar governance of Harrogate 25

Figure 2.3: Area-based initiatives operating in Burnley and Harrogate 37

Figure 5.1a: Harrogate representational links 75

Figure 5.1b: Burnley representational links 76

Figure 7.1: District election turnouts in Burnley and Harrogate, 1983–2002 (%) 107

Figure 7.2: District turnout in county council elections in Burnley and Harrogate, 1973–2005 (%) 108

Figure 7.3: Burnley Borough Council elections, 1980–2002, wards contested 109

Figure 7.4: Harrogate Borough Council elections, 1979–2002, wards contested 109

Figure 9.1: Local service providers' publications delivered directly to households – Burnley and Harrogate 158

Tables

Table 1.1: Key indicators of socio-economic contrasts in Burnley and Harrogate 16

Table 3.1: Elected local authorities serving Burnley, 2003/04 41

Table 3.2: Regional quangos serving Burnley, 2003/04   41

Table 3.3: Local public spending bodies serving Burnley, 2003/04   42

Table 3.4: Partnerships, zone boards and other cross-sectoral
bodies serving Burnley   43

Table 3.5: Elected local authorities serving Harrogate, 2003/04   43

Table 3.6: Regional quangos serving Harrogate, 2003/04   44

Table 3.7: Local public spending bodies serving Harrogate,
2003/04   45

Table 3.8: Partnerships, zone boards and other cross-sectoral
bodies serving Harrogate, 2003/04   45

Table 3.9: Estimates of local authority expenditure as a total of all
public expenditure in Burnley and Harrogate   46

Table 3.10: Total budget for core services (FSS), per head of
population, Burnley and Harrogate, 2004/05   46

Table 3.11: Public perception of service provision by district,
county or central government   49

Table 5.1: Comparative remuneration levels, elected councillors
and non-executive directors of local public agencies, 2004/05   73

Table 6.1: Total communications from local residents handled
monthly by one MP's office (average for January and February 2005)   93

Table 7.1: Estimated party membership and party activism in the
Burnley and Harrogate and Knaresborough parliamentary
constituency, 2005   111

Table 7.2: The estimated scale of the voluntary and community
sector in Burnley and Harrogate   113

Table 8.1: Local election turnout compared to estimates of
percentage of electorate engaged by five most popular
consultation and participation mechanisms used by councils
in England, 2001   128

Table 8.2: Percentage of local residents that claim to have ever
attended public meetings of the following organisations   138

Table 8.3: Percentage of Burnley and Harrogate citizens' panel members indicating direct involvement in different aspects of local public services   139

Table 8.4: Percentage of local residents that claim to have attended a consultation event or responded to a consultation exercise undertaken by the following organisations (excludes borough council panel surveys)   141

Table 8.5: Percentage of local residents that claim to have ever made a formal complaint to the following organisations   144

Table 8.6: Complainant contact with public service providers operating in Harrogate 1999/00–2004/05, ranked by average number of complaints received per 10,000 residents   146

Table 8.7: Complainant contact with public service providers operating in Burnley 1999/00–2004/05, ranked by average number of complaints received per 10,000 residents   146

Table 9.1: Record of responses to request for complaints data, made under the terms of the Freedom of Information Act   155

Table 9.2: Local and regional newspapers serving Burnley and Harrogate   161

Table 10.1: People per elected councillor and average population per council, Western Europe   174

Table 10.2: Average turnout at sub-national elections within the EU   175

Case Studies

Case Study 2.1: The Burnley Borough Council website   33

Case Study 3.1: Brian Fenn, Burnley Wood Community Action Group   52

Case Study 4.1: The Council Housing Options process, Harrogate 64

Case Study 6.1: Dunnockshaw and Clowbridge Parish Council vs United Utilities   98

Case Study 7.1: Faith groups and local activism   115

Case Study 7.2: The contribution of 'super-activists'   118

Case Study 8.1: Local democracy and the NHS   126

Case Study 8.2: The Howard Street Community Health Centre   135

Case Study 8.3: Police and Communities Together (PACT)   139

Case Study 8.4: Calico Housing's customer contact system   147

Foreword

As this book was being finalised, George Galloway's decision to participate in Channel 4's Celebrity Big Brother 2006 was provoking renewed debate about popular disengagement with the democratic process in Britain. Comparisons between voting figures for Big Brother and turnouts in national and local elections have, of course, been made ever since the first series of Big Brother was screened in 2000. While such comparisons are arguably disingenuous, they are nonetheless dramatic. In June 2003, *The Observer* noted that 'almost twice as many votes were cast in the last series of Big Brother as in May's local elections', when only a third of the eligible electorate took up their right to elect local representatives.

Falling local election turnouts have been the headline indicator of wider concerns about the state of local democracy in recent years. Yet, it cannot be suggested that politicians have ignored or overlooked these issues. The current government has established reviving local democracy and engaging communities in local decision-making as a key objective for Labour's third term of office. Moreover, this commitment to a 'new localism', now spearheaded by David Miliband, as Minister of Communities and Local Government, is echoed across all the principal political parties. A group of 23 leading Conservatives have recently advocated large-scale decentralisation as part of their case for 'Direct Democracy' (2005). Such goals have long been a central plank of the Liberal Democrats' policy programme.

Any degree of political consensus about the need for greater local control and local democracy is a rare event in British party politics. Inevitably, closer inspection of the proposals being advocated by the three main parties indicates that there are significant differences of opinion about how to respond to the 'crisis' of local democracy. Yet, the common agreement about the need for urgent action to revive local political engagement and promote greater local autonomy is striking.

Based on in-depth research in two northern towns – Burnley and Harrogate – this book examines the state of local democracy in England today, and assesses the strengths and weaknesses of the competing proposals for future reform. The book seeks to offer a comprehensive analysis of local democracy in action, assessing not only the democratic role of local authorities, but the extent of local democratic control over all public service provision. The book makes a number of key recommendations for policy, as well as a plea for constructive, cross-party working on the issue of local democracy.

The research project on which this volume is based was funded by the Joseph Rowntree Charitable Trust, for whom the condition of local democracy in the UK has become a major concern, particularly given evidence of increased alienation from the political process among parts of the electorate. The project was carried out by Stuart Wilks-Heeg and Steve Clayton of the University of Liverpool over a period of 20 months – from April 2004 to December 2005.

Thanks to the Trust's generous financial support, the project team were able to undertake detailed fieldwork in both towns, spending two working months in each. The fieldwork involved building a comprehensive political profile of the two towns, based on an extensive mapping and analysis of the full range of organisations involved in policy-making and service delivery locally. The research also benefited enormously from the level of support and assistance provided by local organisations in Burnley and Harrogate, including community groups, to undertake this mapping of local democracy and to assess its operation against established democratic criteria. As such, this book represents a summary of a very large body of work, much of which was used to produce working papers as the project progressed. Detailed individual reports on specific aspects of the research can be downloaded from the State of Local Democracy project website, the address for which can be found on the back cover of this volume.

A project of this scale would not be possible without the assistance of a large number of people. First and foremost, the project could not have been undertaken without the financial assistance of the Joseph Rowntree Charitable Trust and the constant support, advice, insight and encouragement provided by Stephen Pittam and David Shutt. The project was served throughout by an Advisory Group, which included representatives from the Trust, senior councillors and officers from the respective borough councils, academic specialists, and other co-opted members. A central feature of the advisory group has been that it includes representation from each of the three main political parties. The input of the advisory group to the project had been invaluable throughout, and this book has benefited greatly from their input. The members of the group are listed in appendix 1.

We are especially grateful to Burnley and Harrogate Borough Councils for their cooperation throughout the project and for allowing us to utilise their respective citizens' panels. Thanks should also be extended to all those people who gave up their time to be interviewed – far too numerous to mention – and particularly those who agreed to participate more than once. We owe a great debt to our series of short-term interview transcribers – Lee Threlfall, Dave O'Brien, Adam McHugh, Caroline Room, and James Milton – who undertook a relatively tedious task in exchange for modest financial reward. Additional thanks are due to Dave for helping to finalise draft reports, and particularly to James, who was heroic in his role as copy editor for the final manuscript for this volume. As ever, full responsibility for what the book contains rests with the authors alone.

Stuart Wilks-Heeg, University of Liverpool
January 2006

Glossary

ABI	Area-Based Initiative
BCN	Burnley Community Network
BNP	British National Party
BVPI	Best Value Performance Indicator
BVPP	Best Value Performance Plan
BWCAG	Burnley Wood Community Action Group
CABE	Commission for Architecture and the Built Environment
CBM	Community Beat Manager
CPA	Comprehensive Performance Assessment
CPO	Compulsory Purchase Order
CVS	Council for Voluntary Services
EU	European Union
DETR	Department for Environment, Transport and the Regions
FOI (Act)	Freedom of Information (Act)
FSS	Formula Spending Share
HBC	Harrogate Borough Council
HMIC	Her Majesty's Inspectorate of Constabulary
GONW	Government Office for the North West
HMRI	Housing Market Renewal Initiative
IDeA	Improvement and Development Agency
IPCC	Independent Police Complaints Commission
IVR	Institute for Volunteering Research
LAA	Local Area Agreement
LGA	Local Government Association
LGIU	Local Government Information Unit
LPSB	Local Public Spending Body
LSP	Local Strategic Partnership
MORI	Market and Opinion Research International
NDPB	Non-Departmental Public Body
NHS	National Health Service
NYCC	North Yorkshire County Council
OECD	Organisation for Economic Cooperation and Development
ODPM	Office of the Deputy Prime Minister

NIMBY	Not In My Back Yard
PAC	Public Administration Committee
PACT	Police and Community Together
PALS	Patient Advice and Liaison Service
PCG	Primary Care Group
PCT	Primary Care Trust
PSU	Police Standards Unit
RDA	Regional Development Agency
RSL	Registered Social Landlord
SHA	Strategic Health Authority
SRB	Single Regeneration Budget
VCF (sector)	Voluntary, Community and Faith (sector)
VCO	Voluntary and Community Organisation
VCS	Voluntary and Community Sector
YOT	Youth Offending Team

1
Whose Democracy? Whose Local?

I am convinced that the most fruitful field before reformers at the present time is to be found in an extension of the functions and authority of local government. Local government is near the people. Local government will bring you into contact with the masses. By its means you will be able to increase their comforts, to secure their health ... to lessen the inequalities of our social system and to raise the standard of all classes in the community.
Joseph Chamberlain, 1885

1.1 Introduction

Much has changed since Joseph Chamberlain's campaign to persuade progressive reformers in late nineteenth century Britain to see local government as the primary agent of social change. Local government control over services has diminished, the British state has become more centralised, local public service provision has become more complex and fragmented, and the number of unelected public bodies operating locally has proliferated. Many would argue that the scope for a local politician today, even one as visionary as Chamberlain, to use the powers and resources available to them locally to pursue a 'big idea' for a town or city has all but evaporated. As Sheena MacDonald (2005) recently put it on Radio 4, with the possible exception of the mayor of London, Ken Livingstone, 'those motivated by civic duty or the celebrity of high civic office have melted away, their role increasingly taken over by central government – direct rule from the House of Commons, the Treasury and Downing Street'.

While power has been seen to have drained away locally, the transition from local govern*ment* to local govern*ance* described above has also been portrayed as fundamentally undemocratic. There is much sense in this basic proposition. Yet, we would also argue that the changing status of elected local government points to a need for any analysis of local democracy to look beyond the world of elected local governments, local elections and local politicians. Local public service provision no longer arises exclusively, or even primarily, from the processes of political decision-making associated with elected local councils. The notion of a local democratic deficit must therefore be subjected to closer and more comprehensive scrutiny. We have attempted such an analysis through consideration of the full range of mechanisms through which local public bodies in two northern towns, Burnley and Harrogate, relate to local residents. Moreover, in trying to assess the quality of local democracy under such conditions of fragmented local service provision, we have sought not to lose sight of the 'bigger picture' of how a town works. Under the current arrangements, can local leaders, representing places with strong local identities, come anywhere close to realising Chamberlain's notion of local democracy as 'the most fruitful field before reformers'?

Before dealing with such questions directly, there are of course important conceptual issues to consider. Inevitably, there are competing interpretations and forms of 'democracy', as well as complications of using the prefix, 'local', to study democracy at a sub-national level. This introductory chapter therefore begins by considering further how to define 'democracy' within the context of the changes in local governance outlined above. As we demonstrate, the contested character of both democracy and local democracy poses significant questions for any attempt to assess 'the state of local democracy'. Our response to the dilemmas raised is to opt for as comprehensive a definition of local democracy as possible, based around the notion of a 'local democratic mix' (c.f. Haus and Sweeting, 2003). At the same time, this discussion also raises the issue of geographical scale in local democracy and, in particular, whether there is a link between the quality, or even quantity, of democracy and the scale at which democracy operates. Finally, this chapter also briefly introduces the research project and the two case study towns, before outlining the structure of the book as a whole.

1.2 Re-conceptualising local democracy

While we have already outlined the case for a broader conceptualisation of local democracy, it will be useful to elaborate on what we see as the three principal reasons for this approach. First, as was noted above, local councils can no longer claim to be the primary providers of local public services. Since the 1980s there has been a clear trend towards a proliferation of public and semi-public bodies at the local and regional level in the UK. As is shown in chapter 3, less than half of local public expenditure in the two towns we examine is controlled by local councils. To a significant extent, this diversification of local public service provision has come about as a result of the transfer of functions from elected councils to non-elected bodies. Moreover, in many cases, this shift to non-elected bodies has arisen from central government attempts to realise their policy objectives through a bypassing of elected local authorities. Paradoxically, recent attempts to overcome the problems of fragmentation that arose from such dynamics have added to this plethora of local public bodies. This has produced a country-wide growth in the number of local partnership bodies, some generated from local initiatives promoting collaboration with the private and voluntary sectors, but many arising from central government requirements aimed at promoting local multi-agency working. As we highlight in chapter 2, local democracy must now be identified from an alphabet soup that encompasses everything from ABIs (area-based initiatives) to YOTs (youth offending teams).

Second, although these trends are widely recognised among academic researchers and policy-makers, their implications for the study of local democracy is often overlooked. Certainly, the emergence of complex, fragmented networks of local policy-making and service provision has been captured by the widespread use of the term 'local governance'. As such, the concept of local governance has come to imply a clear distinction from the notion of 'local government', under which local councils were unequivocally regarded as the principal providers of local public services. Yet, it is important to recognise that there is a significant degree of arbitrariness about which services are under the control of elected local bodies. For instance, why do local elections in the UK impact upon social services but not upon health services? Does the simple absence of local electoral accountability in the NHS mean that health care should be excluded from any discussion of local democracy? Any judgement as to what practices and institutions should be most central to such an analysis will depend upon which wider principles are attached to the term 'democracy'.

Third, new forms of service accountability and citizen participation have been introduced into local governance alongside traditional mechanisms of representative democracy, which appear to have declined in significance. The growth of non-elected local agencies (quangos) and the widespread introduction of private-sector auditing techniques, in particular, have weakened the extent of direct democratic control, while also introducing diverse forms of service accountability. As we show in chapter 8, most formal local public bodies share local councils' experience of opening up aspects of decision-making to new forms of public and organisational participation, as well as the introduction of new mechanisms designed to render them more responsive to individual 'customers' or users. Such reforms reflect the growing influence of theories of Public Choice and New Public Management, with new accountability and 'customer feedback' mechanisms based on private sector models generally introduced at the behest of central government. While the adoption of market-based models has often provoked concerns that their underlying purpose is simply one of 'cost-cutting', these trends also indicate a shift in notions of accountability away from democracy as a collective process to a more individualistic, market-based concept designed to make service providers more responsive to their users. At the same time, patterns of local involvement have also diversified via attempts to promote wider forms of citizen engagement, such as direct involvement in services, representation on partnerships, and an array of new consultation processes.

A definition of local democracy is therefore required that recognises that while local authorities remain the only local agencies elected via a universal local franchise, they operate alongside a host of other agencies locally that provide a range of means through which local residents can seek to influence their decision-making. Yet relatively few attempts have been made to analyse the implications of the transition to local governance for the quality of local democracy. What, for instance, are the democratic implications of local strategic partnerships (LSPs), introduced in 1999 to promote joint working between local public agencies, the private sector and the voluntary sector?

If the study of local democracy lags behind the study of local governance, much the same can be said in relation to the diversification of citizen/customer engagement with local public bodies. Recognition of the diverse forms of involvement that local democracy now takes and the connections and tensions between these competing 'models' raise crucial questions. For instance, have new forms of service accountability and public consultation/participation helped to redress shortcomings in the local democratic process? Or have they contributed, even if only indirectly, to the growing sense of alienation to the political process among large sections of the population? Is there a danger that focusing on how individuals experience, and relate to, specific public services militates against local political leaders advancing a 'big idea' or 'strategic vision' for their locality?

1.3 Whose democracy?

No questions are more difficult than those of democracy.
Williams, 1983, p.97

Few people would disagree that the basic definition of democracy derives from the original Greek words 'demos' (people) and 'kratos' (rule); democracy thus represents 'rule by the people' or 'government by the people'. Accordingly, the Concise Oxford English Dictionary defines democracy as 'a system of government by the whole population, usually through elected representatives'. Unsurprisingly, it is with the interpretation of such 'basic' definitions that the difficulties really start: much of the disagreement arises from the emergence of powerful, but competing, normative cases for democracy. As Williams (1983) has elaborated, there are essentially two competing modern meanings of democracy, derived respectively from the liberal and socialist traditions. The former sees democracy as defined by the openness of elections, the existence of freedom of speech and the protection of basic democratic rights. The latter tradition, however, defines democracy more in terms of popular power and control by the majority. As a result, little consensus exists about either the basic meaning of 'rule by the people', or the mechanisms through which it can be achieved. While 'freedom' or 'liberty' is the cornerstone of liberal accounts of the rule of the people, 'equality' is at the heart of most socialist conceptions of democracy. Likewise, whereas liberal definitions of democracy focus heavily on 'indirect', or representative, democracy, socialist and anarchist traditions make the case for greater 'direct', or participatory, democracy.

More recently, a third distinction has emerged, which we may term 'public choice'. Since the 1980s, notions of 'consumer sovereignty', derived from conventional economics and promoted by advocates of public choice theory, have become increasingly influential in the analysis and practice of democracy (Dunleavy, 1991). Contrasting sharply with socialist conceptions of democracy, in particular, public choice theory takes the individual, rather than the collective, as the key unit of analysis. Additionally, while both the liberal and socialist traditions view individuals as 'citizens', public choice accounts of democracy see the individual as a 'rational consumer' in a political 'marketplace'. The increasing influence of public choice theory is seen, for instance, in the widespread use of customer complaints mechanisms and expanding 'competition' and 'choice' agendas in the public services. Thus, while liberal and socialist traditions are largely concerned with the capacity of citizens to exercise power through 'voice', public choice theory stresses the importance of individuals having powers of 'exit' in relation to public services. As such, public choice accounts of democracy are focused on the quality of public services and freedom of choice, rather than on the quality and freedom of public debate. Likewise, notions of equality among citizens are essentially absent from public choice accounts of democracy.

Within these wider debates about the meaning and practice of democracy, particular significance has often been attached to *local* democracy. As Dearlove (1979) notes, in 'orthodox' accounts there is not only a strong normative case made for local democracy as a foundation of democracy within the nation state, but local government has often been seen to be *especially* democratic. Moreover, elements of the different democratic traditions identified above – such as representative democracy, participatory democracy and user democracy – are all inescapably present at the local level. As Pratchett (2004, p.361) suggests 'it is at the local level that the relationship between representative democracy and widespread citizen participation makes most sense'. Long-run concerns about the decline of local democracy have been central to attempts to augment traditional representative democracy at the local level with multifarious additional forms of representation, participation and consultation in local governance (Haus and Sweeting, 2003). As such, localities constitute the key site in which the various competing notions of democracy coexist in practice and where the interplay between the competing conceptions of democracy outlined above is arguably clearest. In this regard, Haus and Sweeting (2003) offer a comprehensive categorisation of local democracy, as well as a set of analytical categories that offer a useful basis for empirical research. Drawing on the work of Frieder Naschold (1997), Haus and Sweeting suggest that contemporary local democracy is effectively characterised by a 'local democratic mix', made up of four distinct forms of local democracy:

◆ *Representative democracy*, comprising local councils run by politicians elected by universal suffrage among local residents;

◆ *Network democracy*, constituting forms of functional representation, through which decision-making is influenced by organised interests, such as employers or trade unions, or decisions are reached in concert with other local agencies, as in local partnership arrangements;

◆ *User democracy*, involving mainly customer and consumer feedback models that seek to connect service providers more closely to individual users of those services. These include 'market research' and 'customer satisfaction' type surveys, definition of service standards, the provision for customer choice in public services and the introduction of customer complaint mechanisms;

◆ *Participatory democracy*, embracing a variety of means of involving local people in decision-making, including forms of direct democracy, such as local referenda, as well as deliberative opinions polls and consultations, public meetings, citizens' juries, and tenant participation in social housing. The key factor distinguishing participatory democracy from user democracy is its more *collective* orientation, generally involving public debate and deliberation, rather than agencies responding to expressions of *individual* preference or concern.

Our approach to local democracy therefore highlights the importance of considering the relative significance of each of these elements of the overall democratic mix, while also seeking to identify and disentangle the interconnections between them. Figure 1.1 illustrates, using the case of Burnley, how this notion of the local democratic mix can be applied to the range of public bodies operating in the town. At the same time, however, we recognise that local democracy cannot easily be divorced from national democracy. Serious problems arise from any attempt to 'privilege' the quality of local democracy or to analyse local democratic processes in isolation from those of the nation state. Dearlove's (1979) seminal critique of the conventional orthodoxies of local democracy remind us that the activities of political parties, organised interests and national government all tend to militate against democratic principles and practice at the local level. As such, the study of local democracy cannot take place in isolation from analysis of the broader political system in which it operates. Moreover, whatever the character of the local democratic mix, a core concern in this book is whether the character and operation of local democracy today renders it more or less difficult to pursue a 'big idea' locally. For all these reasons, the research on which this book is based involved not only detailed fieldwork in two localities, but also a wider analysis of the positioning of local democracy within the British political system.

Figure 1.1: The local democratic mix in Burnley

	Representative	Network	User	Participatory
Burnley Borough Council	Annual election (3 years in every 4) of Borough Councillors, representing individual wards	Consultation with other local bodies on key policy issues; Partnership working, especially Local Strategic Partnership	User satisfaction surveys; Citizens' panel; Consultation surveys; Formal complaints procedure, with recourse to local government ombudsman, if required	Public meetings (e.g. on Neighbourhood Action Plans, housing market renewal); Local Agenda 21
Lancashire County Council	Election of county councillors every 4 years	Consultation with other local bodies on key policy issues (e.g. Building Schools for the Future); Partnership working, especially participation in district-level local strategic partnerships	Monthly SMS consultation programme (via mobile phones); Formal complaints procedure, with recourse to local government ombudsman, if required	Cabinet in the Community; Local Agenda 21
Calico Housing	Elections for tenant board members; Role of elected members on governing board		Customer satisfaction surveys; Customer contact meetings	Focus/interest groups; Tenants and residents associations
Burnley College	Elections for staff and student board members; Role of elected members on governing board	'Stakeholder' views provided by head teacher representative and private sector representatives on	Student evaluation questionnaires	

(Continued)

Figure 1.1: The Local Democratic Mix in Burnley (continued)

	Representative	Network	User	Participatory
		governing board; Regular liaison with key partners, e.g. University of Central Lancashire		
Lancashire Constabulary	Role of elected members on Lancashire Police Authority	Partnership working; Joint police/ council scanning meetings (weekly)	Local residents can contact community beat officers directly by mobile phone; Complaints procedure – either direct to police force or to Independent Police Complaints Commission	Independent members of police authority; Police and Communities Together (PACT)
Burnley Pendle and Rossendale Primary Care Trust	None	Partnership working; Attendance at local authority scrutiny committees	Patient satisfaction surveys; Patient Advice and Liaison Services (PALS); Independent Complaints Advocacy Service (ICAS)	Patient and Public Involvement Forums (PPI); Expert Patient Programme; Diabetes Empowerment Group; Occupational Therapy's Patient Story Project; Patient Experience Team
Burnley Action Partnership (BAP)	Participation of elected members; Elections of Burnley Community Network representatives	BAP operates primarily, if not entirely, on the basis of network democracy	Consultation on community plan	

The implications of the changing character of central–local relations for local democracy are explored in detail in chapter 4. However, it is important to note at this juncture the crucial tensions inherent to the relationship between local democracy and local autonomy (Pratchett, 2004; Beetham *et al.*, 2002). As Pratchett (2004) notes, while local democracy and local autonomy are seen as virtually synonymous concepts, the relationship between them is, in reality, far more complex. Local autonomy is generally seen as a pre-requisite for local democracy and local democracy, in turn, is widely held to be a pre-requisite for democracy within the nation state. At the same time, however, high levels of local autonomy are likely to result in significant variations in democratic practice, and in the standards and comprehensiveness of public services, resulting in potentially enormous inequalities of citizenship. In socialist traditions, in particular, such inequalities would be interpreted as profoundly undemocratic. It is therefore evident that 'democracies need to find an effective balance between equal citizenship throughout their territory and the demands of distinctive regional and local autonomy' (Beetham *at al.*, 2002, p.247). This question of how such a balance can best be struck, raises a complex set of issues concerning which policy function and what levels of policy autonomy should operate at which geographical scale. For the study of local democracy, this is essentially a question of 'whose local'?

1.4 Whose local?

The biggest curse of local government is its large size that generates remoteness. Time to think small.

Malcolm Dean, 2005

The relationship between democracy and the size of political units has been debated ever since the first democratic state was established in Athens in 508BC. Indeed, the view that 'democracy truly flowers in communities and in small areas' originated in Ancient Greece, where 'Plato calculated the optimal number of citizens as 5,040, and Aristotle thought even this number too large' (Dearlove, 1979, p.32). This basic proposition that smaller units of government are more democratic has been examined extensively since the publication of Dahl and Tufte's classic (1973) book *Size and Democracy*. Dahl and Tufte postulated that defining an optimal size for a democracy was impossible, since trade-offs between democracy and efficiency are likely as political units increase in size. In this view, democracy is indeed fostered by smaller units of government, but such units are likely to experience severe difficulties providing the range of functions expected in a modern democracy. Conversely, larger units of local government are likely to experience a decline in 'democratic quality' but are likely to enable the achievement of a number of 'scale economies', thereby allowing a broader range of public services to be delivered more effectively and at lower cost to the taxpayer.

Far from dispensing with the question of whether there is an 'optimal size' for local authorities, Dahl and Tufte's work prompted renewed interest in where the balance could best be struck between democracy and efficiency. Moreover, the assumption that larger units of local government produce economies of scale, while smaller units promote greater democracy and accountability continues to shape international debates about whether there is an optimal size for local authorities (Dahlberg *et al.*, 2005). As we show in chapter 10, national and international research evidence points consistently to a strongly *negative* relationship between size and democracy, while equivalent studies examining the evidence for economies of scale have generally failed to uncover any clear *positive* relationship between size and efficiency. Despite such evidence, however, it is a particular feature of UK political debate that an assumed democracy vs. efficiency trade-off provides a powerful justification for larger units of local government and other local public bodies.

This 'conventional wisdom' has appeared to some observers to be almost immune to any counter-argument or evidence, even if the source is an official governmental inquiry. In 1969 the Royal Commission on Local Government in England 'came to the only possible conclusion – namely that neither research nor submitted evidence has proved that any particular size of authority was best for any function' (Morton, 1970, p.59, cited in Dearlove, 1979, p.71). Three years later, the Local Government Act of 1972 introduced provisions for amalgamating local authorities in England and Wales, reducing the number of county councils from 58 to 47 and replacing the 1,250 municipal boroughs, urban districts and rural districts with 333 district councils (Wilson and Game, 1994, p.52). Dearlove (1979, p.65) argued that this apparent gulf between research evidence and policy response could be traced back to the nineteenth century, with the 'economies of scale' argument generally going untested ever since, 'as constant repetition has given the rule the status of obvious common-sense'. As Dearlove (p.66) goes on to note 'practically no one has stood outside a broad acceptance of the idea that larger local authorities were the key to increased efficiency'.

In the context of this powerful 'conventional wisdom', those arguing for the retention of smaller local authorities in the UK have, therefore, tended to be viewed as lone voices. Yet, such voices can still be heard. Speaking in the House of Lords in a debate on local government and regional assemblies, Lord Greaves, also an elected member of Pendle Borough Council, argued on the basis of turnout in the 2004 local elections in North West England that the 'figures show a clear correlation between the size of the local authority and turnout'. Lord Greaves went on to argue that the correlation reflects 'how close the councillors who represent them are to the people living in those areas'. He continued that:

Within the shire districts, on average, one councillor represents 1,000 to 1,500 people. In the metropolitan districts, it is four, five, six, seven times that number. People are far less likely to know their councillors and the candidates who are trying to get elected. A Government who are on record weekly as saying that they want to increase turnout in elections as one of the fundamental improvements they want to make to our democratic system must take this on board: the more local the people or the councillors who stand for election, the higher will be the turnout of people who will vote for them

Lords Hansard, 16 June 2004, Column 824

Although Lord Greaves' conclusions are derived solely from a 'snapshot' of a single region in a single year, wider evidence supports his case. Analysis of ward level turnouts in all English local elections in shire districts, metropolitan boroughs and London boroughs from 1973–1999 clearly demonstrates that turnout is 'systematically higher' in shire districts and 'systematically lower' in metropolitan boroughs (ODPM, 2002c, p.78). The same report notes that there is a clear tendency for both wards with a larger electorate and wards electing a single member to experience lower levels of turnout. In other words, there is good reason to pay further attention to Lord Greaves' argument that a smaller ratio of electors per councillor will tend to mean higher turnout in local elections. However, policy-makers have paid scant attention to the possibility that creating larger local authorities may diminish the quality of local democracy. Instead, it is generally assumed that any danger of larger councils being more 'remote' can be compensated for by the introduction of the executive/scrutiny split in local government, requirements for local authorities to consult local residents, and the introduction of mechanisms such as neighbourhood forums.

At the same time, it is largely assumed that any 'loss' of democracy will be more than compensated for by an increased quality of, and satisfaction with, local services. This reasoning is clearly underpinned by a progressive redefinition of what is meant by 'local democracy'. We have already noted how traditional conceptions of representative democracy have been augmented, and increasingly, substituted by, notions of user democracy, in which the citizen is recast as a 'consumer' of public services. Such an approach effectively reduces local democracy to issues of producing and consuming local services. Once redefined as 'consumers', local residents are more or less automatically assumed to 'want' the benefits of efficiency, economy and effectiveness that larger units of local government are assumed to bring.

In this context, it is highly apparent that national government has come to assume that 'bigger is better' for most local public services. Long-running debates about the size for local authorities are increasingly paralleled in other key areas of local public service provision, most notably health care and policing. At the time of writing, government proposals are on the table that will reduce the number of primary care trusts (PCTs) from 300 to 100, and discussions are underway looking to reduce the number of police forces from 43 to less than 30. In both cases, a key driving force behind the 'merger mania' (Bojke *et al.*, 2001) is the concern of national governments to raise public sector productivity and to reduce differences in performance between localities. Yet, almost without exception, the conclusions reached in research studies about the scope to secure benefits from creating larger units of local government, primary health care or police stand in stark contrast to the arguments being made in favour of amalgamation. Meanwhile, widespread concerns have been expressed about the scope for larger police forces and PCTs to sustain the progress that they have made in engaging with local people. In short, 'whose local?' has become perhaps the most significant question in understanding the operation of democracy within contemporary local governance.

1.5 The research project

The aims, objectives and research methods employed in this study reflect the issues raised by the above discussion of the nature of contemporary local democracy. The principal aims of the study were to explore the strengths and weaknesses of democratic processes in the two towns, assess the extent to which these dynamics are typical of elsewhere in the UK, and to identify potential local and national policy recommendations for strengthening local democracy. As such, the research involved working closely with a range of local stakeholders in Burnley and Harrogate, particularly the respective district councils, over an extended period, to undertake a comprehensive mapping and audit of local democracy, assessing its operation against established democratic criteria. As such, the study sought to build a comprehensive political profile of the two towns, based on an analysis of the full range of organisations involved in policy-making and service delivery locally. In simple terms, the research set out to answer the following key questions:

◆ Who does what locally?

◆ To whom are local agencies accountable?

◆ How are local policy priorities arrived at?

◆ To what extent do citizens participate in local affairs?

◆ To what extent are local people involved in running services and holding them to account?

◆ How much money does each agency spend locally and how do they determine how to spend it?

◆ How much of a say do local residents have in relation to these decisions?

◆ Is it any longer possible to develop a 'big picture' for a town?

The research was carried out in three principal phases. These comprised: first, a detailed mapping of governance structures in Burnley and Harrogate; second, a broad ranging 'audit' of local democracy in the two towns; and, third an assessment of how local democracy in the UK measures up against established democratic criteria, and in comparison with other European countries. The project was carried out over a period of 20 months, from April 2004 to December 2005. Detailed fieldwork was undertaken in both Burnley and Harrogate, including interviews with some 200 politicians, policy-makers, community activists and residents across the two towns. The research team also attended a cross-section of 26 public meetings of local councils, health care trusts, police authorities and other public bodies. The research findings also include data derived from survey questions put to a weighted sample of local residents via the Burnley Citizens' Panel and the Harrogate District Panel. In total, the project team spent more than seven working weeks in each town over the life of the project, including a number of extended stays. A fuller account and discussion of the research methods used, as well as details of the interviews conducted and meetings attended are contained in appendices 1–4.

The decision to undertake a comparative study of Burnley and Harrogate was made for a number of reasons. The core towns are of a roughly similar size, and form part of wider districts, comprising a mix of urban and rural areas, operating within a two-tier local government structure. In addition, both towns are of sufficient distance from a major city for them to exhibit a strong sense of self-identity. At the same time, the choice of Burnley and Harrogate as case study areas offered an opportunity to consider the impact of contrasting socio-economic conditions on local democracy. It would scarcely be possible to identify two medium-sized towns in northern England which differ as greatly in relation to core social, economic and demographic indicators. As Table 1.1 shows, Harrogate's residents are considerably more likely to have high-level qualifications and to work in professional occupations than their counterparts in Burnley, while experiencing a quarter of the level of domestic burglary, and typically living in properties whose market value is four times that in Burnley. However, while influential, such contrasts should not always be read at face value. Our analysis of ward level data for the two districts suggests that socio-economic contrasts *within* Burnley and Harrogate are as great, if not greater, than contrasts *between* them. Moreover, relative affluence can create its own local policy problems, as the case of affordable housing in Harrogate demonstrates (see chapter 4).

Table 1.1: Key indicators of socio-economic contrasts in Burnley and Harrogate

	Burnley	Harrogate
Total population (2001)	89,500	151,300
Unemployment (%) (Nov. 2005)	2.2	1.0
Share of jobs in higher occupational grades: 1–3 (%) (2003)	22	48
Residential burglaries per 1000 of population (2001)	15	4
Adults with no qualifications (%) (2001)	36	22
Educated to degree level or above (%) (2001)	13	25
Proportion of dwellings classified unfit (%) (2003)	23	4
Average property price (2004)	£46,417	£195,887

Sources: 2001 Census of Population, Local Labour Force Survey, Annual Business Inquiry, Land Registry.

1.6 Structure of the book

The remaining nine chapters of this book present the principal research findings arising from the project, organised around a number of specific themes relating to local democracy. Chapters 2, 3 and 4 set out much of the context for the research findings. Thus, chapter 2 maps the array of bodies involved in public service delivery in Burnley and Harrogate – 'from ABIs to YOTs' – to provide an initial picture of local governance in the two towns. The various types of public bodies operating in the two towns, their scale of operations and their 'closeness' to local residents are mapped out. Following on from this analysis, chapter 3 presents and analyses data on relative levels of public spending by these bodies. Although the data present some limitations, it is found that only around half of all public spending is under the control of elected bodies, with the district councils accounting for only five per cent of total local public spending. This chapter also discusses the role of social capital in shaping decision-making in local public services and the direction of public spending. In chapter 4 we turn to examine some common pressures faced by all local public agencies that militate against local autonomy and, by extension, local democracy. Drawing on our fieldwork, we highlight the particular influence of the universal drive towards centrally defined performance criteria and targets. It is argued that meaningful local democracy requires a far greater degree of local autonomy than currently exists.

The role of local elites and popular participation are assessed in chapters 5, 6 and 7. Chapter 5 addresses questions concerning the representativeness and accountability of the wide array of public bodies now governing local service provision. We show that unelected public bodies demonstrate considerable variation in the ways their governing bodies are appointed, with local councillors playing a significant role on some bodies and very minor roles on others. These issues are taken further in chapter 6, which focuses specifically on the role of elected politicians in local democracy. While the primary focus is on the role of district councillors in Burnley and Harrogate, attention is also paid to three other groups of politicians operating locally – parish councillors, county councillors and members of parliament. In chapter 7 we focus on the importance of political participation and civic engagement to vibrant local democracy. The chapter engages directly with the proposition that there is a crisis of political and civic involvement. A key finding is that local activists appear to be spreading themselves more thinly, across increasingly diverse forms of engagement. We argue that the decline of political parties has reached a crucial point if meaningful electoral competition is to be sustained at the local level.

Chapters 8 and 9 turn to consider the role of key contemporary trends in local democracy, associated with the rise of the 'citizen as consumer' and the increased emphasis on communications in relations between local public agencies and the population they serve. Chapter 8 asks whether the decline of party politics has been countered by increased citizen participation in other elements of the 'local democratic mix'. It is argued that, if local democracy is to be enhanced by diversifying the forms of engagement open to citizens, it is crucial that such reforms are embedded more fully in core principles of democracy. Chapter 9 then turns to examine the way public bodies communicate with the people they serve. We find that reforms over the past decade have vastly improved the way such bodies communicate with the public and greatly increased the availability of information about public bodies. However, it is suggested that there appears to be some degree of 'information overload' deriving from this new openness. For ordinary citizens, digesting and making sense of the information can be a daunting and time-consuming process. How useful much of this information is to the majority of the public without some guidance is highly questionable.

The final chapter of the book seeks to place the research findings in a broader context and outlines a set of proposals for reviving local democracy. We assess the quality of English local democracy in comparison with other European countries and in relation to the European Charter of Local Self-Government. We also consider the extent to which the competing proposals for reform offered by the main political parties in England would be likely to address the concerns identified in the book as a whole. It is argued that the greatest threat facing local democracy is the spectre of 'continuous reform' from the centre. To this end, the book concludes with a series of recommendations that are felt to maximise the potential for individual localities themselves to foster a process of local democratic renewal.

2
From ABIs to YOTs:
Digesting the alphabet soup

To involve yourself in civic life locally, regionally or nationally is to
bathe deep in a swamp of jargon in the depths of acronym hell.
Simon Fanshawe, 2005

2.1 Introduction

A series of brief texts runs along the top of the walls in the main council chamber in Burnley Town Hall. These feature key dates in the history of the council, such as the granting of the First Charter for a Market and Fair in 1293/4, but also when the council acquired control over specific public functions: the waterworks in 1854, the cemetery in 1855, the gasworks in 1861, the tramways in 1901, and so on. One Burnley councillor has prepared a parallel series to be placed along the base of the walls, providing the dates when most of these functions were transferred from Burnley Borough Council to higher-tier local authorities and, more frequently, to private companies and unelected quangos. This 're-allocation' of functions to other bodies has prompted considerable fragmentation in local public service providers and, for many local residents, the most obvious outcome will be the resultant 'alphabet soup' of abbreviations and acronyms. From area based initiatives (ABIs), through local area agreements (LAAs), to youth offending teams (YOTs), such abbreviations litter the everyday speech of those working in and with the public sector, such that books like this demand a glossary to aid the reader's digestion.

This chapter maps out the alphabet soup of public bodies operating in Burnley and Harrogate and in doing so raises some key issues to be explored further in subsequent chapters. These issues relate to the increasing fragmentation of public service provision represented by the alphabet soup and its implications for public accountability. The chapter provides a 'map' of the various public bodies serving the two towns, their scale of operations and an initial (and rough) index of their closeness to local residents. It points to an increasing tendency for the 'scaling up' of service provision, driven by supposed economies of scale, with a weaker 'scaling down' of a limited set of functions. The latter is particularly clear in the area of neighbourhood management. Combined with the increasing role of partnership working and the expansion of the voluntary and community sector in service provision, questions of precisely how these various bodies are accountable, and to whom, are increasingly important.

2.2 Types and functions of sub-national public bodies

Although local authorities remain the principal multi-functional providers of local public services, alongside them is an array of usually single-purpose agencies, ranging from small housing associations to primary care trusts with budgets rivalling those of the largest local authorities. These bodies are frequently labelled 'quangos' due to their common feature – they operate with varying degrees of independence from the formal structures of local democratic political control. There are six functional categories in which 'quangos' have a particularly significant role locally:

◆ *NHS bodies*: Strategic health authorities, primary care trusts, hospital trusts, health care trusts, ambulance trusts;

◆ *Criminal justice system*: The police, probation services, community safety partnerships, magistrates' courts;

◆ *Education, early years and young people*: Sure Start programmes, Connexions, Learning and Skills Councils, further education colleges, locally managed schools;

◆ *Economic development, regeneration and housing*: Regional development agencies, housing associations, Small Business Service, local regeneration partnerships;

◆ *Arts, culture and sport*: Arts Council regional offices; North West Vision; Screen Yorkshire; Sport England North West; Sport England Yorkshire; North West Cultural Consortium; Yorkshire Culture;

◆ *Utilities and public transport*: Privately provided but publicly regulated services, primarily railways, buses, water, electricity, gas and telecommunications.

A simple, if crude way, of mapping public bodies operating in Burnley and Harrogate would be to distinguish between elected bodies and such unelected 'quangos.' However, the term 'quango' is increasingly contested. Some observers stretch the category to encompass all of those listed above, including highly localised bodies, such as grant-maintained schools. Others reject the notion of regarding all the bodies listed above as quangos and instead restrict the term to non-departmental government bodies. In order to provide a full analysis of local democracy in the two towns, we suggest a more nuanced analysis of unelected local agencies is required. To this end, we employ the categorisation provided in the House of Commons' Public Administration Committee report *Mapping the Quango State* (PAC, 2001). This offers a comprehensive analysis of the quango state and provides the following typology of quangos:

◆ *Non-Departmental Public Bodies (NDPBs)*: Executive or advisory bodies with a UK remit, relating specifically to one of the constituent countries of the UK or to a specific English region, e.g. the BBC, the Countryside Agency, the British Potato Council and regional bodies serving the national regulators such as Ofwat or Ofcom. There are about 1,000 NDPBs, and national governments typically seek to restrict the definition of quangos to this category;

◆ *Task Forces*: Defined as 'temporary advice giving bodies', 295 Task Forces were established in the first 18 months of Labour coming to power in 1997, with 52 of them operating for two years or longer;

◆ *Regional and devolved quangos*: Includes a number of executive and advisory bodies that pre-dated the Labour administrations and a number established under the Labour government's devolution agenda. Although many are specific to Scotland, Wales or Northern Ireland, a number also operate across all the English regions, e.g. Regional Development Agencies, Regional Chambers, and regional arts boards and cultural consortia;

◆ *Local public spending bodies (LPSBs)*: Primarily bodies in the education, housing and health sectors, including higher education institutions, further education colleges, the Learning and Skills Councils, foundation schools, city technology colleges, housing associations, primary care groups, primary care trusts, and NHS trusts;

◆ *Partnerships, Zone Boards and other local cross-sectoral bodies*: A broad category covering bodies prevalent in policy areas characterised by multi-agency or short-term area-based initiatives, such as regeneration, crime and drugs, e.g. New Deal for Communities partnerships, Single Regeneration Budget partnerships, Sure Start, Health Action Zones, Youth Offending Teams, Drug Action Teams.[1]

As the bodies in the last three categories are often responsible for shaping local services, either strategically or in terms of delivery, and the LPSBs are often some of the biggest local public spenders, these are the highest profile 'quangos' in our research.

2.3 Scales of operation in local governance and 'closeness' to local residents

The governance of both Burnley and Harrogate thus requires consideration of a large number of bodies serving much larger geographical areas and populations than is represented by the two towns. If we include the principal sub-national bodies with a bearing on local governance in the two towns, eight spatial scales can be identified, of which five are 'above' the district scale (see figures 2.1a and 2.1b). This depiction of the 'multi-scalar' character of governance illustrates six important issues arising in both towns.

First, few bodies operate within boundaries co-terminous with the two district councils, and those that do tend to be restricted to either partnerships in which the district councils are the lead partners, or to bodies established independently from the district councils following the removal of functions from their direct control. Second, a significant proportion of agencies have county-wide decision-making structures. This arises directly from the 1974 reorganisation of local government, which created a strong tendency for local government functions to move upwards from the district to the county level. The shift of powers and

---

1   Many of the bodies in this category have very close links with elected local authorities, have budgets managed by local authorities, exist as part of a legal requirement placed upon local authorities or are managed by local authority staff. While the PAC defines them as quangos, they clearly fit somewhat uncomfortably within this 'typology' of quangos.

functions upwards to county councils has been widely felt to render local government more remote. Notably, Lancashire County Council has sought to provide at least a partial counter-balance to this tendency by introducing decentralised structures intended to provide direct links between districts and County Hall. These include significant investment in district partnership offices. Third, while moves to introduce a more powerful regional tier have been stalled by the electorate's rejection of proposals for an elected regional assembly for the North East, the introduction of both regional development agencies and regional chambers/assemblies has strengthened the regional scale.

Fourth, a number of bodies have been created due to district council functions being 'hived off' to private companies, e.g. bus companies, or 'third-sector' organisations. For example, Calico housing was created as an independent registered social landlord (RSL) following the transfer of Burnley Borough Council's housing stock in March 2000. Unlike elected authorities, such organisations tend not to be restricted to a geographically specific area of operation. Consequently such bodies tend to operate on an inter-regional scale, with major housing associations and bus companies providing local services across the North of England. A similar pattern is evident for Calico Housing and Burnley College. While both continue to primarily serve the district council area, their independence increasingly enables them to seek to operate across a larger territory. Calico's desire to expand into neighbouring districts strongly influenced the decision to re-brand the company, which was initially called Burnley and Padiham Housing. Similarly, Burnley College's widening catchment area partly results from it offering a range of higher education programmes on behalf of the University of Central Lancashire.

Finally, partnership structures such as LSPs require district councils to work principally with bodies that typically serve much larger geographical areas. The districts' partner organisations within LSPs do not necessarily have organisational structures or decision-making procedures relating specifically to Burnley or Harrogate district. While economic development is a key function for both district councils, there is a strong tendency for local economic development partnerships to be 'scaled upwards', with districts seeing a powerful rationale for collaboration that enables the achievement of greater 'critical mass'. The opportunities that such cooperation provides for local action are also reinforced by the preferences of Regional Development Agencies to work with sub-regional and sub-county partnerships, rather than single district partnerships. Again, the movement is towards a county-level structure. Thus, the East Lancashire Partnership was formed by the six East Lancashire districts in 1997 and, during 2005, was merged with the Lancashire West Partnership to form a single Lancashire Economic Partnership.

Figure 2.1a: The multi-scalar governance of Burnley

Scale	Public Body	Initial Index of closeness*	Direction of movement
Inter-Regional Two or more standard English regions	Accent Housing North British Housing Limited Burnley and Pendle Buses±	– – –	↑ ↑ ↑
Regional One standard English region	North West Development Agency Government Office for the North West North West Regional Assembly Arts Council North West North West Cultural Consortium	1: 448,951 – 1:84,122 – –	= = = = =
Sub-regional Two or more English counties	Cumbria and Lancashire Strategic Health Authority	1:146,333	=
County One standard English county	Lancashire County Council** Lancashire Constabulary† Lancashire Care NHS Trust† Calderstones NHS Trust† Lancashire Fire and Rescue Service† Lancashire Connexions Ltd† Lancashire Probation Service† Lancashire Ambulance Trust† Lancashire Learning and Skills Council† Lancashire Economic Partnership	1:14,917 1:83,219 1:117,894 1:354,278 – – 1:88,420 – – –	= ↑ ↑ = = = = = = ↑
Sub-county Two or more standard districts or unitary authorities	Burnley Pendle and Rossendale Primary Care Trust East Lancashire NHS Trust Elevate	1:17,414 1:37.036 –	↑ = =
District/Unitary One district or unitary authority	Burnley Borough Council Calico Housing Burnley College Burnley Action Partnership Initiative Burnley	1:1,989 1:4,972 1:5,594 – –	= ↑ ↑ = ↑

(Continued)

Figure 2.1a: The multi-scalar governance of Burnley (Continued)

Scale	Public Body	Initial Index of closeness*	Direction of movement
Sub-district Two or more parishes or neighbourhoods within a district or unitary authority	SRB 6	–	
Parish/ Neighbourhood One parish council or clearly defined neighbourhood	Parish councils Sure Start local programmes	– –	= =

Notes

* This initial index is a ratio of the representatives on the governing body of the organisation (pro rata for those above district level) to the population of the district.
± Part of the Blazefield Group, which owns 5 bus and coach companies across the North of England, including Harrogate and District
** Excludes unitary authorities of Blackpool and Blackburn with Darwen
† Includes unitary authorities of Blackpool and Blackburn with Darwen

Figure 2.1b: The multi-scalar governance of Harrogate

Scale	Public Body	Initial Index of closeness*	Direction of movement
Inter-Regional Two or more standard English regions	Accent Housing North British Housing Limited Harrogate and District Buses±	– – –	↑ ↑ ↑
Regional One standard English region	Yorkshire Forward Government Office for Yorkshire and the Humber Yorkshire and Humber Regional Assembly Arts Council Yorkshire Yorkshire Cultural Consortium	1: 332,220 – 1:134,675 – –	= = = = =
Sub-regional Two or more English counties	North and East Yorkshire and Northern Lincolnshire Strategic Health Authority Tees, East and North Yorkshire Ambulance Service	1:125,551 1:20,148	= =
County One standard English county	North Yorkshire County Council** North Yorkshire Constabulary† North Yorkshire Fire and Rescue Service† North Yorkshire Connexions Ltd† North Yorkshire Probation Service† North Yorkshire Learning and Skills Council†	1:7,698 1:44,162 – – 1:53,625 –	= ↑ = = = =

(Continued)

Figure 2.1b: The multi-scalar governance of Harrogate (Continued)

Scale	Public Body	Initial Index of closeness*	Direction of movement
Sub-county Two or more standard districts or unitary authorities	Craven, Harrogate and Rural District primary care trust	1:12,810	↑
District/Unitary One district or unitary authority	Harrogate Borough Council Harrogate College Harrogate LSP Harrogate & District NHS Foundation Trust	1:2,803 – – 1:4729††	= ↑ = =
Sub-district Two or more parishes or neighbourhoods within a district or unitary authority	SRB 6	–	
Parish/ Neighbourhood One parish council or clearly defined neighbourhood	Parish councils Sure Start local programmes	– –	= =

Notes
* This initial index is a ratio of the representatives on the governing body of the organisation (pro rata for those above district level) to the population of the district.
± Part of the Blazefield Group, which owns 5 bus and coach companies across the North of England, including Burnley and Pendle
† Includes unitary authority of City of York
** Excludes unitary authority of City of York
†† Includes 13 members of Board of Directors plus 19 members of Board of Governors

A number of policy dynamics are leading to the formation of increased capacity at the sub-district level, for instance parishes and neighbourhoods. These include numerous area-based initiatives, the drive to introduce neighbourhood management, and the quality council scheme to promote parish and town councils taking on additional roles. The (re-)establishment of Padiham Town Council in May 2002 is a clear illustration of a potential revitalisation of this lowest tier of local government. This increasing localisation is rarely a mechanism for bypassing district councils, but casts them in a new role. For instance, the introduction of neighbourhood management in Burnley involves the district council playing a greater role in managing and coordinating a wide range of initiatives targeted at, or devolved to, individual parts of the borough. Likewise, a possible bolstering of parish councils will have important implications in the Harrogate district, where there are 73 active town and parish councils.

This analysis indicates an overwhelming tendency for local governance to be 'scaled up', with a simultaneous, but probably weaker, tendency for some functions and interventions to be scaled down to a very local level. This is a continuing process, as shown by current national moves to create significantly larger police forces and primary care trusts (PCTs). Similarly, the initial recommendations of the Boundary Committee's review of the structure of local government in the North of England, since 'shelved' as a result of the decision to postpone referenda on regional assemblies, clearly favoured creating larger basic units of local government, underpinned by enhanced structures at the neighbourhood and/or parish scales. These dynamics raise important questions regarding the level of capacity remaining at the district scale, which we discuss further below. At the same time, the fragmentation of local governance, the 'silos' created by local agencies being funded and overseen by separate central government departments and agencies, and the lack of co-terminosity between the geographical areas that public agencies serve, have all led to concerted attempts to promote 'joined-up' government at the local level. This is most notable in the growth of partnership working, through statutory bodies (e.g. crime and disorder reduction partnerships) and non-statutory bodies (e.g. local strategic partnerships), as well as locally driven initiatives (e.g. Ripon City Partnership, Burnley and Padiham Community Alliance). In addition, programmes such as Elevate and the Housing Market Renewal Initiative (HMRI) in East Lancashire indicate, at least in theory, how a sub-regional programme can be delivered at a neighbourhood level, with the district council acting in a key strategic and policy role, as well as the crucial link between individual residents and a sub-regional policy agenda.

Despite such practice, however, the growing concentration of public agencies at the regional, county and sub-county scales, generally justified with reference to economies of scale, suggests that public agencies are becoming increasingly remote from local residents. Figures 2.1a and 2.1b also offer an initial (and admittedly crude) ranking of the 'closeness' of public agencies to the populations of Burnley and Harrogate. This index, based on the ratio between the pro rata number of representatives on each organisation's governing body and the district population, points to a clear pattern in both towns. Local residents are best served, in terms of the number of representatives per head, by their district councils. County councils also score relatively well and those LPSBs responsible for former district council functions also come near the top of the list. However, regional bodies are, by this measure, highly remote from local residents. Although a little artificial, this 'quantitative' measure of closeness appears to confirm common sense notions of which public bodies citizens have most contact with. These ideas are explored further, with reference to a wider range of indicators, in chapter 8.

2.4 Partnership working: Re-joining policy agendas?

As was noted in the typology of quangos, partnerships, zone boards and other local cross sector bodies have become increasingly prevalent in policy areas characterised by multi-agency working. In addition, local strategic partnerships (LSPs) have been established across the UK since 2001, with the aim of bringing together 'public, private, voluntary and community interests to provide a strategic framework within which partners can work together more effectively to secure the economic, environmental and social well being of the area and those who live and work there' (ODPM, 2005, p.5). LSPs oversee the production and implementation of community strategies and neighbourhood renewal strategies (in funded areas), but have discretion in how they organise themselves, the issues they focus on and how they conduct their business. A key difference between the LSPs in Burnley and Harrogate is that of financing. As Burnley is one of the 88 most deprived local authority areas, its LSP receives additional funding through the Neighbourhood Renewal Fund (NRF), currently £1.2 million per annum. One result of this is that Burnley's LSP is accountable for NRF expenditures to the Government Office for the North West, through the Neighbourhood Renewal Unit (NRU). However, in general it remains unclear to whom LSPs are accountable. When asked in interviews to identify where accountability lies, members of both LSPs provided a range of answers, from the ODPM/central government, to the Government Office, the council or 'the partners'. Many were altogether unclear, with one senior official noting 'I think that the lines of accountability are completely blurred, frankly'.

A recent ODPM evaluation report, while presenting an overall positive view of LSPs, notes mixed levels of engagement with public sector partners, which are often constrained by tensions between centrally driven priorities and local considerations. The report also points out that the success or failure of LSPs depends on the attitude and leadership of the local authority, and more specifically that 'aligning the LSP positively with councillors' roles and responsibilities is often a difficult issue but one which goes to the heart of issues of legitimacy and democracy in local governance' (ODPM 2005, p.8). The report also highlights difficulties in establishing effective governance structures and recommends that LSPs should clearly set out their mechanisms for accountability and that 'attention should be given ... to the relationship of the LSP to the democratic accountability of the local authority' (*ibid.*: 10).

More recently, the Audit Commission have produced a more critical report on partnerships, *Governing Partnerships: Bridging the Accountability Gap* (2005), which urges local public bodies to take a much harder look at the partnerships they are involved in, especially in terms of their accountability. The report notes that partnerships are a highly significant aspect of public service delivery, with around 5,500 partnerships in the UK accounting for approximately £4 billion of public expenditure. Although partnership working is seen to be valuable, the report points out that it brings risks as well as opportunities. Neither does partnership working automatically deliver 'value for money', suggesting that public bodies need to ask searching questions of the partnerships they are involved with. It also emphasises that problems in partnerships 'arise when governance and accountability are weak: leadership, decision-making, scrutiny and systems and processes such as risk management are all under-developed in partnerships' (Audit Commission 2005, pp.2–3). Thus, the report contends, clear accountability is needed between partners to produce better public accountability – especially when things go wrong. These issues surrounding accountability are explored in further detail in chapter 5.

2.5 The expanding role of the voluntary and community sector

In recent decades the role of the voluntary and community sector (VCS or 'Third Sector'[2]) in public service delivery at the local level has grown steadily. In a cross-cutting review of the sector in 2002, the then Chief Secretary to the Treasury, Paul Boateng, commented that the sector has key roles to play in the reform of public services, reinvigorating civic life and building a bridge between the needs of individuals in communities and the capacity of the state to improve their lives (HM Treasury 2002a, p.3). Following the review, the Treasury established *future*builders, a one-off investment fund of £125 million to build capacity in the sector through loans and grants. A later review of the sector, while noting the diversity of types of organisations within the sector, made strong claims concerning the advantages VCS organisations have over both public and private sector bodies in service delivery. These included being highly user-focused, having the skills and knowledge to tackle difficult social issues and meet complex personal needs, the ability to build users' trust, and to be flexible and offer joined-up service delivery (HM Treasury 2004, p.3). Both reviews also pointed to the potential for the Third Sector to operate in those circumstances where trust between individuals and communities has been eroded, or where 'democratic pressures' constrain the response of the public sector (for example in its provision to drug users or asylum seekers) (*ibid*.: p.30). As the government is encouraging the sector to expand its role in local service provision, it is another important aspect of the map of local service providers in the two towns.

The increased role of the voluntary and community sector is evident in both Burnley and Harrogate, albeit with significant differences between the two towns. In Burnley, the sector comprises upwards of 350 individual organisations, of which about half are clubs, societies and informal groupings and 42 per cent are registered charities. The sector accounts for an estimated 1,410 full-time and 1,050 part-time employees in Burnley and, taking into account 8,500 volunteering positions, is estimated to be worth £42 million to the local economy (WM Enterprise, 2003. See

---

2   In Burnley the sector is normally referred to as the voluntary, community and faith sector. For clarity, we use the government's term 'voluntary and community sector', which includes faith-based organisations.

also chapter 7 for further discussion).[3] VCS organisations draw their income from various sources, including grants from local public sector agencies, contracts for the delivery of public services, membership fees and donations and National Lottery grants. Of these, National Lottery funding is the most readily calculable flow of public money to the sector locally. Although the National Lottery database shows just over £2.5 million of 'Charitable Expenditure' Lottery grants have been made in Burnley up to November 2005, inclusion in the national Fair Share initiative indicates that Burnley has generally received a below-average proportion of total lottery funding.[4]

The sector is represented by three umbrella organisations locally: Burnley, Pendle and Rossendale Council for Voluntary Services (CVS), the Community Alliance and the Burnley Community Network. The most established and – in the eyes of some local organisations – the most traditional, is the local CVS, set up in 1935. In contrast, the other two umbrella groups are more recent and specifically represent VCS organisations in the Burnley district. The Community Alliance was constituted in 1999, while the Burnley Community Network, formed in 2002, is the most recent addition. There are strong links between the three bodies and, to a large extent, their co-existence represents a positive local response to the fragmented partnership and consultation arrangements that characterise local governance. Thus, the Community Alliance was created specifically to foster community involvement in regeneration initiatives locally, particularly the Single Regeneration Budget programme in Burnley. Likewise, the Burnley Community Network was specifically established to operate alongside Burnley's Local Strategic Partnership, the Burnley Action Partnership, and provide VCS input into the LSP's work.

The Harrogate VCS is represented by two umbrella organisations, Harrogate and District CVS and Ripon CVS, which are closely connected and, where possible, work jointly. The formation of two CVS branches is both historical, with Ripon established first, and a reflection of differences

---

3   There are strong grounds for questioning WM Enterprise's estimates for the size of the sector in Burnley, details of which are contained in Chapter 7.

4   The National Lottery Fair Share initiative provides guaranteed funding via the Community Fund and the New Opportunities Fund to 77 disadvantaged areas of the UK that have secured lower than average levels of lottery funding. Figures for lottery allocations to Burnley were obtained from: http://www.lottery.culture.gov.uk/PreSearch.asp?id= lauth_AB (as of 18-10-2005).

between the largely rural areas represented by the latter and the more urban areas represented by the former. The two CVS branches have upwards of 200 member organisations with nearly 3,500 volunteers, serving around 360,000 beneficiaries and an annual income of over £7.5m (Dowson et al., 2000. See chapter 7 for further discussion). The Borough Council has a Voluntary Sector Forum which acts as an interface between the sector and the Council, and provides core funding for a limited number of VCS organisations. However, North Yorkshire County Council Social Services Department has stronger links as it contracts many of the VCS organisations to provide services. Harrogate has eighty per cent more lottery funding than Burnley (£28m compared to £15.3m), including twice as much in 'Charitable Expenditure' grants (£4.9m compared to £2.5m). Harrogate has also secured over twice as many awards in number (532 compared to 240) (ibid.). Despite this, Dowson et al.'s study indicated some scepticism about lottery funding for the sector partly because Harrogate lacked areas of 'deprivation.'

2.6 Locality: The changing position and politics of district councils

As noted above, both borough councils operate at scales significantly smaller than those served by most other public sector agencies and partnerships operating locally. Moreover, there is a strong drift of functions upwards and an apparent partial counterbalance to this tendency provided by a pull to more local areas, through a resurgence of parish councils and the growing emphasis placed upon neighbourhood management, rather than a bolstering of the district councils' roles. The analysis clearly suggests that the district tier is being squeezed, a scenario also highlighted by the progressive loss of functions at the district scale (see Case Study 2.1). Indeed, virtually all interviewees viewed the continuation of district councils within a two-tier local government structure as unsustainable. In the words of one Burnley Council representative:

The borough council [is] *dead keen on directly elected regional assemblies,* [its] *got a big policy position on that, and* [its] *also dead keen on becoming a unitary authority based on bigger boundaries. So,* [its] *dead keen on not existing anymore.*

Case Study 2.1: The Burnley Borough Council website (Accessed December 2004)

Burnley Borough Council's website provides a '12 bar' menu down the left hand side. Of these 12 bars, seven constitute key policy areas – education, environment, health, housing, leisure, social care, transport and streets. By following these bars, the user will be directed to Lancashire County Council as the key service provider in three instances (education, social care, transport) and to the Primary Care Trust in another (health). In a fifth case, housing, the user is told that the Borough no longer has any housing stock. Only the bars for environment and leisure navigate the user through to services provided primarily by Burnley Borough Council itself.

One the one hand, this use of the Council's website to route the visitor consistently elsewhere, captures the removal of functions from district councils such as Burnley. If Burnley County Borough had had a website 50 years ago, it would have provided local residents with information on what their local council was doing in relation to most, if not all, of the functions listed above and probably several more besides. On the other hand, it can be seen as underlining the continued significance of district councils, and their role as the first port of call for many local residents. Frequently confused about who provides what services, local people will often approach the 'closest' unit of local government in the first instance. Indeed, interviews with elected councillors indicate that many local residents believe that Burnley District Council continues to have a role in health, education, housing and public transport.

At the time of writing, the future of the district tier is unclear. Although put briefly on hold, following the *de facto* abandonment of the government's policy of moving towards elected regional authorities, the government announced that the issue of local government structure would be re-visited during 2006. In line with many of the conclusions reached by previous reviews, interviewees from across the public, private and voluntary sectors raised concerns about the capacity of district councils to deliver services effectively due to their limited abilities to achieve economies of scale and critical mass. Indeed, throughout the research, virtually no challenge to the case for amalgamating district councils was offered from any quarter, reflecting the historical dynamics of policy debate outlined in chapter 1. However, there was one significant dissenting view, provided by David Curry, the Conservative MP for Skipton and Ripon, who served as Minister for Local Government from 1993–97:

I think people's loyalty is a lot more to the district council than to the county council [...] Britain is very underrepresented by councils; we have fewer councils in this country. In many ways the district councils are still very remote. I'm inclined to say we need more councils, and more elected councillors, and we need to push it on to American style democracy, the parish and the community.

Although this is clearly a minority view, there are strong grounds to support it, as we shall see in chapter 10. Nonetheless, local government interviewees tended to be well-versed in the arguments in favour of larger, unitary authorities. Both district councils have retained their policy positions, adopted in light of the Boundary Committee review of 2003–04, stating their clear preference for amalgamation with surrounding districts in order to create larger, unitary authorities. Moreover, this viewpoint found much support among several interviewees beyond the respective district councils, who voiced concerns about the quality of elected members and council officers at the district scale. While these concerns are not supported by the Comprehensive Performance Assessments for the two councils, there is some evidence that the 'upward drift' in local governance applies to personnel as well as to functions. While a full analysis has not been possible, numerous instances were cited by interviewees of senior district council officers and members moving on to higher-tier local authorities or roles in other public sector bodies. The extent of this trend, and whether it represents a significant loss of skills at the district scale is questionable. However, it does reinforce the significance of district councils as a real-life 'training-ground' for those seeking a representative, and generally better remunerated, role in larger public bodies. As one interviewee described it:

With people moving on to the governing structures of larger organisations, like NHS bodies for instance, it tends to be a one-way traffic [...] the people that make those appointments regard, I think, having served on a local council as proof that you are capable of operating in that sort of environment.

Despite the apparent consensus in favour of creating larger unitary authorities, even within the existing district councils' boundaries, there is evidence that local people feel aggrieved by a perceived 'remoteness' of council decisions affecting their areas. Significant tensions exist between towns and neighbourhoods within the two districts. The existing geographical scale of the Harrogate district, at over 500 square miles, is already a source of tension between areas with distinctive identities, although it is at least significantly smaller than the territory covered by North Yorkshire County Council, a territory described by one interviewee as 'three times the size of Luxembourg'. In the case of Burnley, in particular, there is clear evidence of residents mobilising to challenge council decisions on a neighbourhood and even street-basis, a tendency described by one interviewee as a proliferation of 'the ultra-micro, local groups'. In some instances, such dynamics have been seen as virtually paralysing local decision-making, as one Burnley interviewee explained:

One of the problems that we've had in Burnley has been this tension between different neighbourhoods and particularly about the direction of spend. And some people predating the BNP have used that focused spending as an opportunity to say "if they're having it, why can't we have it" and that has been a theme of local politics for the last 5 or 6 years in Burnley. And I think a weaknesses in the political leadership has been to follow that line, instead of saying "look we're here for Burnley as a whole, we're not here for Burnley Wood, Duke Bar, Stoneyholme, Daneshouse, Accrington Road [...] we want to see the town prosper". But I expect that some of that is inhibited by the funding requirements of SRB, and European area-based initiatives.

During the late 1990s, regeneration schemes and other area-based initiatives became a significant factor in increased intra-borough tensions in Burnley. During this period, an independent councillor raised questions about the apparent targeting of funds on wards with a high percentage of Asian households (Brooks, 2002). Issues about the distribution of regeneration funds and council grants subsequently became a key element of the BNP's local campaign. The attention paid to this issue arguably reflects a widespread misconception about the scale of regeneration funds; in reality, area-based initiatives account for a very small proportion of total public expenditure in any locality. However, the visibility of such programmes, as well as their tendency to apply strictly within what many regard as apparently arbitrary boundaries, often makes them a key focus of local political conflict. There are currently 18 government sponsored area-based initiatives operating in Burnley, three times the number in Harrogate (see Fig 2.3). This is not an indicator of a relative lack of area-based initiatives and partnership working in Harrogate as this refers only to externally-funded schemes, which are mostly targeted at areas with high levels of deprivation and for which Harrogate simply does not qualify. Nonetheless, this contrast is highly significant, as such initiatives tend to have a multi-dimensional impact upon local politics. Not only can area-based initiatives become a focal point for local political conflict, they also draw local authorities into additional sets of relationships to government offices in the regions and central government departments in Whitehall. As we discuss in chapter 4, such relationships can cut both ways in relation to local autonomy.

2.7 Conclusion

This chapter has mapped out the range and scales of public bodies operating in the two towns, an exercise which indicates both an increasing level of fragmentation of service provision and an overall 'scaling up' of local governance. As such, we may describe local democracy as being subjected to twin pressures of both 'moving out' and 'moving up' from the district councils that had previously been the undisputed centres of local political power. The chapter has also highlighted the expansion of quangos, the increasing role being played by the voluntary, community and private sectors and, by extension, the growing significance of partnerships. These trends raise three central issues for local democracy that are explored in subsequent chapters. First, the shifts identified raise questions about both the representativeness and accountability of local service providers to the public they serve, issues that we explore in more detail in chapter 5. Second, the fragmented nature of local governance and the shift of power away from Burnley and Harrogate town halls, reiterates our concern that such towns may lack any clear source offering the capacity and leadership required to develop a 'big picture' for their respective futures. Finally, the analysis presented here again raises the question of whether arguments for increasing the size and scale of local service providers, rooted in assumptions about economies of scale, may come at the cost of local democratic control and public engagement.

Figure 2.3: Area-based initiatives (ABIs) operating in Burnley and Harrogate

Name of ABI	Sponsoring Department(s)	Burnley	Harrogate
Building Safer Communities	Home Office	●	●
Capital Modernisation Fund to Assist Small Retailers in Deprived Areas	Home Office	●	
Community Cohesion Pathfinder	Department for Education and Skills/ Home Office	●	
Excellence in Cities	Department for Education and Skills	●	
Fair Share	Big Lottery Fund/Department for Culture, Media and Sport	●	
Framework for Regional Employment and Skills Action	Department for Education and Skills/ Department of Work and Pensions/ Department of Trade and Industry	●	●
Healthy Living Centres	Big Lottery Fund	●	
Healthy Schools Programme	Department for Education and Skills/ Department of Health	●	●
Market Renewal Pathfinder	ODPM	●	
Market Towns Initiative	Countryside Agency/Department for Forestry, Rural Affairs and Agriculture/ Regional Development Agencies	● (Padiham)	●
Neighbourhood Renewal Fund	ODPM	●	
Neighbourhood Wardens	ODPM	●	
New Entrepreneur Scholarships	Department for Education and Skills	●	
Single Community Programme	ODPM	●	
Single Regeneration Budget	ODPM	●	●
Step-up	Department for Work and Pensions	●	
Sure Start	Department for Education and Skills/ Department for Work and Pensions	●	
Youth Music Action Zones	–	●	●
TOTAL	–	18	6

Note: The table refers to area-based initiatives funded by central government departments/agencies or the national lottery. It does not provide an overview of all area-based initiatives in the two boroughs. It should also be noted that the geographical scales at which the initiatives operate vary enormously, and that not all of these ABIs have been in operation simultaneously.

3
Votes Count, Resources Decide

Stein Rokkan's aphorism – 'votes count, resources decide' – is a keen reminder that inequalities in resources can undermine political equality. Tackling social exclusion and other 'wicked issues' ... will only occur if resources can be mobilised that are commensurate with the problem-solving tasks that these issues entail.

Stone, 2002, p.13

3.1 Introduction

Stein Rokkan's famous phrase 'votes count, resources decide' points to a crucial issue for local democracy – the significance of financial, organisational and social resources to political outcomes. Following on from the previous chapter's analysis of the range of public bodies operating in the two districts, this chapter presents and analyses data on the relative levels of public spending by these bodies. It also considers the significance of another, unevenly distributed, local resource – social capital – to the operation of local democracy. Although the data present some limitations, a number of key issues are highlighted in relation to local public expenditure. In both districts, only around half of all public spending is under the control of elected bodies, and district councils account for only five per cent of all local public spending. That unelected bodies account for a significant share of total public expenditure, and by extension public employment, in both Burnley and Harrogate is perhaps unsurprising given the previously noted 'scaling up' of functions. However, evidence on public perceptions indicates that most residents view district councils as having far wider responsibilities for local service provision and public spending. Moreover, the second half of the chapter suggests that, given the apparent lack of direct democratic control over around fifty per cent of local public spending, wealth and social capital are increasingly influential in directing local public services and public spending.

3.2 Estimating the relative significance of elected and unelected bodies

Here we provide an assessment of the relative importance, in terms of public spending, of each distinctive type of public body in Burnley and Harrogate respectively. We have taken spending data for public bodies from their annual summary of accounts and used this to produce a rough map of public expenditure in the two towns. To create this rough map, we first identified the principal public agencies operating regionally, sub-regionally and locally along with their respective total budgets and total staff base. Then an estimate was made of the proportion of each organisation's expenditure in the relevant districts, based in most instances on the simplistic and problematic assumption that spending is distributed on an equal pro-rata basis across the territory that each organisation serves. In two cases, Lancashire County Council and Lancashire Police, a more precise calculation of district level spending was made available by the agencies concerned. Finally, using the relevant parts of the typology put forward in chapter 2, each organisation was assigned to one of four categories: i) local authority; ii) regional quango; iii) local public spending body; or iv) partnerships, zone boards and other public sector bodies.

Aside from the difficulty of establishing a robust means of calculating local public expenditure (Bramley *et al.*, 1998), the data presented here have a number of further limitations. First, we were unable to obtain complete information for all the bodies identified. Second, wherever possible data for the 2003/04 financial year were used, with data for earlier years being used where this did not prove possible. Third, diversity in presentation of public sector agencies accounts meant that determining the total expenditure of each body was not always straightforward. Fourth, adding together the total budgets of the various public bodies identified would in a number of cases involve significant double-counting of expenditure. For example, in the health sector the budgets of strategic health authorities and primary care trusts are primarily allocated to individual health care trusts or used to 'purchase' specific services from them. Fifth, using assumptions of equal pro-rata public spending to determine the approximate level of total public spending in Burnley and Harrogate is clearly a crude measure, and should be regarded as providing only an initial indication of the extent to which there is local democratic control over public expenditure. Finally, all calculations exclude local spending accounted for by the Benefits Agency, which will constitute a major spender in both districts.

Despite these methodological limitations, the results (Tables 3.1– 3.8), reveal a number of important characteristics common to public spending and governance of both towns, as well as some important differences. It is evident in both towns that the district councils are in many ways the 'poor relations' in the two-tier local government structure. The two district councils have similar net budgets: £15m in Burnley and £20m in Harrogate, based on the ODPM's 'formula spending share'. On this measure, as Table 3.9 shows, the two district councils account for just 5 per cent of local government expenditure within their own boundaries. However, Harrogate's gross budget, comprising total revenue expenditure, is over £86 million and, under this definition, accounts for a much higher proportion of the county share (23 per cent) than in Burnley (7 per cent). Harrogate's £86 million gross budget arises from a combination of unique local circumstances. The Harrogate district has a larger population than Burnley and, unlike Burnley, has retained its housing stock, which generates significant rental income. Furthermore, additional income is generated by Harrogate International Centre, wholly owned by the district council, but operating as an 'arm's length trading division'. Once due account is taken of the size of Harrogate's population in comparison to Burnley's, it is notable that the former operates on a much smaller level of service spending per head of population: £130 compared to £176.

Table 3.1: Elected local authorities serving Burnley, 2003/04

Name of public body	Area served	No. of staff	Total budget (£000s)	Approx. pro rata staff	Approx. spend in Burnley (£000s)
Burnley Borough Council	Burnley District	700	*Net*: 15,600[1] *Gross*: 20,100[2]	700	*Net*: 15,600 *Gross*: 20,100
Lancashire County Council	Lancashire County	38,000	1,080,000	2,997	99,000[3]
Town and parish councils (8)	8 parishes within Burnley*	–	–	–	–
TOTALS		38,700	1,095,600	3,697	114,600 (119,100)

Notes
* *Only active town and parish councils have been included. These are Briercliffe, Cliviger, Dunnockshaw and Clowbridge, Habergham Eaves, Hapton, Igenthill, Padiham and Worsthorne. Their spending and staffing are negligible.*
1 *Based on ODPM's formula spending share (FSS).*
2 *Total revenue expenditure.*
3 *Estimate provided by Lancashire County Council.*

Table 3.2: Regional quangos serving Burnley, 2003/04

Name of public body	Area served	No. of staff	Total budget (£000s)	Approx. pro rata staff	Approx. spend in Burnley (£000s)
North West Development Agency	North West England	350	311,000	5	4,136
Government Office North West*	North West England	402	14,500	5	181
North West Regional Assembly	North West England	78	2,326	1	31
TOTALS		830	327,826	11	4,348

Note
* *Figures are for 2001/02. The figure given is for running costs only, to avoid double counting – much of GONW budget is transferred to other bodies (Hansard 8th January 2001, Column 383w)*

Table 3.3: Local public spending bodies serving Burnley, 2003/04

Name of public body	Area served	No. of staff	Total budget (£000s)	Approx. pro rata staff	Approx. spend in Burnley (£000s)
Cumbria and Lancashire Health Authority	Cumbria and Lancashire	100	438,176	5	20,594
Lancashire Care NHS Trust	Lancashire	2,500	117,449	158	9,226
Calderstones NHS Trust	North West England, but primarily Lancashire and Greater Manchester	1,390	34,301	32	1,613
East Lancashire Hospitals Trust	East Lancashire	7,000	231,430	1,208	39,944
Burnley, Pendle and Rossendale PCT	Burnley Pendle and Rossendale	1,300	259,091	477	95,112
Burnley College	Burnley	*326	**12,700	326	12,700
Calico Housing	Burnley	200	12,561	200	***15,224
Lancashire Constabulary	Lancashire	5,289	284,700	335	26,000
Lancashire Probation Service	Lancashire	550	18,600	35	1,176
TOTALS		18,329	1,396,308	2,776	221,589 ††(170,806)

Notes
* 1999
**2002/03
*** Calico registered a trading deficit in 2003/04, financed by borrowing
†† Total calculated to minimise double counting by subtracting from the total the figures for:
Lancashire Care NHS Trust, Calderstones NHS Trust and East Lancashire Hospital Trust

Table 3.4: Partnerships, zone boards and other cross-sectoral bodies serving Burnley

Name of public body	Area served	No. of staff	Total budget (£000s)	Approx. pro rata staff	Approx. spend in Burnley (£000s)
Burnley Action Partnership	Burnley	4	1,200	4	1,200
Elevate*	East Lancashire	–	50,000	–	7,500
SRB6	Brunshaw, Trinity, Bankhall & Rosegrove	–	2,857	–	2,857
Sure Start programmes (3)**	See note below.	–	–	–	–
TOTALS			54,057		11,557

Notes
* Elevate's full programme commenced 2004/05
** Sure Start programmes are located in Daneshouse & Stoneyholme, Duke Bar – Burnley Wood, and South West Burnley

Table 3.5: Elected local authorities serving Harrogate, 2003/04

Name of public body	Area served	No. of staff	Total budget (£000s)	Approx. pro rata staff	Approx. spend in Harrogate (£000s)
Harrogate Borough Council	Harrogate District	1,220	*Net*: 20,031[1] *Gross*: 86,400[2]	1,220	*Net*: 20,031 *Gross*: 86,400
North Yorkshire County Council	North Yorkshire County	30,000	436,000	7,971	115,829
Town and parish councils (73)	73 parishes within Harrogate	–	–	–	–
TOTALS		31,220	522,400	9,191	135,860 (202,229)

1 Based on ODPM's formula spending share (FSS).
2 Total revenue expenditure.

Table 3.6: Regional quangos serving Harrogate, 2003/04

Name of public body	Area served	No. of staff	Total budget (£000s)	Approx. pro rata staff	Approx. spend in Harrogate (£000s)
Yorkshire Forward	Yorkshire and Humberside	–	300,000	–	9,111
Government Office Yorkshire and Humberside	Yorkshire and Humberside	435	12,800	13.22	388
Yorkshire and Humber Regional Assembly	Yorkshire and Humberside	45	2,577	1.36	78
TOTALS		480	315,377	14.58	9,577

Table 3.7: Local public spending bodies serving Harrogate, 2003/04

Name of public body	Area served	No. of staff	Total budget (£000s)	Approx. pro rata staff	Approx. spend in Harrogate (£000s)
North and East Yorkshire and Northern Lincolnshire SHA	North and East Yorkshire, North and North East Lincolnshire	84	65,821	7.85	6,154
Craven, Harrogate and Rural District PCT	Craven and Harrogate	736	188,099	543	138,886
Harrogate Health Care NHS Trust	Harrogate	1,809	67,554	1,809	67,554
Harrogate College	Harrogate	*255	**8,255		8,225
North Yorkshire Police	North Yorkshire†	2438	93,453	492	18,838

(Continued)

Table 3.7: Local public spending bodies serving Harrogate, 2003/04 (Continued)

Name of public body	Area served	No. of staff	Total budget (£000s)	Approx. pro rata staff	Approx. spend in Harrogate (£000s)
North Yorkshire Probation Area	North Yorkshire†	***200	–	40	–
Tees, East and North Yorkshire Ambulance Service	Tees, East and North Yorkshire†	1,432	44,350	150	1,233
TOTALS		5,067	459,277	1,233	236,087 ††(168,533)

Notes
† Includes unitary authority
* 1995-96, full-time equivalent
** 1995 figures
*** Estimate from website
†† Total calculated to minimise double counting, by subtracting from the total the figures for Harrogate Health Care NHS Trust

Table 3.8: Partnerships, zone boards and other cross-sectoral bodies serving Harrogate, 2003/04

Name of public body	Area served	No. of staff	Total budget (£000s)	Approx. pro rata staff	Approx. spend in Harrogate (£000s)
North Yorkshire Youth Offending Team	North Yorkshire†	202	1,973	41	397
Local Strategic Partnership	Harrogate	0	0	0	0
SRB (Ripon City Partnership 2000-05)	Ripon	–	2,600	–	2,600
TOTALS		202	4,573	41	2,997

Note
† Includes unitary authority

Table 3.9: Estimates of local authority expenditure as a total of all public expenditure in Burnley and Harrogate

	A. Total public spending in district*	Total county and district council spending as % of A	District council total revenue expenditure as % of A	District council FSS** as % of A
Burnley	294.2 million	40%	7%	5%
Harrogate	380.3 million	53%	23%	5%

Notes
*The figure for total public expenditure has been adjusted so as to minimise double-counting of local health expenditure and includes the full income/turnover of the respective district councils. Partnerships, zone boards and other bodies have not been included as the budgets of these organisations are often held by local authorities.
**Formula Spending Share – a formula representing spending needs which is the main determinant of the Revenue Support Grant (RSG) and includes data on the demographic, social and physical characteristics of an area.

Table 3.10: Total budget for core services (FSS), per head of population, Burnley and Harrogate, 2004/05

	Burnley	Harrogate
Service expenditure (FSS)	£15,789,000	£20,031,000
Population	89,000	154,000
Service expenditure per head	£176	£130

The share of public expenditure by LPSBs in both towns clearly rivals the share under the control of democratically elected bodies. This is particularly evident in Burnley, for which we have more complete data on LPSBs. As Table 3.9 illustrates, 53 per cent of public expenditure identified in Harrogate is under the control of elected local councils, compared to just 40 per cent in Burnley. If restricted to core service expenditure (represented by FSS), as little as five per cent of local public spending is accounted for by the district councils. In the case of Burnley, the district council is estimated to be only the sixth largest spender in the district and has a core budget not much larger than two bodies it was previously responsible for – Calico Housing and Burnley College. Harrogate's own position as the third largest spender in the district partly arises from the fact that it has not transferred its housing stock, as has already been noted.[5]

Based on these calculations, regional quangos do not account for a significant share of public expenditure or public employment in the two towns: we estimate that they comprise in the region of 1.5 to 2.5 per cent of local spending. However, a number of regional bodies, including the Environment Agency and the Countryside Agency, have not been included in the analysis, due to difficulties obtaining accurate data. The data are therefore likely to represent an under-estimate of the significance of regional quangos. While the data on partnerships, zone boards and other cross-sectoral bodies remains incomplete, it is clear that they have a far larger role in Burnley than in Harrogate, as was shown in the list of area based initiatives in the two towns in Figure 2.3.

It is clear then that in both towns a substantial proportion of public spending is in the hands of unelected bodies. Most of these are funded through central government departments and can thus be said to have an indirect link to the democratic process. Nonetheless, in terms of local democracy, their governing bodies, unlike elected local authorities, are not democratically accountable to the communities they serve. In later chapters, we discuss how some of these bodies employ other aspects of the democratic mix to provide some level of representation, participation and consultation for citizens in their areas. Elected local authorities employ a similar mix of methods to engage with their communities, but remain unique in that their governing body – the members of the elected council – can be (and often are) dismissed by the people they serve. As we show in chapters 9, there is a clear tendency within the local media in both towns to focus on covering the business of the district council rather than that of the county council.

There is also strong evidence of a huge mismatch between the resources local agencies control and the attention they are respectively accorded by local residents. National survey evidence indicates that, in areas with two-tier local government structures, there is a relatively high degree of confusion amongst the public over who is responsible for the provision of particular local services. As Table 3.11 indicates, depending on the function in question, anything between a third and two-thirds of local residents are unable to specify correctly the tier of government

---

5   Harrogate Borough Council estimated spending on housing and housing services for 2003/04 is approximately £19.3m (Harrogate Borough Council, 2003).

responsible. Thus, 14 per cent of those surveyed thought schools were a district responsibility, 15 per cent plumped for 'central government', while 65 per cent correctly answered that it is a county responsibility (highlighted in bold). This degree of confusion can result in the majority of the public viewing 'The Council' (effectively meaning the district council) as the primary public service spender and provider in an area, regardless of whether this matches the actual levels of spending and service provision. The problem is, without doubt, exacerbated by the fact that, while district councils bill local residents for council tax, they subsequently re-allocate around 80 per cent of this revenue to other bodies – primarily county councils and county-level police forces.

The tendency for local residents to be unclear about where service responsibilities lie is particularly evident in Burnley, where many district councillors report that 50 per cent or more of approaches made to them by their constituents concern county council functions. These factors place elected members (and to a lesser degree, officers) under public scrutiny through the local media and through public awareness of 'The Council' to the extent that one councillor referred to it being a 'goldfish bowl life.' While the local media have made attempts to counter such misconceptions, their scant coverage of county council issues (see chapter 9) is likely to sustain popular misconceptions, and there is little indication that the chief executives or boards of the non-elected public bodies in the two towns are placed under a similar level of public and media scrutiny.[6] At the same time, coverage of local issues in the letters pages of the local press is a further indicator and driver of the popular confusion that sour relationships with local politicians and council officers. As one long-standing councillor noted: 'When I read the Burnley Express and read letters saying that Burnley Council is responsible for education policy, or for education failures, it drives me around the bend'.

---

6   There are, of course, important exceptions. The front page of the *Burnley Express* on November 8th, 2005 carried the names and photographs of the East Lancashire Hospital NHS Trust Board, urging them not to move services, such as intensive care, from Burnley to Blackburn.

Table 3.11: Public perception of service provision by district, county or central government

	District %	County %	Central Government %
Schools	14	**65**	15
Council housing	**62**	27	4
Support for elderly/mental health/ disabled people	39	**35**	16
Public transport	28	45	14
Refuse collection	**69**	22	4
Pre-school and nursery education	26	**44**	15
Libraries	27	**63**	3
Sports and leisure facilities	**57**	29	3
Social security payments	13	17	**60**
Fire service	16	**60**	18
Trading standards	16	**34**	32
Parking/ public car parks	**66**	23	4
Protecting children at risk from harm	19	**39**	26
Looking after roads, pavements and street lights	48	44	6
Household waste sites (tips)	59	**32**	2

Note
The tier of government that is actually responsible in each case is highlighted in bold, i.e. Districts are solely responsible for just four of these functions: council housing; refuse collection; sports and leisure facilities; and parking/public car parks.
Source: ODPM 2002b: 10

3.3 Wealth, social capital and democracy

As a rough rule of thumb, if you belong to no groups but decide to join one, you cut your risk of dying over the next year in half. If you smoke and belong to no groups, it's a toss-up statistically whether you should stop smoking or start joining.

Putnam, 2000, p.331

Rokkan's observation that 'votes count, resources decide' was made in the mid-1960s and was used, in the main, to refer to organisational resources. Yet, had Rokkan been writing more recently, he would almost certainly have also made reference to the importance of personal and group resources signified as 'social capital'. Although the meaning and usefulness of the concept of social capital has been widely debated, following Putnam (1995, p.67), we may define it as 'features of social organisation such as networks, norms and social trust that facilitate coordination and cooperation for mutual benefit.' Thus, for Putnam, communities 'rich' in social capital are characterised by members who engage in mutually beneficial collective action. Social capital, thus defined, can operate in different communities in a positive fashion to encourage civic engagement and promote more effective community development and governance. As the above quotation from Putnam illustrates, it is even claimed that civic participation will significantly benefit an individual's health.

Subsequently, it has been proposed that social capital can be formed and expanded, especially in communities where it is lacking, in order to transform them (Stone, 2002). However, there may also be a less positive side to social capital, using this definition. As it refers to 'networks, norms and social trust' it may also be a source of social power and influence for those who are within these networks, share (largely) the same norms and have existing bonds of social trust. At the same time, this may make it difficult for those outside to enter into the network and may thereby marginalise their interests. This may produce a system of local governance mechanisms which reflect the norms, values and interests of a relatively narrow social network or loosely established local elites. While we have not had the time or resources to complete a detailed analysis of whether this is the case in either Burnley or Harrogate, we can point to a set of indicative findings which suggest that social capital, as discussed here, is potentially influential in local governance in the two towns. Some of these issues are discussed in more detail in subsequent chapters.

A regular theme in interviews conducted for this research with individuals from a range of public bodies and voluntary and community organisations were the problems associated with what they referred to as 'the usual suspects.' This term was used in three ways. First, it was suggested that consultation and community engagement processes often faced the problem of consistently gaining responses from, or engagement with, the same groups of people within the community. Other groups (most notably the young and members of ethnic minorities) were defined as being very difficult to connect with. We discuss this aspect of 'the usual suspects' problem in more detail in Chapter 8. However, it is clear that if consultation or engagement processes are failing to include particular groups of people within communities, then their voices and views will not even potentially influence the formulation and implementation of policy. Likewise, if these processes are dominated, even if unintentionally, by groups of people from a relatively narrow demographic range, then it is likely that their voices and views will have an unrepresentative influence on policy processes.

The second way in which the term, 'the usual suspects', was used was captured in an acronym coined by one interviewee – SOFA or 'same old faces again.' This particular interviewee was pointing out a problem with community engagement as, in his area, he could name the fifteen or so people from 'the community' that turned up regularly to meetings or events or who were most closely engaged with the processes as 'community representatives.' Similar concerns were expressed by those individuals attempting to get representative groups of people on residents or tenants committees. One Harrogate councillor mentioned that she felt that the pressure for representativeness on their tenants' forum was coming from the government rather than the tenants themselves. She also felt that, even if the forum members were elected, it would be highly unlikely that they would become more representative of Harrogate's tenants, as it would probably be the same people who would stand for election.

That only a narrow range of people are prepared to take part in these formal processes parallels wider problems of a general absence of civic engagement among up to fifty per cent of the population (see chapter 7). Evidently, the scale of non-engagement represents a mixture of citizen apathy and, for specific sections of the population, the existence of significant barriers to participation, including language, cultural norms and values, disabilities and other factors. The paucity of local residents willing and able to seek involvement in local governance can, unsurprisingly, result in the same person being recruited to serve in multiple roles, as is shown in the case study below.

The third connotation of the 'usual suspects' is the way in which the 'same old faces' are members of a wide variety of boards and committees across a range of service areas. We discuss this aspect of 'the usual suspects' issue in more detail in chapter 5, where we examine the various methods of recruitment of individuals to the governing boards of public bodies, and how, and to whom, these governing boards are accountable.

Case Study 3.1: Brian Fenn, Burnley Wood Community Action Group

Brian is a retired lorry driver, who described himself as not well educated, but who has recently taken courses at the local further education college. He had no background in community activism, until he became involved in the Burnley Wood Community Action Group, which was formed in October 2003 in response to the Council's Neighbourhood Action Plan. Brian now chairs the organisation. He described how, once he had become chair of BWCAG, he became involved with, and was elected to positions on, other local bodies. He helped to establish the Police And Communities Together meetings in Burnley Wood, which helped BWCAG to get funding for improved street lighting in the area. He became BCWAG's representative on Burnley Community Network, joined the Community Alliance (and later became finance director) and was invited onto the Burnley Action Partnership (the LSP) and Burnley Regeneration Management Committee. He is also a community member of the Council's Housing Scrutiny Committee and Masterplan Committee, is on the Neighbourhood Management panel and is involved with the East Lancashire Community Health Group. He has attended Lancashire Police Authority meetings, as a community representative, and has also established close relations with the local police. He is vice-chair of the Board of Governors of Whittlefield Primary School, and has been appointed shadow governor to two new schools being built under the Building Schools for the Future initiative. Brian, through his work with BWCAG, also has close links with the Accent Housing Group, who provided one of their properties for use as a drop-in community centre. He has also provided written evidence to the House of Commons ODPM Select Committee, and is regularly asked for comments on community and regeneration issues by the local media.

3.4 Conclusion

From the financial mapping of public bodies undertaken, it is clear that a substantial proportion of local public spending is in the hands of unelected bodies. As we detail in chapter 8, many of these bodies are using a variety of public consultation and engagement processes to seek to enhance their accountability to the people they serve. However, as we explore in more detail in chapters 5 and 6, their governing bodies are largely unelected and are usually accountable upward to central government targets. The increasingly narrow range of people being recruited to the governing boards of these bodies raises further questions about the extent to which this narrowness is influencing the formation and implementation of policy locally. We have also argued that the uneven distribution of social capital can have a significant impact upon local decision-making, particularly in light of the diversification of the local democratic mix. In some instances, social capital becomes little more than a foundation for so called NIMBYism. For instance, the social capital of particular individuals and groups, plus their abilities to access the 'right' people and information, can become highly evident when it comes to mobilising protests against particular local planning applications. We explore these concerns in more detail in the chapters which follow.

4

Between the Devil and the Deep Blue Sea?:

Can there be local democracy without local autonomy?

Targets are the reduction to absurdity of the centralist state. They are the tool of Lenin's Gosplan ... All the checks and balances in the constitution: local democracy, professional autonomy, parliamentary oversight, civil service independence, all are outflanked by the new control.

Simon Jenkins, 2005

4.1 Introduction

As we noted in chapter 1, there are a number of tensions inherent to the relationship between local democracy and local autonomy. This chapter focuses on a set of common pressures faced by all local public agencies that, we argue, militate against local autonomy and, by extension, local democracy. Drawing on detailed fieldwork in the two case study locations, the overwhelming factor that we identify as undermining local autonomy is the universal introduction of centrally-defined performance criteria and targets, driven in part by attempts to define and achieve national standards. This target culture, moreover, has been applied following decades of progressively tighter controls over local public spending, such as the tendency to 'ring-fence' elements of budgets, and to allocate funds on a competitive basis for specifically defined purposes. We also highlight that there is a pattern of national government engaging in persistent reforms of the administrative and management structures of local public bodies.

Yet, there is a great paradox to this observed centralisation. The forms of centrally-driven change identified clearly diminish local autonomy, yet they have taken place alongside greater central requirements for local public bodies to ascertain and respond to the views of local residents and users. Given this context, this chapter makes two principal arguments. First, current frameworks of central–local relations undermine basic notions of local autonomy and local democracy. They are also inherently flawed: citizens' expectations are raised, while the capacity of local agencies to respond is diminished. Second, local democracy requires a far greater degree of local autonomy than currently exists. Local democracy can only be enhanced if there is not only an acceptance, but also a celebration, of variations in services between different localities.

4.2 Local democracy and the 'target culture'

The balance between central government direction and local control has been a constant theme of local government debates since the late 1970s (Dearlove, 1979) and the same themes can even be traced back to the 1950s (West Midland Study Group, 1956). Moreover, despite the widespread currency of the concept of the 'new localism' in contemporary debate, growing concerns have been expressed in recent years regarding the extent of central control and the limits on local autonomy. However, today's concerns about diminishing local autonomy can be distinguished from those expressed in previous decades in that they are heard not only from local authorities, but from all bodies delivering local public services. Interviewees in local councils, health care trusts, police forces, further education colleges and a range of other local bodies consistently pointed to similar mechanisms that have served to increase central control over the local delivery of services. At the heart of this *de facto* 'new centralism' has been the proliferation of centrally defined targets for local authorities, NHS bodies, police forces and other organisations. As such, the following comment was made during an interview concerning policing, but with minor amendments could have been taken from any number of interviews with local councillors, council officers, NHS managers and others:

> [Central government are] *all about quantitative measurement, so it's "reduce burglary, reduce auto crime, increase detections, narrow the justice gap, do this by that". And all of that micro-management goes on, and dominates policing to a large degree. We are measured to within an inch of our life. And there is increasing sophistication by central government and increasing*

willingness to intervene where numbers on a page don't meet with their expectations [...] There's a real sort of regime that schools will be familiar with [...] It's the same idea [...] First of all you get a letter, and then you get a bit of support, and then ultimately down the line, somebody knocks on your door and says "I'm here to take your job".

It is not possible here to elaborate in detail upon the vast and complex audit arrangements that have become the focal point for relations between central government and local public agencies. Building upon measures introduced by previous Conservative administrations, Labour governments since 1997 have sought to underpin their programmes of public sector reform by linking comprehensive spending reviews with public service agreements. Current public service agreements, operational for the period 2003/04–2005/06, define 130 targets for central government departments intended to improve governmental coordination, enable delivery of key reforms, tackle deprivation and provide for greater accountability (HM Treasury, 2002b). In turn, central government departments have established performance indicators and targets for the central agencies and local public bodies charged with implementing government policy. As a result, virtually all public sector bodies, ranging from local councils and health care trusts to police, probation services and prisons, are assessed regularly against nationally-defined performance targets. In many cases, indicators have been used to grade and often rank the relative performance of public bodies, with 'league table' style rankings being extended from the education sector to local authorities, hospitals and even prisons. Monitoring and analysis of statistical data is, moreover, backed up by inspection visits carried out by independent 'quality assurance' and monitoring teams. The significance and reach of these comprehensive systems of audit for local public bodies may be illustrated with reference to the arrangements currently covering local authorities, health care trusts and police forces:

◆ *Local authorities*: The performance of local authorities is measured via a combination of Best Value Performance Indicators (BVPIs) and the Comprehensive Performance Assessment (CPA). There are in excess of 100 BVPIs, a selection of which are used as part of the annual CPA performance assessment. In several policy areas financial penalties may be incurred by under-performing councils and/or financial rewards provided to those performing well against the criteria;

◆ *Health care trusts*: The 10 year NHS Plan, published in July 2002, established a comprehensive set of targets for the NHS. Performance indicators for individual health care trusts are, in turn, set by the Healthcare Commission. Primary Care Trusts and Acute and Specialist Trusts are currently assessed against 40 performance indicators, while 28 indicators apply to Mental Health Trusts and 21 to Ambulance Trusts. Based on these indicators, each NHS Trust is given a 'star rating' ranging from 0 to 3 stars. Trusts achieving 3 star status are eligible for 'earned autonomy', i.e. greater freedoms are granted in return for high performance. These freedoms include less frequent monitoring from the centre and, in the case of Acute and Specialist Trusts, the opportunity to apply for Foundation Trust status;

◆ *Police forces*: Since October 2002, the web-based iQuanta system has constituted the principal means of monitoring police performance nationally. Police forces are required to submit monthly returns relating to the indicators established by the Policing Performance Assessment Framework. The data is monitored by the Home Office and the Police Standards Unit (PSU) as the basis for deciding where intervention by the PSU may be required.

There is nothing new in this insistence that local councils and other local public bodies must direct their efforts towards the attainment of national policy goals: the growth of the welfare state was founded on such principles. Moreover, contemporary audit controls are essentially an extension of Thatcherite concerns to increase public sector 'productivity'. During the Thatcher years, however, the emphasis was more firmly on reducing and containing public expenditure. As a result, much of the focus in the 1980s amounted to 'input controls', with a particular emphasis on containing local authority expenditure. Thus, during this period, new budgetary techniques were introduced to control local government expenditure (rate-capping, standard spending assessments) and to ensure that central grant allocations were spent for specific purposes (ringfencing, competitive bidding). The 1988 Local Government Finance Act represented the ultimate expression of this approach (Atkinson and Wilks-Heeg, 2000). Under the terms of this Act, best known for introducing the doomed Community Charge, local authorities were compelled to work within highly restrictive budgetary constraints, with very little scope for raising additional revenue through local taxes. These restrictions have largely been left in place ever since.

Meanwhile public service outputs also became a growing focus for Conservative governments during the 1990s, resulting in measures designed to assess 'value for money' and 'effectiveness' in public policy. Under New Labour, however, the monitoring of performance has taken on at least two additional dimensions. First, there has been a particular concern that any additional government spending, for instance in the NHS, should demonstrably translate into additional service output and improved performance. Second, the use of targets is increasingly linked to the desire of national government to reduce inequalities both in service provision (the so called 'postcode lottery') and in socio-economic conditions across the country. Thus, in outlining the current set of public service agreements, HM Treasury (2002b) emphasises the significance of performance indicators to the government's commitment to improving socio-economic conditions in the most deprived neighbourhoods, since: 'this relies on government departments delivering improvements in public service outcomes in these areas' (HM Treasury, 2002b). As such, contemporary regimes of performance management can be argued to represent a step change from previous arrangements. Indeed, to some commentators, central direction and control have become so pervasive that they represent a reinvention of Soviet-style democratic centralism:

The result of this centralisation [is] *inevitable. Ministers want schools run their way. They want to dictate the curriculum, exams, teacher pay, discipline. Ministers behave likewise towards local planning, local housing, local roads, local parking fines. Add all this to central government's 500 or so quangos, its hospitals, prisons and farm regimes, and you have by far the largest and most comprehensive bureaucratic machine in the free world – one which in range and depth is not unlike that of the old Soviet Union.*

Jenkins, 2005

This shift to increasingly comprehensive systems of performance management over the past decade has profound implications for local democracy. Performance targets not only result in over-dominant central government but also diminish the scope for local choice. The defining purpose of the monitoring systems outlined above is, after all, that they push all local councils, health care trusts, and police forces towards prioritising the same set of issues. Since many performance targets carry some form of wider implication for the organisation concerned –

whether a reward, such as additional resources or greater autonomy, or a punishment, such as financial penalties or 'naming and shaming' – there is an inevitable tendency for public bodies to focus their efforts on meeting central targets, thereby eroding the scope for local choice. In the view of many local policy-makers, the contemporary focus on targets and performance indicators has thus created a 'one size fits all' mentality within the civil service.

This model also creates enormous paradoxes in local service delivery. The danger of centrally imposed targets having unintended consequences and possibly working counter to improving public services dramatically entered the public consciousness during the 2005 General Election campaign. Questioned on live television by a member of the public about how NHS targets are preventing patients from booking non-urgent appointments with GPs more than 48 hours in advance, Tony Blair was visibly surprised, declaring: 'That's news to me ... The whole purpose of this was that people used not to be able to get an appointment within 48 hours. Obviously, it shouldn't work that way, because it would be absurd' (cited in The Times Online, 2005). However, such absurdities are less unusual than the Prime Minister might suppose. Examples such as rural police forces having to prioritise virtually non-existent local problems, such as car crime, because of the need to respond to centrally defined targets, have proliferated since the late 1990s. Within the NHS, senior managers and board members highlight how targets imposed on hospital trusts and PCTs have created conflicts over resource allocation. Recently, the former leader of Liverpool City Council, Cllr Mike Storey, suggested that the council is required to collect data on as many as 1,500 performance indicators, with contradictory and counter-productive outcomes frequently arising. For instance, because Liverpool's planning department performed well in previous years against Best Value targets, a higher level of Planning Delivery Grant was obtained. The additional resource obtained subsequently caused an automatic decline in the council's performance on the measure of 'planning cost per head' (Liverpool Daily Post, 22 September 2004).

However, the impact of 'the target culture' on local democracy goes further: in some instances, performance targets directly erode the role of elected councillors as decision-makers. The case of planning and development control again provides a dramatic example. The Best Value framework establishes a number of performance indicators (BV109 a-

c) measuring and setting targets for the proportion of different types of planning applications processed within specified time frames. Thus, local authorities are to aim to process 60 per cent of major applications in 13 weeks (BV109a), 65 per cent of minor applications in 8 weeks (BV109b) and 80 per cent of other applications in 8 weeks (BV109c). It has widely been noted that a consequence of these targets is that local authorities have sought to minimise the extent to which planning applications become the subject of public debate, with fewer and fewer cases being debated by elected councillors. Indeed, local authorities are effectively precluded from even attempting to meet the targets for planning applications while maintaining a significant role for elected members, since BV188 specifies a target for the percentage of decisions delegated to officers. In areas such as Harrogate, where planning decisions have increasingly become a focal point for public engagement with the local democratic process, the consequences of the performance indicators have created a clearly paradoxical situation for local democracy. As the chief reporter on the Harrogate Advertiser explained:

> [...] *more and more planning decisions are being made by the Director of Housing, and this is the same across all councils.*[7] *At the back of the agenda for the planning meeting there will be many pages again, if not more, of lists of planning applications that have been decided by the Director of Housing or are being deferred to the Director of Housing. They do not contain full notes; they do not include notices of letters of objection and things like that [...] John Prescott has many a time said he wants to see more deferred decisions by planning authorities so we can get them through. I mean, Harrogate for a time had one of the worst records for deciding planning applications within I think it was the thirteen week deadline. And they've sort of clawed that back and they're now doing quite well. But they're only doing that by delegating more and more decisions to officers, and that's not good, that's not good for local democracy.*

Disquiet about central controls is almost to be expected from local policy-makers and it is important to consider how performance monitoring is regarded by MPs and civil servants. Inevitably,

---

7   Technically, such decisions would generally be made by the Council's Head of Planning, deputising for the Director of Development Services.

interpretations of central–local relations among MPs vary according to the political party they represent. Government ministers tend to take the view that the setting of targets is perfectly consistent with notions of 'new localism', since targets do not imply any sense of the centre dictating *how* things are to be done locally. In this view, targets are merely an attempt to specify a minimum level of performance that is expected as an outcome of relatively autonomous decisions made at a local level within the context of overall government policy. This perspective is communicated by many civil servants, including those working at the regional level. Asked to respond to the sense that some council officers have of experiencing 'micro-management' from central government departments, one civil servant replied:

Ministers downwards are increasingly anxious to see real evidence of the gap in disadvantage being tackled and narrowed. And there isn't any […] and if we put anyone under pressure, well forgive me, but that's what we're going to do. We want the evidence. That is not telling them how to do it, which is what I would say is micro-management.

Moreover, the relationship between performance and autonomy is becoming increasingly important. Where performance is very strong locally, provision has been made in many areas for the granting of greater freedoms and flexibilities for local public bodies, reflecting the concept of 'earned autonomy'. Where performance appears weak, local policy-makers will come under growing pressure. Unsurprisingly, such interpretations are not generally shared by opposition MPs. When asked where he felt power lies locally, the answer provided by the MP for Harrogate and Knaresborough was absolutely unambiguous:

With the government – full stop. There's nothing locally. You know, I meet the PCT, the PCT say, "We would love to do that, Phil, but the government says these are our priorities". Again, if you look at policing, we are a low crime area, so therefore our priorities are significantly different to what you would find in Bradford or Leeds, the big metropolitans […] and yet we are having to dance to the same tune in terms of priorities. I do think we have to rethink all that really, and if we are serious about actually having local decision-making and local prioritisation, then we really have got to be much more serious about letting the levers of power actually go down.

4.3 Differential autonomy?

The influence of central government targets and controls is felt strongly at a local level. For instance, it is evident that, within the respective district councils, there is a clear sense that non-statutory services, such as provision of leisure facilities, are those in which there is greatest freedom from central diktat, but also greatest constraint in generating the resources to act locally. This combination of statutory local government services being driven by central government requirements and non-statutory activity being squeezed by a lack of local capacity, leaves very little scope for a district council to pursue a 'big idea'. Thus, it was felt strongly by representatives of Harrogate Borough Council that the organisation would no longer be able to embark upon a visionary policy agenda of the order that had established Harrogate as a major conference venue after the Second World War.

At the same time, however, one of the strongest, and unexpected, contrasts emerging from the Burnley–Harrogate comparison is an apparently greater sense of local policy choice among council officers in Burnley. There may, however, be good grounds for this contrasting perception of local autonomy between two district councils. Given the widespread view that local policy choices are being powerfully shaped by centrally defined targets, it seems evident that policy-makers' perceptions of the constraints on local autonomy will depend, in part, on the degree of fit between local, regional and national policy priorities. Where local priorities 'go with the grain' of national and regional priorities, policy-makers may well feel that there is greater scope to induce change locally. In this sense, the area-based initiatives listed in Figure 2.3 (chapter 2) are an important indicator of the extent to which the two districts are able to draw upon additional central government resource in order to pursue local policy objectives. As was noted, there are four times as many nationally-funded area-based initiatives in Burnley as there are in Harrogate, with most of those applying in the latter being very modest in resource terms.

In the case of Burnley, the availability of additional resource via national programmes such as Elevate and Building Schools for the Future, is also likely to enhance the sense of local policy-makers having scope to make an impact. The extent to which central government and regional bodies have made resources available to programmes in the town obviously reflects social and political developments in Burnley over the past four years, as well as its evident economic problems. Moreover, such government support tends to come with an inevitable requirement to report progress regularly to Government Office North West and central government departments. Indeed, some Burnley council officials report a sense of civil servants attempting to micro-manage high-profile policy initiatives from Manchester or London. However, the fact that policy-makers in Burnley have been drawn into a much closer relationship with central government clearly cuts both ways. There is undoubtedly a greater sense of scrutiny from the centre, but also a greater sense of optimism that the borough council and its partners have the capacity to direct a process of social and economic renewal in Burnley. As one interviewee observed:

> There is very high-level interest in what's going on in Burnley. How is the council responding to all that? How clear and organised is our control and direction of it? Are we doing the right things? Are we moving forward? ... All that's very much on the top table agenda [...] If I was honest I would say that we probably saw it as a threat initially, it felt a bit scary that a little district council like this would be under that sort of scrutiny. But we don't see it that way these days – we see it as a sort of window of opportunity that we've got to get help, advice, resources, from the centre that will help us deal with some issues and that, without that sort of help, we might struggle.

By contrast, local policy priorities in Harrogate do not readily map onto those identified by regional bodies or national government. In some instances, this lack of fit means the council is required to invest in specific forms of provision, despite the fact that its consultation processes indicate that local people's priorities clearly rest elsewhere. In other cases, the lack of fit means that local policy-makers are effectively stuck 'between the devil and the deep blue sea', unable to address local policy priorities, because there are so few, if any, regional or national resources that can be drawn in to help address them.

The political dynamics restricting local policy choice in Harrogate can be illustrated via consideration of the example of affordable housing, seen almost universally as the key local policy issue in Harrogate currently. It is evident that any action the district might wish take to promote affordable housing locally is tightly constrained by regional and national policy frameworks. Given the lack of affordable housing in Harrogate, the council currently see advantages in retaining its housing stock, a standpoint that emerges in part from a decision to respect the overwhelming view of tenants, expressed on three occasions, despite the fact that it goes against the grain of government policy, which has strongly encouraged stock transfer (see Case Study 4.1 below). At the same time, however, the 'right to buy' is resulting in a steady erosion of the council's housing stock, while any attempt to increase the supply of social housing will require the council to work in partnership with housing associations. Social housing development is therefore largely dependent upon using development control mechanisms to part-fund the construction of social housing from any 'planning gains' negotiated as part of private housing construction schemes locally. In turn, the scope for such planning gain agreements to be realised, or indeed for new housing of any kind to be built locally, is tightly restricted by the regional planning framework. The regional plan emphasises the need to boost housing markets in areas of low demand, particularly in parts of South Yorkshire and Humberside, to be achieved in part by imposing strict limits on the amount of new housing that can be built in counties such as North Yorkshire. In short, there is virtually nothing that Harrogate District Council can do, either unilaterally or together with its partners on the District LSP, to take action in relation to the key policy priority that has been recognised by the full range of public agencies, community groups and voluntary sector organisations operating locally.

Case Study 4.1: The Council Housing Options process, Harrogate

During 2005 Harrogate Borough Council and their tenants were undergoing the Council Housing Options process for third time since 1993. The reasons for this reflect tensions between particular central government policy imperatives.

Harrogate Borough Council has approximately 3,800 properties, making it the largest provider of affordable housing with a larger stock than all the RSLs operating in the district combined. The 2000 Housing Survey states that 1798 new homes a year are needed over the next five years in order to meet all identified affordable housing needs, but currently the district is producing about 100 per year and losing about 120 through 'right to buy'.

The first options process was conducted in 1993, when the tenants, through consultation, indicated clearly that they wanted to stay with the council.

(Continued)

> **Case Study 4.1: The Council Housing Options process, Harrogate (continued)**
>
> A measure of the strength of feeling was that they also voted in favour of a 25 per cent rent increase to pay for services in order to stay with the council.
>
> In 2000 the process was undertaken again. This time the council had selected stock transfer as their preferred option, had selected a partner organisation, worked up a proposal and were on the point of sending an offer document out to tenants. When council members eventually decided not to pursue that option, the decision was taken, in part, due to tenants again being in favour of remaining with the council.
>
> During 2004, the government instructed the council to go through the process again, but this time a much lower participation rate was evident and tenants were unclear as to why they were being 'consulted' on this issue yet again (many experiencing this for the third time). The consultation process has not shown any shift in tenants' preferences.

4.4 Conclusion

The title of this chapter asks whether there can be local democracy without local autonomy. Based on our research in Burnley and Harrogate, our answer to this question is an unequivocal 'no'. However, it is also important to turn this question around: can there be local autonomy without local democracy? Under the current system, local partnerships are often constrained in their capacity to act as a result of the demands placed upon their constituent partners by government targets and central direction. Although there is growing evidence that central government recognises this problem, there can be little doubt that it has been a major barrier to enabling partnerships to show local leadership, rooted in local accountability. As one LSP representative explained:

> *The lack of joined-up government* [nationally] *just makes joined-up local government really difficult, because all the different organisations are working to different government offices, different structures, different accountabilities and different centrally imposed priorities as well. So whatever we agree locally is a priority* […] *if the Home Office tell the Community Safety Partnership – which they do! – that actually something else is a*

priority and they've got to have their own performance management structure, it hardly helps the joint working across the partnership.

The growing role of partnerships in local governance has been highlighted elsewhere in this book. Clearly, such partnerships can experience centralisation as a 'double-bind' in restricting the scope for local autonomy. At the same time, however, the prospect of such partnerships operating with greater freedom raises important questions for local democracy. Should local bodies be granted greater autonomy if they are not subject to recognised mechanisms of local democratic control? We return to these issues in the following chapter.

5
Who's in Charge Here?:

Representation and accountability in local governance

If one meets a powerful person ask them five questions: "What power have you got? Where did you get it from? In whose interests do you exercise it? To whom are you accountable? And how can we get rid of you?" If you cannot get rid of the people who govern you, you do not live in a democratic system.

Tony Benn, 2001

5.1 Introduction

In this chapter, we explore the extent to which the fragmentation of public service provision described in previous chapters has affected accountability and representation in local governance. As Tony Benn's famous five questions indicate, democratic systems ultimately rest on the power of the electorate to appoint people to, and remove them from, positions of power. Yet, as local public service provision has become increasingly fragmented, there has been a similar diversification of forms of governance among public bodies, which raises key questions about how accountable these bodies are. The question of how representative governing bodies need to be of the people they serve is also important, as is indicated by such policies as all women short lists for political parties and efforts at increasing diversity in public bodies (detailed below).

Unelected public bodies demonstrate considerable variation in the ways their governing bodies are appointed, with local councillors playing a significant role on some bodies and very minor roles on others. Recent reforms have led to greater transparency in the appointment procedures of unelected bodies; however, despite efforts to increase diversity, their governing boards remain dominated by a largely male, largely white and largely middle-class minority. This raises important questions of the extent to which such bodies effectively represent the public which they serve. There is also evidence of some degree of overlap in membership of the governing boards of these bodies, although the strongest inter-agency links in terms of representation occur because of the multiple roles played by elected councillors.

An increasing number of local partnerships have emerged over recent years reflecting an attempt to 'join up' local service provision. This form of network democracy appears to be an increasingly powerful element of the local democratic mix. However, there are obvious concerns about how structures such as local strategic partnerships (LSPs) are locally representative and democratically accountable. The lack of transparency in LSP decision-making, and their tenuous links with local residents, suggest that they are hugely out of kilter with the trends described elsewhere in this book in relation to individual public sector agencies.

5.2 Representation: Elections and appointments in local agencies

As noted in chapter 2, local public bodies can be crudely divided into two distinct forms of governance: local authorities governed by democratically elected representatives; and LPSBs and some regional quangos governed by boards made up of appointees. However, three important caveats provide some nuance to this distinction. First, a direct link to the formal local democratic process is provided in those LPSBs, such as police and fire authorities and further education colleges, which have a statutory duty to include a specific number of elected local councillors on their boards. Many local partnerships, particularly local strategic partnerships, also tend to include elected councillors, with the Leader of the Council acting as the chair of the Harrogate LSP and the vice-chair of the Burnley LSP. Second, procedures used by different LPSBs to appoint board members differ greatly according to specific statutes or government guidance. In some cases, procedures vary according to the type of board member being appointed. In others, such as tenants' representatives on housing associations or student representatives on college governing boards, board members are elected by the people whom they are to represent. Similarly, some LSP representatives are elected, such as those of the voluntary, community and faith sector on the Burnley Action Partnership (see below for details). Third, a possible new model of local public sector governance is exemplified by foundation hospital trusts, such as Harrogate & District

NHS foundation trust, in which the board of governors are directly elected by the trust's 'members', with membership open to all local residents and trust staff.

In recent years, appointment procedures have become significantly more transparent. Following the Nolan reports (see, *inter alia*, Nolan Committee 1995, 1996, 1997a, 1997b), appointments to public bodies, including regional quangos and LPSBs, now involve positions being publicly advertised, with appointments being made on the basis of individual applicants' skills and specialist knowledge. Likewise, a range of measures, such as reformed remuneration levels, covering childcare costs, making the times and frequency of meetings more family friendly, and setting recruitment targets for women and minorities, have been implemented to encourage diversity among appointees. However, despite increased transparency and other measures, the boards of public bodies remain largely unrepresentative and are often perceived by the public as the preserve of the privileged minority (PAC, 2003, p.21). The Public Administration Select Committee, although noting progress made in recruiting more women and minorities onto boards, emphasised that socio-economic background is a significant barrier, not only affecting women and minorities, but producing an unduly narrow recruitment of white males. In addition, the Committee noted regional differences and age are also diversity issues (*ibid*.: p.33). Merit-oriented criteria for recruitment can also act as a barrier to diversity; as one witness to the Committee pointed out, the reason that non-executive NHS board members were mainly white and middle-class is because recruitment concentrates on 'knowledge and skills [which] preclude[s] large numbers of people who we believe would have the competency to carry out the role' (*ibid*.: 41). In assessing the Committee's Report, Democratic Audit (n.d. 1) has argued that what is required is a profound cultural shift in government to overcome long-established traditions which favour elite ideals and distort efforts to widen recruitment.

Appointments to the boards of those public bodies identified as involved in governance of the two towns generally take one of three forms. First, in LPSBs which maintain a strong connection to local authorities, members are elected or appointed by a combination of methods, although there is always a role for elected members directly nominated by local authorities. The primary examples of such bodies and the range of election and appointment procedures used are:

◆ *Fire and Rescue Authorities*, which are composed entirely of councillors nominated from local authorities. In areas such as Lancashire and North Yorkshire, which are made up of both county and unitary authorities, fire and rescue authorities are constituted as joint committees, with the constituent authorities nominating members on a proportional basis;

◆ *Police authorities*, which are comprised of 17 nominated members as follows: 9 local authority elected members, 3 magistrates and 5 independent members directly appointed by the other members after a procedure of public recruitment and Home Secretary approval. As above, elected members are nominated by both the respective county councils and the unitary authorities that were formerly part of the county;

◆ *Calico Housing (Burnley)*, which is a stock transfer housing association currently governed by an 18 member board comprising 6 tenant representatives, 6 elected councillors, and 6 independent members. Tenants' representatives are elected directly by tenants; elected members are nominated by Burnley Borough Council and independent members are appointed on a competitive basis;

◆ *Burnley College*, which has an 18 member governing board serving 6 distinct constituencies, appointed through a mix of election, direct appointment and nomination. Two staff governors are directly elected by the staff body, while a student governor is directly elected by the student body. Three local authority representatives are nominated by Burnley Borough Council (2) and Lancashire County Council (1), fulfilling the statutory requirement that college boards must include at least two elected members. Local head teachers nominate one representative and one is co-opted by the Vice-Chancellor of the University of Central Lancashire. Six business governors are recruited via public advertisements and direct approaches to business organisations. The remaining members comprise the College Principal and co-opted members.

Second, appointments to local NHS bodies, such as strategic health authorities, primary care trusts and NHS trusts, are governed by specific appointment procedures. Appointments of Chairs and non-executive Directors to NHS boards (around 4,000 positions) were taken out of the hands of ministers with the establishment of the NHS Appointments

Commission – technically a quango itself – in April 2001. Although not seen as representing local people, all such appointees are laypersons and are supposed to reside within the area being served by the body in question. The balance between executive and non-executive directors varies according to the type of body. On strategic health authorities, there are eight non-executive members (including the Chair) and five executive directors, while the balance on primary care trusts is five non-executive and five executive directors. As with other public appointments, the primary emphasis is on appointing people with relevant skills, although the Department of Health also sets targets for the representation of women and minority groups. All positions are remunerated, with chairs of NHS bodies receiving £16,417–£20,930 and non-executive directors £5,436 per annum. In 2004 the NHS Appointments Commission ran recruitment campaigns for 580 posts, which produced 29,000 expressions of interest and 11,000 applications, and made 1,360 local and national appointments.

Third, post-Nolan, appointments to the 22,000 places available on a total of more than 1,000 public bodies nationally are expected to be made on the grounds of merit, using a formal selection procedure. As noted above, the government has issued recruitment targets to improve the under-representation of women, ethnic minorities and people with disabilities on these public bodies. Where 'ministerial appointments' are made the process is monitored by the Officer of the Commission of Public Appointments. Relevant public bodies in this category include regional development agencies and local probation boards. Local probation boards, as established by the Criminal Justice and Court Services Act 2000, comprise 13 members, with 12 appointed by the Home Secretary and 1 appointed by the Lord Chancellor. As with other public bodies, appointments are expected to take place via 'an open process of public recruitment and selection. Members are appointed on the basis of their individual skills and experience that they bring to the Board' (Lancashire Probation Service, 2004, p.20). Board members are paid an hourly rate of £14 per hour. In the case of the Lancashire Probation Board, this resulted in 12 board members receiving £5,000 or less in 2003/04, and one board member receiving £15–20,000.

A striking aspect here is that competition for local public appointments appears to be significantly greater than for local council seats. As one interviewee noted, there were 50–60 applications for the five non-executive positions on the Primary Care Trust Board, whereas his experience of selecting candidates for local council elections is that 'you struggle to find people'. Financial reward may form part of the explanation for the greater competition for non-executive positions on LPSBs, as the 'cash incentives' are considerably greater for non-executive directors on LPSBs than they are for (backbench) district councillors. Table 5.1 presents findings regarding levels of remuneration across a range of public agencies, ranked according to basic payments to either non-executive board members or ordinary elected members. Among those agencies which provide remuneration, district councillors receive the lowest payments. In addition, whilst non-executive NHS board members are only required to spend two and a half days per month on board business, a survey of Harrogate councillors undertaken in 2001 found that the average member spent 57.5 hours per month on council business, the equivalent of 7–8 working days per month. Although only supported by anecdotal evidence, it is possible that individuals, who in the past would have contemplated serving on district councils, are instead being recruited into non-elected public agency positions. These individuals may also see such positions as providing a more influential and clearly defined role within the agency than they might have within a district council.

Recent reform of public appointments, as well as the number of positions reserved for local people, may well have increased the pool from which representatives are drawn. Nonetheless, there is a strong possibility that such bodies will be characterised by overlapping representation. This partially occurs as a result of the attempt to maintain a link with the formal local democratic process by requiring numerous local public bodies to have local authority councillors on their boards. At the same time, however, there remains an obvious danger of public appointments being dominated by a relatively small local elite, with some individuals playing multiple roles. These may also be local authority elected members. An example is provided by one of our interviewees who is an elected member of both the county and the district councils, a member of the police authority, a board member of the regional Learning and Skills Council, a director of Business Link, a non-executive director of the regional tourist board, an executive member of the Local Government Management Board, as well as serving on the board of a college in a neighbouring region.

Table 5.1: Comparative remuneration levels, elected councillors and non-executive directors of local public agencies, 2004/05

Organisation	Chief Executive or equivalent (£ p.a.)	Chair, or equivalent (£ p.a.)	Non-executive Director, or equivalent (£ p.a.)
County Council	National average 118,000	Lancashire Leader 35,020 Deputy 27,140 Executive 21,890	Lancashire Member – 8,755
		North Yorkshire Leader 27,237 Deputy 18,993 Executive 17,619	North Yorkshire Member – 8,001
Police Authority	–	Lancashire Chair 20,795 Vice-Chair 15,400	Lancashire Member 8,800
		North Yorkshire Chair 15,298 Vice-chair 11,473	North Yorkshire Member – 7,649
Regional Development Agency	112,000	51,000 (2days/week) Deputy 15,000 (1 day/week)	7,775
Strategic Health Authority	150–155,000	Up to 21,882 (3.5 days/week)	5,673 (2.5 days/month)
Primary Care Trust	90–95,000	Up to 21,882 (3.5 days/week)	5,673 (2.5 days/month)
Health Trust	85–90,000	Up to 21,882 (3.5 days/week)	5,673 (2.5 days/month)
Probation Service	Chief Officer 55–60,000	–	Board members £14/hour plus discretionary travel allowance and other expenses
District Council	National average 82,000	Burnley, Leader 6,460 Deputy 2,584	Burnley, Member – 1,292
Learning and Skills Council	–	–	Expenses inc. child care (12–15 days/year)
Regional Assembly	N/a	Yorkshire and Humber 5,250 (50 days/year) Vice-chair 3,150 (30 days per year) Executive members 1,050 (10 days/year)	Yorkshire and Humber Member – expenses

Figures 5.1a and 5.1b capture the inter-relationships between the governing bodies of organisations operating in Burnley and Harrogate. The diagrams locate the main organisations operating at the district, sub-county and county scales, with the thickness of the lines connecting them indicating the number of representatives they share.[8] In line with the analysis in chapter 2, these diagrams capture the extent of concentration at the county level: in both cases the strongest inter-connections are between those bodies operating primarily or exclusively at the county level. In particular, because of the role for elected members on fire and rescue authorities and police authorities, the strongest links are between these bodies and the respective county councils. It is noticeable, however, that the mapping of overlapping representation reveals a much more complex web of relationships in Harrogate than it does in Burnley, with North Yorkshire County Council being linked to a larger number of local bodies via its elected members. This representational link extends to Harrogate District Council, with six district councillors also serving as county councillors. It is also clear that there is a stronger set of representational links at the district level in Burnley, again reflecting the roles of elected members on the governing boards of Burnley College and Calico Housing. In the case of Burnley there is a distinct lack of representative links between the district authority and agencies operating at the county level – for example, the police authority. In this instance, the linkages indicate something of a local 'accountability gap'. Moreover, while police authorities are attempting to include district councillors in their governance processes, current plans to amalgamate police authorities are likely to weaken this link even further.

---

8   For example, the line between NYCC and NYPA represents the seven county councillors that are members of the NYPA. A single line, such as between Burnley Action Partnership and the PCT, indicates one representative in common.

Figure 5.1a: Harrogate representational links

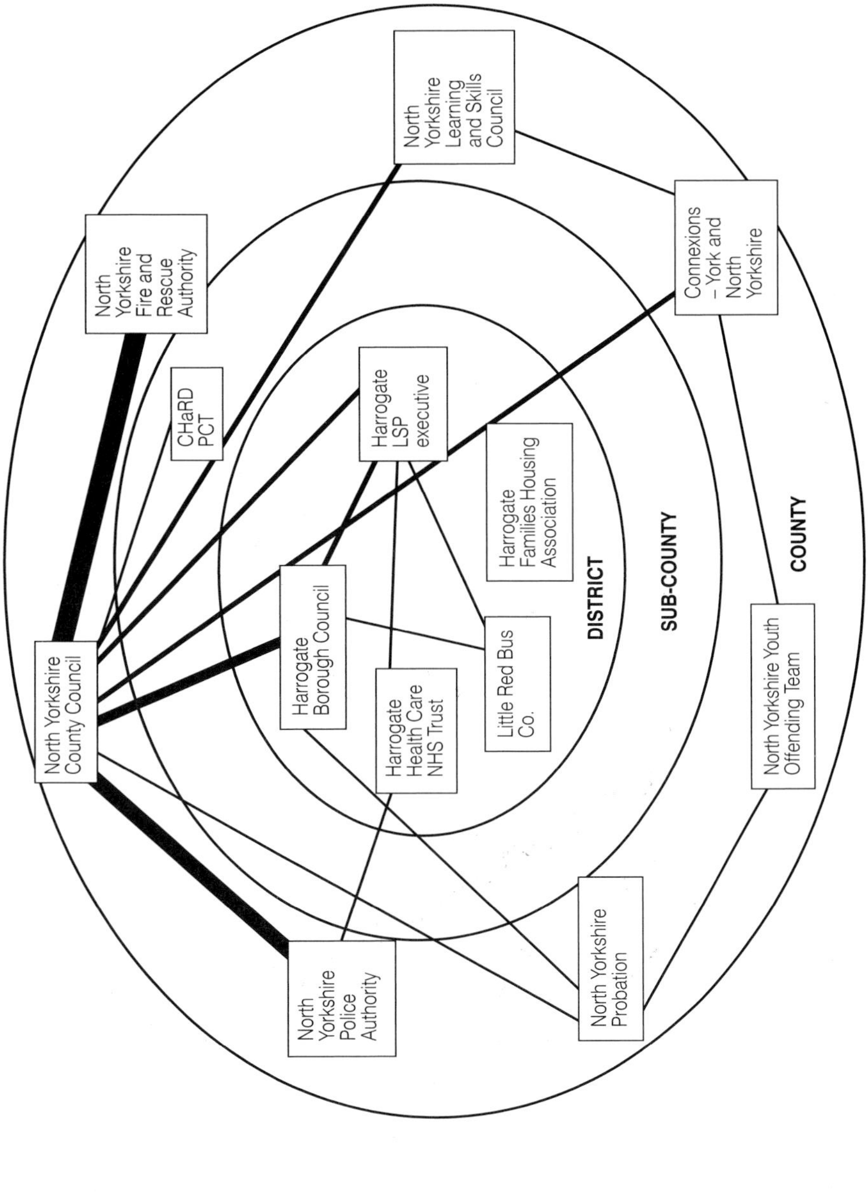

Figure 5.1b: Burnley representational links

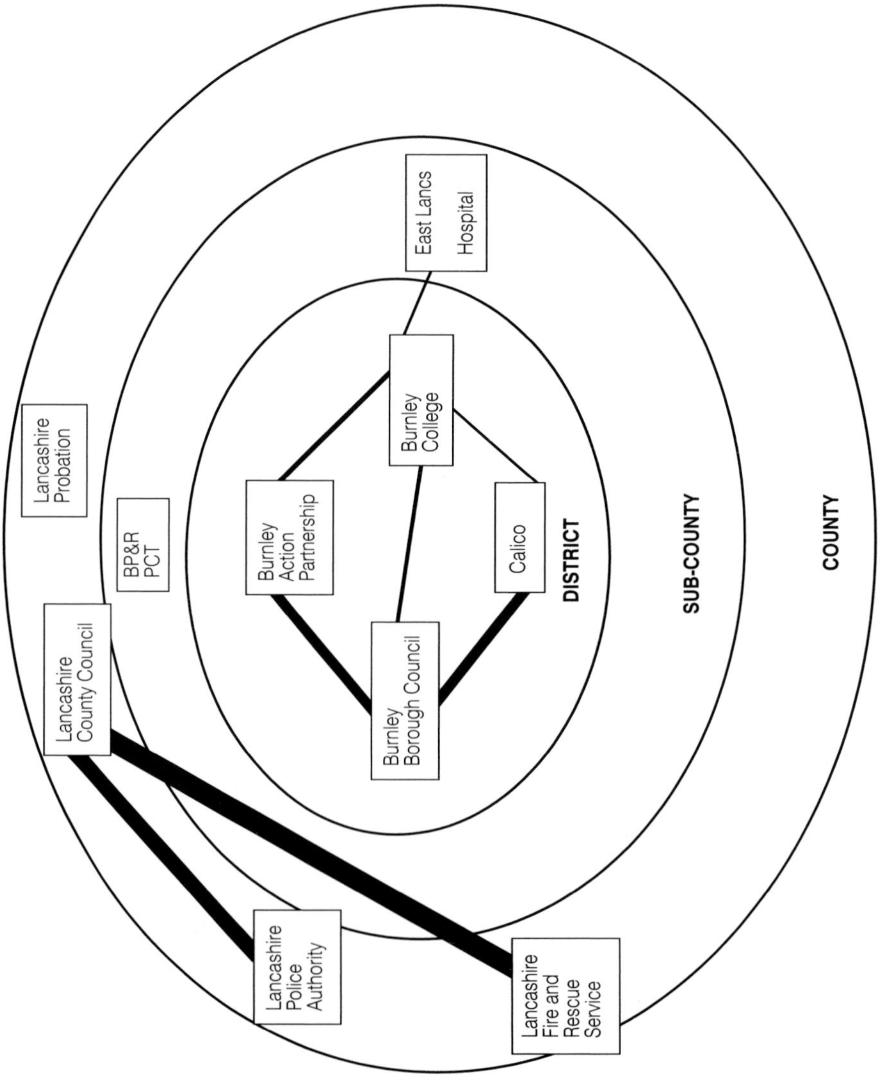

East Lancs Hospital

Lancashire Probation

BP&R PCT

Burnley College

Burnley Action Partnership

Calico

DISTRICT

Lancashire County Council

Burnley Borough Council

SUB-COUNTY

COUNTY

Lancashire Police Authority

Lancashire Fire and Rescue Service

5.3 Accountability, community representation and local partnerships

Under the terms of the Local Government Act (2000) and the Health and Social Care Act (2001), the role of elected members in holding other local bodies to account is also intended to extend beyond nomination to the boards of such organisations. The primary means through which councillors are expected to engage with other local bodies in this way is the provision for scrutiny committees, which can be established not only to hold the council's leadership to account but also to scrutinise the activities of external bodies. For instance, Lancashire County Council has two scrutiny committees that operate in this latter sense. First, the external overview and scrutiny committee reviews and makes recommendations on those services or activities, other than health, carried out by external organisations and which affect Lancashire's inhabitants. Second, the health equalities overview and scrutiny committee scrutinises and reviews the operation of the national Health Service in Lancashire, along with local services provided by the council and other agencies that affect health improvement and health equality. It includes 12 co-opted members representing each district council in Lancashire.

Much doubt has been expressed about the operation of scrutiny arrangements and there is clearly a great deal of variation nationally as to the success of local councillors in adapting to this new role. In general, interviewees at the district level in both Burnley and Harrogate took the view that, while they offered a potentially potent mechanism, scrutiny arrangements were rarely, if ever, working as envisaged. There are indications that overview and scrutiny committees are finding useful roles to play, but these are not generally the roles envisaged in the government legislation that established them (see chapter 6 for further discussion). Moreover, given the considerable emphasis that central government has placed upon multi-agency working at the local level, there is clearly a danger that councillors may sometimes be reluctant to show their teeth when it come to scrutinising external bodies.

The proliferation of partnership and inter-agency working at the local level indicates that there has been a significant growth in 'network democracy' as part of the local democratic mix in recent years. To define partnership working and inter-agency collaboration as part of local democracy may seem counter-intuitive; in many ways partnership working is the very antithesis of what is commonly understood as democratic. However, it can also be argued that partnership working represents a particular form of functional representation, through which decisions are reached through debates conducted among representing counter-balancing organisations that, taken together, represent a broad cross-section of local people. In the view of one interviewee in Burnley, local strategic partnerships represented a form of 'democracy by representation' which contrasts to local government 'ballot box democracy' mainly in terms of its tendency to result in decisions that reflect the interests of town as a whole, rather than individual wards. Other interviewees endorsed this perspective, arguing that the LSP's members represent Burnley as a whole, rather than narrow interests within it.

The flip-side of this argument, of course, is that it is not automatically clear why or how an unelected group of local residents will reach a common understanding of what best serves the town as a whole. Indeed, one interviewee offered a particularly trenchant critique of the democratic deficit arising from bodies such as local strategic partnerships in response to the decision made by its members not to allow the press to attend LSP meetings:

This is public money that is being discussed, it should be held in a public arena and they want to keep the doors closed. And in some respects with LSPs, it's going back almost to the nineteenth century, isn't it, where the great and the good of the local town would sit and discuss its affairs [...] and this is a similar sort of thing. Local businessmen sitting around discussing the town and preferably without the press or the public there. It's going back in history.

Given the attempts to render the local 'quango state' more open, transparent and accountable in recent years there is, indeed, something of an irony in the apparent absence of such principles in relation to LSPs. In the main, it has been assumed that provision for community representation on LSPs and other partnership bodies, alongside leadership from elected local authorities, will mitigate such concerns. Yet, this logic merely raises another thorny issue – the issue of how the direct representation of the voluntary and community sector (VCS) can best be achieved, in keeping with democratic principles. The Treasury (2004) review of the sector noted three main forms of governance and accountability:

◆ *Membership-based organisations*: Members (drawn from a particular section of the community, particular area or from beneficiaries) elect a management board (or similar) which runs the body on a day-to-day basis;

◆ *Stakeholder-based organisations*: These have an executive board or committee constituted, appointed or elected by and accountable to stakeholder organisations. This may be in addition to an individual membership or may be the only form of wider accountability. This type of organisation is often used where a number of bodies (sometimes including public bodies) seek to form a partnership to carry out particular activities;

◆ *Independent self-governing organisations*: These have independent executive boards or committees normally only accountable to the organisation's constitution, and funders with no wider accountability to a membership or to stakeholder organisations. Many charities and voluntary organisations take this form (HM Treasury 2004, p.21).

While VCS representation on regeneration programmes and other forms of partnership working has been strongly encouraged since the early 1990s, a number of problems and shortcomings have been identified in the arrangements that have typically been adopted. A common approach in many localities has been to allocate one or two places on partnership boards to senior local CVS staff as 'representatives' of the sector as a whole. The VCF sector in Harrogate is a fairly typical example of this arrangement, with the two CVS directors (for Ripon and Harrogate) being widely seen as representatives of the whole sector, and also having been elected by the local Voluntary Sector Forum to the executive of the LSP. Dowson *et al.* (2000) note that some statutory sector officers' criticised VCS representatives in North Yorkshire as a whole for failing to attend meetings regularly, for being reluctant to represent the sector as a whole and for not responding quickly.

It is important to note, however, that the assumption that the local CVS can represent the whole sector has been criticised by virtually all concerned, not least by CVS staff themselves, on four main grounds. First, it is seen to be at best, unrealistic, and, at worst, highly misleading, to assume that such a diverse sector can be represented by one or two people. Local CVS directors therefore emphasise that they are there to provide the sector with a voice, not to be the representative of it as a whole. Second, in most localities the CVS accounts for only a proportion of local VCF organisations, leaving many grassroots organisations unaccounted for. Third, reducing the sector to a very small number of people places an enormous burden on a single individual, who typically becomes a member of multiple partnerships, joint committees and various sub-groups. As both the Ripon and Harrogate CVS directors pointed out, they are understaffed and under-funded, and the increasing number of partnership meetings and other forums they have to attend results in them being even more stretched. Fourth, such mechanisms for community representation are widely seen to reproduce the 'usual suspects' syndrome in the representation of local communities.

The formation of the Burnley Community Network in relation to the local LSP points to a conscious attempt to overcome such problems. Based on the WM Enterprise Audit of VCF organisations, the Burnley Community Network has been constituted as a relatively comprehensive membership organisation for the sector in the town. Within the Network, 6 sub-groupings have been identified, with the organisations within each sub-grouping electing representatives to the LSP. In total, the Network elected 19 representatives to the 51-member LSP, using a system of 'one organisation, one vote'. Elections are conducted annually and have so far been carried out in 2003, 2004 and 2005. This procedure is widely recognised to have overcome many of the more serious concerns about the legitimacy and representative claims of VCF participants, while also bringing a number of 'fresh faces' into the local policy process. The strength of VCF representation has also transformed the experience of participating in partnership arrangements for many of those involved. In the view of one of the Network's representative on the LSP, the arrangements have reversed the 'us and them' mentality previously seemingly inherent to VCF participation in partnership working: 'I always say, it's not them, it's us'. Participants in the Burnley Community Network also point to its influence within the LSP on specific issues, such as the LSP's response to the county council's consultation on the Building Schools for the Future programme in Burnley.

Inevitably, the innovative approach to VCF representation on Burnley's LSP cannot overcome all concerns about the extent to which local people are represented and participate in local decision-making. The Burnley Community Network is, for instance, probably no more successful in engaging young people in the local political process than any other body, despite the fact that its membership includes both the Burnley Youth Theatre and the Burnley Youth Council. Furthermore,

BCN's influence is largely restricted to the LSP, and while this has proved significant on a number of occasions, many community representatives were of the view that key Burnley Council proposals had not always been referred to the LSP for the elected community and voluntary sector representatives to consider. What is arguably most significant about this claim is that it illustrates how the Burnley Community Network reflects a wider tendency, observed elsewhere in this book, towards the emergence of 'hybrid' forms of local democracy. In this case, the Burnley VCF sector has adopted a mix of representative and participatory democracy in relation to the LSP, resulting in its representatives claiming legitimacy to scrutinise decisions made by the local council, which in turn operates according to longer established norms of local representative democracy.

5.4 Conclusion

In answer to Tony Benn's fifth question 'how can we get rid of you?', the majority of public bodies looked at for this research would have to answer: 'you – the public – cannot'. As we have detailed above, recruitment to public sector governing boards is increasingly made on the basis of what the individual can 'bring' to the organisation in terms of knowledge, skills and experience – although these are often quite narrowly defined. As we have noted, this increases the possibility that local governance is in the hands of a narrow local elite. However, there remains an indirect link to democratically elected bodies through councillors serving on the governing boards of a number of public bodies. Moreover, attempts have been made to respond to the possibilities of a lack of representativeness and accountability on the boards of non-elected public bodies by introducing a range of means of public consultation and engagement. We evaluate the democratic credentials of these mechanisms in more depth in chapter 8.

6

In Defence of Politicians?:

The role of elected representatives in local democracy

Brace yourself. You are about to hear something unusual, quite possibly unique. Something that is going to be positive – well, largely positive anyway – about one of the most downtrodden and despised groups in society. You are about to hear a piece of reporting that is going to be positive about our hard-working, and often exasperated, British politicians.
Philip Cowley, 2006

6.1 Introduction

Despite the growth of unelected agencies and the diversification of forms of local democratic engagement, elected politicians remain the focal point of local democracy. The purpose of this chapter, therefore, is to consider how local politicians relate to their constituents through campaigning, casework and other forms of contact, and to assess the extent to which they are able to respond to issues raised by local residents. Given that Burnley and Harrogate operate within two-tier local government structures and that both have rural hinterlands with active parish councils, our analysis involves consideration of the respective roles of district, county and parish councillors, with a particular emphasis on the first of these three groups. However, we do not restrict our analysis to local councillors: we also consider the role of members of parliament as politicians with a key role in local democracy. The analysis presented in this chapter suggests that district and parish councillors have the closest relationships with local residents. However, the chapter also argues that the introduction of new political arrangements in local government in 2000 have so far done little to strengthen local democracy, despite the bold claims that were made for them and the way in which they would redefine the role of local councillors. The chapter also suggests that the role of MPs in local democracy requires greater recognition.

6.2 The role of elected councillors

Writing before the introduction of new political arrangements in local government, Wilson and Game (1994) considered whether it was possible to define a 'job description' for local councillors. While noting the enormous variations in the tasks undertaken by local councillors, Wilson and Game suggested that it was nonetheless possible to identify four core areas of activity encapsulating the work undertaken by councillors. Thus, while the balance would vary from one councillor to another, an elected member would typically:

◆ Represent and be accountable to the electorate;

◆ Formulate policies and practices for the authority;

◆ Monitor the effectiveness of those policies;

◆ Provide leadership for the community.

Despite the fact that research studies have consistently found that local councillors give enormous, and increasing, time commitments to fulfilling these roles, there is also clear evidence of growing disconnection between the local electorate and councillors. Low levels of turnout in local elections are paralleled by a very poor level of knowledge amongst people about their local political representatives. A MORI survey carried out just prior to the 2002 local government elections found that 64 per cent of those polled could not name one of their local ward councillors. Accordingly, weak relations appear to exist between local voters and local councillors. In the same MORI survey, 67 per cent said that they have never met their local councillors, with this figure rising to 82 per cent in Greater London.

Such findings have led to growing calls to redefine the role of local councillors as part of a wider process of democratic renewal. In particular, significant attempts have been made to redefine the role of elected councillors via the 'modernising local government' agenda pursued by the current Labour government, spearheaded by two White Papers (DETR 1998, 1999) and the Local Government Act 2000. At the heart of these reforms has been the requirement placed upon councils to abandon the committee system, condemned as 'an inefficient and opaque structure' in which decision-making was not only slow, but which was also seen as a democratic façade. In particular, the increasing politicisation of councils was felt to lead to 'real decisions being taken elsewhere, behind closed doors, with little open, democratic scrutiny and where many councillors feel unable to influence events' (DETR 1998: 1.15). This was also viewed as leading the electorate to 'lose confidence in their council's decisions, individual councillors become disillusioned with their ability to influence local decisions, and people are discouraged from standing for election' (DETR 1999: 1.14).

Under the new political arrangements introduced by the Local Government Act, the committee system has been replaced by new political management structures based on the separation of the executive function. These new executives, powers are intended to provide clear political leadership and strategic direction for councils along with clarity in decision-making. For all local authorities, other than very small district councils, the 2000 Act set out three main options for new executive arrangements:

◆ A directly elected mayor with a cabinet (mayor–cabinet model);

◆ A leader with a cabinet (leader–cabinet model); and

◆ A directly elected mayor and council manager (mayor–manager model).

As well as enhancing executive leadership capacity and decision-making efficiency, the new arrangements are also intended to facilitate backbench members expanding and strengthening their roles as community representatives and as council watchdogs on formal scrutiny committees. As the new political arrangements were expected to mean that less time would be spent in council meetings, the White Paper envisaged backbenchers 'spending more time in the local community, at residents' meetings or surgeries' (ibid.: 3.42) and working in the council as 'champion of their community defending the public interest in the council and channelling the grievances, needs and aspirations of the electorate into the scrutiny process' (ibid.: 3.43). These new and enhanced roles were assumed to be less time-consuming, but also more challenging and rewarding, with the intention that they would encourage a wider and more diverse proportion of the population to become interested in serving as local councillors.

Both Burnley and Harrogate District Councils adopted the leader-cabinet model during 2001–02. Sufficient time has therefore elapsed to allow at least some initial judgements to be made about the extent to which a reinvention of the role of local councillors is being realised.

During the course of our research, we interviewed close to 40 district and county councillors about their roles. While we do not have a fully robust 'baseline' against which to measure the impact of the new political arrangements over the past four years, the interviews point to a number of key issues about the roles played by local councillors, and the extent to which they have changed in recent years. Focusing primarily on the two districts, but with some comparisons made with the respective county councils, we present a summary of our findings here under three main headings: (i) candidates for local elections; (ii) campaigning, canvassing and contact with constituents; and (iii) the experience of scrutiny.

Candidates for local elections

Overall, there is little evidence to date that the new political arrangements have helped to generate greater interest in standing for election locally. An 'optimistic' interpretation would be that there are signs that 'new' candidates for office do continue to come forward. Only four of the councillors we interviewed had served for a total of 15 years or longer, while the average, accumulated length of time in office was just over eight years. Just over half of the councillors interviewed had held office for a total of five years or less, and just under half had been members of their current political party for ten years or under,[9] and around a quarter had first become active in local party politics at some point since the late 1990s.

However, such figures must be qualified. Interviews with local party leaders revealed that falling levels of party membership and low levels of party activism, detailed in chapter 7, have tended to mean that candidates for local council elections are generally drawn from a dwindling pool of candidates. Little more than a third of the councillors interviewed had, at any stage in their political careers, faced competition within their own parties to secure a nomination to stand in local elections. Moreover, this figure is quite possibly misleadingly high, as much of the competition for nominations identified occurred as a result of changes to Burnley's ward boundaries, which led to fresh elections for the full

---

9   The number of 'new' party members among councillors in the two towns is somewhat 'artificially' high, due to a number of Liberal Democrat councillors in Harrogate switching to the Conservatives in the past five years.

council in 2002. Moreover, there are few signs that the socio-demographic profile of councillors is becoming more diverse. While there are some signs of parties recruiting new and younger activists who have subsequently become councillors, this is not occurring at the rate required to replace older members. As a result, the average age of councillors in both Burnley and Harrogate has continued to rise, with elected members remaining predominantly middle-aged or retired. Currently, women make up 36 per cent of district councillors in Burnley, while 22 per cent of Harrogate's district councillors are female. Although this is higher, in both cases, than the representation of women in parliament, the proportion of female councillors in the two towns has been remarkably stable since 2001, despite annual elections to district councils.

Campaigning, canvassing and contact with constituents

While there is certainly evidence that councillors are spending a considerable amount of time in their wards, much of this arises from time spent campaigning for re-election and handling casework, rather than from providing 'local leadership'. Clearly, it is difficult to draw a clear distinction between campaigning, on the one hand, and championing local causes and local people on the other. Nonetheless, the time spent by elected members on campaigning tends to be considerable, and is an aspect of the role that is frequently overlooked. The vast majority of councillors indicated that they leaflet and canvass in their wards all year round, and that they are also involved in supporting the campaigns of other elected members, including county council elections and, in general, election campaigns. In the 6–8 weeks prior to elections, the average councillor spends around 15 hours per week canvassing and campaigning. On this basis, we estimate that the average borough councillor in Burnley and Harrogate will spend up to 200 hours annually on political campaigning alone. Moreover, the task of campaigning increasingly rests with councillors themselves, who are able to count upon only limited support. Based on the interviews we conducted, we estimate that elected members account for 40–50 per cent of local activists for almost all political parties in Burnley and Harrogate. The outcome, as one local party leader noted is that the burden of staying in touch with the local electorate falls heavily upon a small number of individuals:

Every ward that we have is having problems finding people who will knock on doors, or even deliver leaflets. There's a problem right across [the local parties]. *And what you have basically are the sitting councillors and prospective candidates who are doing virtually all of the work.*

On top of campaigning, Burnley and Harrogate councillors typically spend a similar amount of time dealing with casework, with the average of around 4 hours per week, or 200 hours per annum, spent dealing with issues raised by individual constituents. However, in contrast to the figures for campaigning, this estimate conceals enormous variations in the levels of ongoing contact between individual councillors and their constituents. Councillors reported spending anything between 1 and 15 hours per week working on casework brought to them by their constituents. Moreover, while there is insufficient data to reach firm conclusions, we would suggest that two distinct patterns can be discerned in relation to the observed variations in casework:

(i) There is a clear tendency for district councillors to receive more contact from local residents and to spend more time on casework than county councillors. Indeed, most of the county councillors we spoke to suggested that their casework amounts to nothing more than a few hours per month. This pattern once again underlines the relative closeness of district councils to local residents highlighted throughout this book; and

(ii) It appears that Burnley district councillors deal with more casework on average than Harrogate district councillors. Moreover, among all councillors, there appears to be a tendency for councillors in inner-urban wards in Burnley to have the highest levels of ongoing contact with their constituents. It is likely that these differences stem from contrasting socio-economic conditions, with more affluent residents experiencing either fewer problems or having the confidence and contacts to pursue issues with local officials directly.

Interviews with local MPs and their caseworkers indicate that a significant amount of casework relating to constituents' problems with local public agencies is handled by MPs and their staff. Whereas MPs tend to run busy weekly surgeries in their constituencies – typically on a Friday or Saturday – virtually every councillor we interviewed that had hosted surgeries had quickly given up. In the words of one councillor:

'Tried it, nobody ever came [...] six weeks, every Saturday morning. Nobody ever came'. As we discuss below, the growing portfolio of casework handled by MPs has been facilitated, in part, by the provision of expenses to MPs enabling them to employ dedicated caseworkers. There would seem to be grounds for examining the 'division of labour' between councillors and MPs in more detail and for investigating the possibility of making similar resources available to groups of local councillors. In part, residents will often approach their MP simply because they are likely to have a higher profile locally than ward councillors. Indeed, one of the clearest impacts of the introduction of Cabinet arrangements in local government was suggested to be that members of the executive become more visible to the general public and, therefore, more likely to be approached by local residents. This tendency stands in stark contrast to what was envisaged in the 1998 and 1999 White Papers:

> It's certainly not true that the non-executive members can relieve the executive members of their constituency roles. The opposite tends to happen. Because the executive members are the ones with their names in the papers, those are the ones that the constituents go to.

The experience of scrutiny

The introduction of overview and scrutiny arrangements under the terms of the Local Government Act of 2000 was motivated by a concern to enhance democratic accountability within local councils and to increase the extent to which elected local politicians are able to hold unelected local and regional bodies to account. A particularly striking feature of the provisions introduced in 2000 is the capacity for scrutiny committees to invite members of other public bodies to give evidence, as well as the specific roles accorded to local authorities in scrutinising the work of external bodies such as health care trusts.

However, in contrast to these intentions, a recent national survey of the impact of overview and scrutiny in local government suggested that 'the majority of members and officers are unable to agree the system in their authority had been successful' (Gains *et al.*: 2004: 11). The lack of consensus appears to reflect a view that councillors have been far more effective in the 'overview' than in the 'scrutiny' role. Hence, there is a widespread sense that 'there had been more success in reviewing service outcomes than in holding decision makers to account' (*ibid.*: 2004: 11). Our interviews with local councillors and council officers reflected a similar level of disagreement about the effectiveness of scrutiny. In particular, our research in Burnley and Harrogate suggests that:

◆ There is limited evidence that the new political arrangements are enabling a redefinition of the role of backbench councillors. It is not clear that backbench members spend less time in meetings under the new arrangements. Analysis carried out by Harrogate Borough Council in 2002 suggested that the scrutiny function had increased the number of meetings by 100 per cent. The majority of councillors interviewed did not feel they spent less time in meetings, with the exception of those who had chosen not to become involved in scrutiny;

◆ While there is a widespread view among senior council officers and many executive members that scrutiny powers are considerable, there is also a clear sense that backbench councillors had yet to recognise their strength as scrutiny members or the power they hold to set their own agendas. While many councillors feel that scrutiny remains in its infancy, it currently has a long way to go if it is to evolve into a stronger and more effective check on the power of the executive;

◆ There is a clear sense at both the district and county levels that overview and scrutiny committees are struggling to operate in the manner envisaged in government White Papers and legislation. There is some agreement that the main contribution of scrutiny thus far has been in the area of policy development, but few councillors view it as effectively calling the executive to account. Frequently cited examples of successful overview and scrutiny committee activity includes visits to neighbouring authorities aimed at identifying potentially transferable 'good practice'. While laudable and valuable activity in itself, such 'fact finding missions' sit somewhat uneasily with the formally defined function of scrutiny;

◆ Very few overview and scrutiny committees have made use of the power to co-opt non-elected members, designed, in part, to enable them to bring in external expertise and knowledge. Only one instance was found of a scrutiny committee using this power, with the co-optee serving for less than a year and generally having little engagement with the work of the committee;

◆ The apparent reluctance of overview and scrutiny committees to 'flex their muscles' is underlined by the fact that they have rarely called-in decisions on any of the four councils examined. This reluctance to call-in decisions does not appear to be a function of the relative stringency of call-in rules in the four local authorities – an assessment that is underpinned by the findings of national research (Gains *et al.* 2004: 12, Stoker *et al.* 2004: 48-50);

◆ For many backbench councillors, particularly those with experience of the committee system, the experience of overview and scrutiny has proved a frustrating one. A long-standing councillor in one authority described her experience of overview and scrutiny in the following terms: 'we feel like a glorified focus group sometimes'. Likewise, in another council, a perceived lack of any clear role or purpose for scrutiny committees was felt to have led to dwindling attendance, with some committees attended by as few as five or six from a total membership of ten.

If academic analysis of the executive/scrutiny split has come to mixed conclusions, the views of local journalists are far less ambivalent. Evidence suggests that local journalists see the new arrangements as restricting the access of reporters to key meetings, decision-makers and information, and thereby compromising the ability of local papers to report openly and accurately on decision-making in local affairs. A survey of 110 local newspaper editors, chief reporters and local government communication officers, carried out by Grant Riches Communication Consultants (2003), found that less than 7 per cent described the introduction of the new political arrangements in local government as 'good for local democracy'. Moreover:

◆ Seventy-five per cent felt council decision-making had become 'less open and transparent' under the new arrangements, while more than 80 per cent felt that a growing number of decisions were 'being made behind closed doors';

◆ Around 75 per cent were of the view that the modernization of local government had failed to render the local democratic process more understandable for the general public;

◆ Under 15 per cent regarded scrutiny as making councils 'more open and accountable', while 66 per cent described scrutiny arrangements as 'a waste of time'.

6.3 The role of MPs

My heart used to sink when people came through my door and said "you are my last hope".

Tony Banks, MP, 2005

Members of parliament are, naturally, seen as the embodiment of national democracy and the role of MPs in local democracy is generally overlooked. Such an interpretation of the role of MPs rests, however, on a highly artificial distinction between national and local democracy. In reality, the distinction between national and local democracy is not so clear-cut, particularly as MPs are elected to represent constituents residing in a specific locality. Indeed, MPs play a significant role in the local democratic process, aided significantly by their office staff, and provide a key link between local and national democratic processes. Based on the interviews conducted with MPs, eight sets of activity were identified through which MPs engage with the local democratic process. While there are clearly significant differences in the extent to which individual MPs are involved in each of the eight forms of activity, there was consensus that these categories capture the ways in which an MP relates to local democracy:

(i)   MPs and their staff handle casework for constituents that concern local public bodies, particularly local councils, police, and health care trusts;

(ii) MPs have close relationships with the local party branch in the constituency they represent;

(i)   MPs will frequently be lobbied by people, organisations, or groups within the locality on specifically local issues such as planning, transport or NHS provision;

(ii) MPs have ongoing relationships with local public bodies, ranging from formal links provided through regular meetings to occasional informal contacts;

(iii) MPs tend to feature regularly in the local media, particularly the local press, and may become heavily involved in specific local media debates;

(iv) MPs may become involved with strategic policy debates within the constituency, for instance through their participation in local strategic partnerships or other partnership bodies;

(v) MPs become involved in lobbying for their constituency and representing it in national policy debate;

(vi) MPs may, in some circumstances, become involved in brokering with central government and regional bodies over issues such as the allocation of additional public investment.

There was agreement among the four MPs interviewed that the first of these roles, handling casework relating to local public agencies, constitutes by far the most significant and the most time-consuming of the eight roles identified. Estimates provided by MPs and their staff suggest that 50–70 person hours per week are spent by MPs' offices in handling casework brought by local constituents. Typically, the management of casework involves the equivalent of at least 1.5 full-time members of staff, with the MP spending at least a further 5 hours per week on casework themselves, including time spent in surgeries. Estimates provided by one MP's caseworker suggest that around 290 'communications' are received by the office from members of the public per month concerning issues or grievances with local or national bodies. As Table 6.1 shows, the largest share of contacts are made via post, followed by e-mail, telephone and attendance at surgeries. Clearly, a significant share of these communications will represent multiple contacts from the same individuals, particular those with ongoing cases.

Nonetheless, the number of communications from local residents being received by MPs' offices is considerable and, almost universally, it was felt that the resources available to support MPs' casework were insufficient. In several instances it was suggested that, were the funding available, an additional full-time member of staff would be justifiable, given the work involved in handling casework. It has been estimated that, whereas MPs in the 1950s received an average of 12–20 letters per week, the volume of post received annually by the House of Commons today translates into 15,000 items per MP (Cowley, 2006). Indeed, the contrast between the constituency demands placed upon modern day MPs and their predecessors is vividly illustrated by Dari Taylor MP's childhood memories of her father, Daniel Jones, MP for Burnley from 1959–83, completing his weekly casework after Sunday lunch:

He was in the dining room and suddenly the table would cover with his papers. And he would hand-write responses to local government officials, his constituents, and in three hours he would go through all that he needed to and respond to them. And then, with a great sense of satisfaction, he'd put his coat on, and he'd walk to the post and he'd post them. That was it – over and done with. That was my father's handling of his parliamentary correspondence.

Taylor, 2005

As noted, the volume of casework handled by MPs contrasts sharply with the reported volumes handled by both district and county councillors. Unlike local councillors, the staffing budgets and other allowances available to MPs enable them to delegate casework to specialist employees. Nonetheless, it is striking that the average number of hours devoted weekly to casework by MPs offices is equivalent to the time spent on casework by approximately 10–15 district councillors. Moreover, in contrast to the district and county councillors we interviewed, where surgeries are virtually unheard of, MPs typically convene three or four surgeries a month in their constituencies, with an average of 10–15 attendees at each. To some extent, such comparisons are disingenuous. Casework handled by MPs does not exclusively relate to local public service provision and only a small proportion concerns the work of local councils. In terms of both casework volume and time spent on individual cases, issues concerning national government departments and agencies tend to dominate. At the time the interviews were carried out, the most common categories were tax credits, immigration and the child support agency.

Table 6.1: Total communications from local residents handled monthly by one MP's office (average for January and February 2005)

Form of contact	Approx. contacts received
Post	100
Email	80
Telephone	50
Surgeries	40
Faxes	20
TOTAL	290

However, as a rule of thumb, casework concerning specifically local public service providers constitutes around half of all casework handled by MPs. Chiefly such casework consists of issues concerned with the following areas of local service provision: housing and housing benefit, council tax, planning, transport, health services, social services, and policing. In such cases, MPs' offices generally become involved after a constituent has initially broached the issue with the local agency concerned. There is also a small, but significant, degree of casework 'referral' between local Citizens Advice Bureaux and MP's offices. Inevitably, there can be some overlap between the roles of MPs and that of elected local councillors in handling casework. In some instances, MPs do take on cases that elected local councillors might be expected to handle initially, although this arises in the vast majority of cases from the decision made by a constituent to contact their MP, rather than a local councillor, in the first instance. Such instances often occur in the context of MPs' surgeries, which are increasingly the principal, if not only, 'drop-in' facility through which local residents can contact politicians. As one MP noted 'if someone had sat down for three hours waiting to see me on a Saturday morning, there is no way I was going to say "go and see Councillor so and so"'. While some MPs nationally run surgeries in conjunction with local councillors, such a model was generally eschewed by the MPs serving the Burnley and Harrogate districts.

It is also likely that a number of 'well informed' local residents have come to find that raising a local issue with an MP, particularly if relating to evidence of injustice or maladministration in local public services, is an effective mechanism of citizen redress. While firm evidence is not available, there is a clear sense among MPs and their caseworkers that intervention from an MP's office tends to provoke appropriate action when genuine problems or grievances are raised. In the view of one interviewee, MPs are particularly effective when they become involved in cases arising from local service provision, where a letter from the MP will tend to 'land on the desk of the chief executive'. Moreover, it was suggested that the smaller and more 'local' the service provider, the greater the impact of MP intervention will be. Thus, a letter from an MP is more likely to lead to a far more rapid correction to a miscalculation or maladministration of housing benefit – a function controlled by district councils – than would be the case for a similar error made by the Inland Revenue in relation to tax credits.

Beyond casework, there is huge variation in the roles played by MPs in the local democratic process. While all MPs interviewed have some degree of involvement with each of the roles outlined above, the balance of activity is different in each case. Each MP described a very different set and balance of relations with local councils, schools, primary care trusts, police and other bodies. To some extent, the variation is a matter of style. Some MPs see it an important part of their role publicly to engage with, and provide a degree of leadership in, local policy debates, while others seek to exert a more subtle influence from 'behind the scenes'. In some cases, MPs take a conscious decision to play a relatively passive role in relation to local democracy, essentially taking the view that the principle of 'subsidiarity' suggests that local, rather than national, politicians should take the lead in seeking to define local policy priorities. Such differences become especially apparent in relation to local planning decisions – the principal issue on which MPs in both Burnley and Harrogate are lobbied by local residents and local groups.

Inevitably, variations in MPs' involvement with local democracy also have a great deal to do with party control of local government. Where the same political party holds both the parliamentary seat and controls the local council, there is an obvious tendency towards close working relations and a relatively high degree of contact between MPs, council leaders and other councillors from the ruling group. However, such relationships are far from automatic, with the extent of ongoing contact between MPs and local councillors varying significantly, even where the same party controls both roles. Where one party holds the parliamentary seat and another party controls the local council, effective working relationships can be extremely difficult to forge, particularly if the area concerned is relatively closely contested in local and national elections. The problems arising from such 'political asymmetry' between parliamentary representation and council control were seen to be of such significance in the view of one interviewee as to represent 'a huge flaw within the system'.

The degree to which MPs see it as part of their role to be involved in lobbying or brokering activity with civil servants and cabinet ministers will, in part, depend upon the type and scale of local problems. In the case of Burnley, where the town's decline was arguably overlooked for decades by those framing national regeneration policy, lobbying central government was a constant feature of the career of the recently retired MP for Burnley, Peter Pike. For instance, Mr Pike indicated in interview that he had raised the issue of housing conditions in Burnley more than three hundred times in the House of Commons during his 18 years as MP. However, the Burnley case also illustrates that there is a relatively narrow line between lobbying and brokering, with the distinction often depending upon whether a local MP is drawn from the ranks of government or from an opposition party. Thus, the election of a Labour government in 1997 was to progressively enhance the access of Burnley's Labour MP to key national decision-makers. As a result, Mr Pike noted how his role changed from one of 'fighting to get money for essential school repairs' to one that enabled him to play a direct role in negotiations concerning the full-scale rebuilding of Burnley's secondary schools under the Building Schools for the Future programme.

6.4 The role of parish councillors

The vision for local government sees an important role for citizen engagement and participation so that they have greater influence over the delivery of public services. There are a variety of possible models to give communities a stronger voice at local level, one of which is through parish and town councils.

Nick Raynsford, MP, to the House of Commons, 2004[10]

Parish and town councils have frequently been overlooked in accounts of local democracy. Limited attention has been paid to parishes for a number of reasons, including the tendency for many parish councillors to be elected unopposed,[11] and the absence of any real parish council powers. Moreover, the coverage of parishes is highly uneven: as was noted in chapter 3, there are 73 active parish and town councils in Harrogate, but just 8 in Burnley. However, as the above quotation highlights, the present government has indicated growing interest in parish and town councils, making provisions for these bodies to acquire greater powers under the 'Quality Parish' scheme. Moreover, as the case of Padiham Town Council illustrates (established in 2002, after what one interviewee described as 'a hard fight'), there is frequently a demand for such highly localised units of local government, even if their

---

10 *Hansard,* 14 Sept 2004: Column 1527W.
11 Edwards *et al.* (2002) suggest that, from 1998–2001, contested elections were required in just 28 per cent of parish, town and community council wards.

resources and functions are highly limited. Arising from this context, our research suggests that there are strong grounds for reconsidering the significance of parish and town councils, and for seeing them as bodies with particular and unique qualities in relation to local democracy. In particular, we have found that:

◆ Despite the infrequency of contested elections nationally, there are many instances of competitive elections to parish and town councils in Burnley and Harrogate, with some instances cited of quite intense, and even bitter, election campaigns;

◆ Public attendance at parish and town council meetings is often far higher than anything achieved by district councils, county councils, primary care trusts or any other local public bodies. For instance, a parish councillor in Briercliffe (Burnley) reported regular public attendance in the region of 12–20 people, with 50 or more attending where particularly controversial local issues, such as pub licensing, were being discussed;

◆ There are particular democratic qualities to parish and town councils that simply cannot be replicated at higher tiers of local government. District councillors that have previously served as parish councillors, or continue to do so, frequently highlighted the closer relationship that they have with local residents in the latter of the two roles;

◆ The view that parish councillors are uniquely close to local people is reinforced by the fact that in areas with parish councils, there is a typically a representative for every 800 residents, whereas in areas where the district council is the lowest tier of local government, the ratio of local politicians to local residents is around 1:2000;

◆ Parish and town councils provide even the smallest of local communities with a close link to higher tiers of local government and, in the view of one interviewee, parishes can operate frequently as 'people often go to the parish council as the first port of call. We're sort of, to use the phrase "a one-stop shop". People come to us even though they know that it's not a parish council responsibility';

◆ There are a number of cases of parish councillors being able to respond highly effectively to concerns raised by local residents, particularly in instances involving the management of parks and children's playgrounds, where parishes often have a direct responsibility, as well as in relation to planning decisions, where parish councils have advisory powers. In one instance, a parish council representing just a few hundred local residents was able to lead a successful campaign to stop a wind farm development proposed by United Utilities and initially supported by Burnley Borough Council (see Case Study 6.1).

We would argue that, despite their obvious shortcomings, there is clear evidence that resurgent parish and town councils could offer significant opportunities to promote public engagement at the most local level, and that parish councillors can play a significant role in countering the remoteness of higher tiers of local government. As a senior county councillor noted:

My predecessor suggested very strongly that I go to all the parish councils. I duly went. I have to say I've been impressed. […] They have no power of course. But I do think they can reflect local views and they are absolutely ear to the ground stuff. They made me aware of concerns that I wouldn't be aware of otherwise […] They drill down quite a long way into the local community.

Case Study 6.1: Dunnockshaw and Clowbridge Parish Council vs United Utilities

During 2002 a proposal was submitted to Burnley Borough Council by United Utilities for planning permission for a wind farm on the hills above Dunnockshaw reservoir, close to the villages of Dunnockshaw and Clowbridge on the south-western outskirts of Burnley District. The proposal came exactly 10 years after the controversy surrounding the eventual building of a wind farm at Long Causeway, in the Cliviger parish of Burnley.

As had been the case with the Cliviger wind farm, the proposed development in Dunnockshaw and Clowbridge was strongly opposed by the local parish council, representing around 500 local residents. The proposed 200 foot turbines at Dunnockshaw were significantly larger than those used in Cliviger, and were memorably described by Cllr Marcus Johnstone of Lancashire County Council as 'two thirds the height of the Blackpool tower'. Moreover, some of the turbines were planned to be located as close as half a mile from people's homes, an issue that raised considerable

(Continued)

Case Study 6.1: Dunnockshaw and Clowbridge Parish Council vs United Utilities (continued)

concern. Despite this opposition, the development was initially granted outline planning permission by Burnley Borough Council and was also supported by Lancashire County Council.

Dunnockshaw and Clowbridge parish councillors immediately set about mobilising local opposition to the development, visiting virtually every house in the parish and declaring confidently that 97 per cent of residents were opposed. At the same time, parish councillors set about building a wider coalition of interests against the development, contacting Burnley district councillors known to be sympathetic, as well as their county council representative. Significantly, the parish council also organised fund-raising events used primarily to generate the funds required to employ a planning consultant. Based on the advice of the planning consultant, a coalition emerged with a unifying concern to oppose the development on the grounds of its impact on the landscape. In particular, the development would have been visible from across the borough and would have involved the destruction of a recently completed memorial tree-planting scheme in the area.

Although the decision to grant planning permission locally was eventually reversed by the council's Development Control Committee in March 2003, the case was subsequently the subject to a public inquiry in February 2004. Despite the resources, specialist expertise and presentational skills that United Utilities were able to deploy at the inquiry, their case was defeated by the parish councils and their allies, who followed a simple and consistent line of criticising the development on environmental grounds. The outcome, which was widely portrayed in the local press as a 'David versus Goliath' scenario, underlines the relevance that parish councils can have in representing their local communities, particularly where they are able to link into the wider structures of local democracy.

6.5 Conclusion

This chapter adds to the conclusions reached in chapter 5 about the central role of elected politicians to local democracy, even in a context where so much public spending is in the hands of unelected bodies. Indeed, given the issues of remuneration highlighted in chapter 5, the significant time that councillors spend campaigning and dealing with casework suggests a major imbalance when compared to equivalent roles on other local public bodies, such as 'non-executive directors' on NHS trust boards. At the same time, however, it is evident that recent reforms intended to bolster the role of elected councillors within their communities and in holding other local bodies to account have had limited impact. While the scrutiny function may take time to develop, we are not persuaded that it currently offers the scope to enable local councillors to realise the sort of impact on local affairs that would persuade more voters to think that local elections 'matter'. At the same time, interviews with local MPs revealed the significant impact that MPs, in conjunction with their staff, can have on the local democratic process. Yet, the relationship of MPs to local democracy is rarely considered in this way. We would argue that active constituency MPs can play an important role in helping to strengthen local democracy, although there is a parallel danger that very strong local MPs may serve to further erode the distinction between local and national democracy. For instance, the tendency for many local residents to approach MPs, rather than councillors, regarding issues concerning local public agencies raises questions about where the 'division of labour' between politicians should lie. Providing local councillors with an equivalent scale of resource to respond to casework could, of course, significantly alter this balance.

Our findings clearly indicate a need to challenge the popular conception of politicians as self-interested, self-serving and lazy. It is perhaps one of the greatest challenges for reformers to find a means of overcoming this myth, which has profoundly negative consequences for the recruitment of candidates for local election, for local election turnouts and for the relationship between politicians and local residents. There is a very real danger that in the face of an overwhelmingly hostile public, local politicians, and even MPs, will retreat from attempting to provide leadership on contentious local issues and instead become largely reactive, attempting to achieve little more than 'survive' in their role. As one experienced local politician remarked:

Politicians, instead of giving a lead, follow. They'll jump on any passing bandwagon to try and get a few cheap votes [...] councillors are increasingly doing not what they think is right, but what they think will win them a few votes and that bodes dreadfully badly for local government.

7
The Party's Over?:

Local political participation and civic engagement

In February 2002, Bath and North East Somerset Council facilitated a public meeting to discuss how to address voter apathy. Only one person attended.

Dolton, 2005, p.1

7.1 Introduction

Few would dispute that political participation is essential to the health of local democracy. Yet, there is little agreement about what constitutes political participation, about whether some forms of participation are more important to local democracy than others, or about whether declining levels of (some forms of) participation constitute a 'crisis' of local democracy. A number of principal trends in political participation are clear. It is well known that there has been a steady fall in local electoral turnout and local party activism. Likewise, it is generally accepted that such trends are, to some extent, countered by stable, and, in some cases, rising, levels of participation in non-electoral politics and various forms of civic engagement. There is also wider evidence of a diversification of political participation in 'mature' democracies, for instance via the growth of various forms of 'identity' and/or 'lifestyle politics', many of which have a specifically local dimension. The crucial question, however, is what consequences do these developments have for the way in which local democracy operates?

In seeking to address this question, this chapter takes a broad view of local activism, ranging from local party politics and pressure groups through to voluntary and community sector activity. Using national datasets as well as our own research findings from Burnley and Harrogate, the chapter engages directly with the proposition that there is a crisis of political and civic involvement. We argue that there has been a diversification, rather than a straightforward decline in local political and civic engagement. However, we also suggest that such diversification raises major issues for local democracy. An increasingly diverse local political and civic infrastructure is being maintained by a minority of the population and there is a pronounced tendency for this 'activist minority' to be drawn from the educated, white middle-classes. This presents particular challenges for elected local government. With local activists spreading themselves more thinly across a broader range of activities, the erosion of local political parties has reached such an advanced state that meaningful party competition is increasingly difficult to sustain at the local level.

7.2 Defining political participation and civic engagement

Definitions of political participation have progressively broadened in recent years, largely out of recognition that forms of political participation have diversified. Political scientists no longer tend to restrict themselves to the study of 'conventional' forms of participation in representative democracy, such as voting, campaigning and standing for office. 'Non-conventional' forms of political participation, such as signing petitions, taking part in demonstrations, engaging in civil disobedience or other forms of 'direct action' are now commonly included in mainstream definitions of political participation (Parry *et al.,* 1992; Birch, 1993). Recognition has also been given to the growth of direct citizen participation in the policy process and in the decision-making structures of public bodies since the 1960s, including tenants' involvement in social housing, parental involvement in the governance of schools and the more recent growth of public consultation in the public services (Birch, 1993; Birchall and Simmons, 2004; Power Inquiry, 2005). To provide for a comprehensive categorisation of political participation, we might also add 'do-it-yourself political activity' (cf. Power Inquiry, 2005), a term that captures a huge variety of 'bottom-up' activism and 'lifestyle politics' ranging from mutual associations to environmentalism, vegetarianism and 'queer politics'. There has also been growing recognition of the symbiotic relationship between political participation and more everyday forms of civic engagement (Putnam 1993, 1996, 2000). In this view, the collective sum of citizen involvement in groups and organisations results in the formation of networks of trust and cooperation, representing the 'social capital' that is crucial to sustaining a healthy democracy. For all of these reasons, we adopt a broad understanding of political participation in local democracy which recognises that:

> *democracy lies as much in the vitality of* [...] *citizens' self-organisation in all aspects of their collective life – what has come to be called civil society – as well as their formal relation to government.*
>
> Democratic Audit, n.d.2

7.3 National trends in political participation and civic engagement

It has been clearly documented that levels of electoral turnout, party membership and party activism have all declined in recent years. The evidence of decline is compelling and is frequently cited by those concerned about the health of national and local democracy in the UK (Power Inquiry, 2005). The following are broadly indicative of the trends that have been identified:

◆ Considerable fluctuations notwithstanding, electoral turnouts in the UK show overall decline since the early 1950s and have slumped in recent years. The 2001 and 2005 general elections recorded the two lowest turnouts since 1918 (Power Inquiry, 2005);

◆ Local election turnouts show similar patterns to those for general elections. All district election turnouts since 1973 have been under 50 per cent. Turnout in local elections fell below 30 per cent in both 1998 and 2000 (Rallings and Thasher 2003);

◆ Disengagement from electoral activity is especially evident amongst social classes DE, younger voters and most ethnic minority groups (Electoral Commission, 2002, 2003a);

◆ Party membership in the UK has been in steep decline since the mid-1960s. Levels of activism among party members have also dropped over the same period (Seyd and Whiteley, 2004).

However, while such evidence suggests to some that there is an escalating 'crisis' of representative democracy, it is also apparent that many forms of political activism are increasing, and that public interest in local affairs remains particularly strong. Despite the decline in electoral activity, surveys carried out since the early 1980s suggest that both public willingness to take political action and reported levels of actual political action remain remarkably stable (Bromley *et al.*, 2001). These polls are borne out by wider evidence that participation in 'pressure activity' has increased in recent years, particularly among the young. Moreover, as we show in more detail in chapter 8, there is widespread public involvement in public services, with notable numbers of people serving as police 'special constables', lay magistrates, school governors, tenants' representatives, and in other similar roles (Birchall and Simmons, 2004). Moreover, if civic engagement is considered in its broadest sense, research suggests that around 22 million adults are involved in some form of volunteering annually, collectively accounting for 90 million hours of voluntary work per week (IVR, 1997).

7.4 The stratification of citizenship

While the trends pointed to above suggest overall levels of local political and civic engagement remain relatively stable, closer examination reveals enormous variations between different sections of society. Assimilating evidence from a diverse range of surveys on political and civic engagement, a picture of 'stratified citizenship' emerges, based around four broad groups of local citizens. These effectively represent a 'pyramid' of political and civic engagement, with a small number of local activists at the peak, and a majority of 'locally disengaged citizens' along the base:

◆ *Core local activists*: Based on national figures for party membership and activism, local party politics is the preserve of less than three per cent of the population. Up to seven per cent of the population participate directly in public service provision (Birchall and Simmons, 2004), and regular volunteering is sustained by a core group of around 12 per cent of the population (Ruston, 2003). We estimate that local political and civic infrastructure is therefore sustained by a relatively small activist minority, constituting up to 15 per cent of the population;

◆ *Regular participants*: Coulthard *et al.* (2002) found that 21 per cent of people had been involved in a local organisation over the previous three years, and 27 per cent had taken some form of action in response to a local problem. These figures are consistent with surveys that suggest around 25 per cent of the population have ever made formal complaints to local public bodies (see chapter 8). On this basis we suggest that up to a quarter of the population (including core activists) are likely to participate to some extent in local affairs on a fairly regular basis;

◆ *The latently engaged*: Survey evidence consistently suggests that around half the population typically express willingness to engage in local affairs. For instance, 55 per cent of people say they would like to be more involved in the decisions made by their local council (ODPM, 2005). Surveys carried out on behalf of the Institute for Volunteering Research suggest that around half of the adult population had been involved in formal voluntary activity in the previous 12 months (IVR, 1997);

◆ *The locally disengaged*: This category constitutes up to 50 per cent of the population, comprising citizens that do not tend to vote in local elections, do not tend to volunteer, do not read a local newspaper, and indicate that they have little or no interest in local affairs.

There is a further sense in which citizenship is stratified. Levels of political and civic activism show strong correlations with age, occupation, levels of education and personal wealth (Parry *et al.*, 1992; Power Inquiry, 2005). Those educated to A-level and above, those in social classes ABC1 and those on above average incomes are far more likely to be active in local affairs in some form (Coulthard *et al.*, 2002). This pattern is particularly pronounced in relation to activism associated with 'new politics', such as environmentalism. At the same time, those showing the lowest levels of local engagement are generally those possessing the fewest formal qualifications and living on the lowest incomes. The broad categories presented above are therefore cross-cut by factors such as age and social class. Moreover, given their contrasting socio-economic circumstances, a comparison of local political and civic engagement in Burnley and Harrogate is therefore likely to reveal some clear contrasts in levels and forms of political and civic engagement. At the same time, national trends would lead us to expect activists to constitute a minority of local residents, particularly in relation to party politics.

7.5 Political representation and participation in Burnley and Harrogate

Given the centrality of participation to local democracy, we sought to undertake a comprehensive audit of political and civic participation in Burnley and Harrogate. There were four main elements to this audit, which comprised: (i) analysis of electoral turnout; (ii) local party membership and activism; (iii) the scale of voluntary and community sector activity; and (iv) patterns of citizen engagement in a wide range of political and civic activities. With the exception of the analysis of election statistics and existing surveys of the voluntary and community sectors, this exercise depended heavily upon original data collection. This data collection included face to face interviews with party leaders and membership secretaries, telephone interviews with local community and voluntary groups, and survey questions put to members of the citizens' panels operating in the two towns. Appendix 1 provides fuller discussion of the methods used and of the methodological issues arising.

Elections

Participation rates in national elections among Burnley and Harrogate voters largely match national trends. Turnouts in Burnley for the general elections of 1997, 2001 and 2005 have been 67 per cent, 56 per cent and 59 per cent respectively, matching the low turnout levels of recent years, and the slight increase (although higher than the national average) of 2005. The borough of Harrogate includes all or part of three constituencies. The turnout for the Harrogate and Knaresborough constituency in 1997 was 73 per cent, falling to 65 per cent in 2001 and rising slightly to 66 per cent in 2005. The other two constituencies overlapping with Harrogate district showed similar results, with 1997 turnouts in the mid-70s falling to just over 66 per cent for the next two elections. The difference in turnouts in Burnley and Harrogate is consistent with our expectations, given the contrasting class structures in the two towns and levels of education among local residents.

Similarly, turnouts at district elections have generally paralleled the national picture, having been normally below 50 per cent and having declined in both districts through the 1990s (see Figure 7.1 below). The decline in Burnley was stronger and deeper than the national average with a low of 24 per cent in 1998. Turnout has since substantially increased, so that in 2002 a turnout of 53 per cent was recorded, the highest locally in a district election since 1983. This may be a result of particular local conditions, specifically the rise of Independent councillors led by Harry Brooks, the subsequent increase in BNP electoral activity, and the response of other local parties to these developments. From 1988 to 2000, turnout in Harrogate was consistently 3–5 per cent above that in Burnley, again consistent with the contrasting class structures of the respective electorates. Harrogate has also shown an increase in turnouts since the nadir of 29 per cent in 1998, and in 2004 the district elections recorded a local high of 55 per cent. Again, specific local conditions may have played a part here, with increased Liberal Democrat-Conservative competition becoming evident in Harrogate from the late 1990s onwards, and local controversy over the costs of refurbishing the Royal Hall reaching its height.

Figure 7.1: District election turnouts in Burnley and Harrogate, 1983–2002 (%)

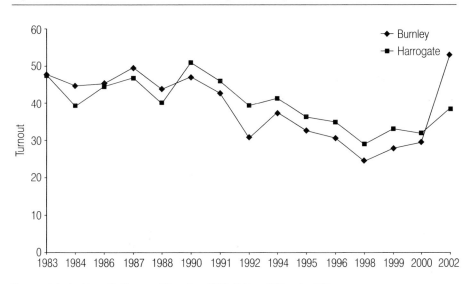

Source: Adapted from Rallings and Thrasher, 2003: Table p.266 and p.322.

The effect of holding local elections on the same day as national elections can clearly be seen in the turnout for county council elections in Burnley and Harrogate. As Figure 7.2 shows, turnouts prior to 1997 were low and declining in both districts. They have been boosted since 1997 by scheduling county elections on the same day as general elections.

Figure 7.2: District turnout in county council elections in Burnley and Harrogate, 1973–2005 (%)

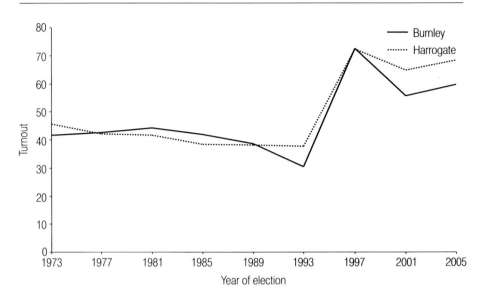

Source: Adapted from Rallings and Thrasher, 2003: p.266, p.322; 2005 figures author's calculation from Lancashire and North Yorkshire County Council website data.

In line with national trends, while turnout levels at local elections have been in decline, the contestation of seats has increased since the 1960s and 1970s. In both Burnley and Harrogate, overall contestation of seats has increased with very few wards either at district or county level being uncontested. However, it appears that, at the local level parties are focusing on wards they regard as 'winnable'. This is most clearly shown in the case of Burnley. Since 1973 only eight wards have ever been uncontested, but from the mid-1990s council elections have increasingly become a two-horse race between Labour and the Liberal Democrats, despite the rise of the Independents and, subsequently, the BNP.

Figure 7.3: Burnley Borough Council elections, 1980–2002, wards contested

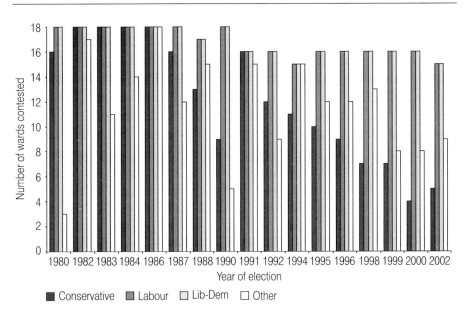

Source: Adapted from Rallings and Thrasher, 2003: p.266.

Figure 7.4: Harrogate Borough Council elections, 1979–2002, wards contested

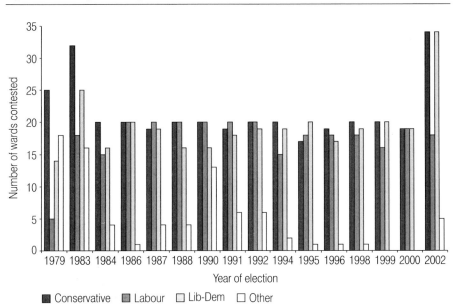

Source: Adapted from Rallings and Thrasher, 2003: p.266.

Party membership and party activism

Taken at face value, the patterns of turnout in general and local elections presented above, and the contestation levels for seats on the respective borough councils, would suggest that electoral participation and party competition are relatively vibrant in the two towns. However, such statistics should not automatically lead us to assume that talk of a crisis of local democracy is exaggerated. Local elections in England are centred on party competition and therefore depend upon political parties to field candidates and organise campaigns. Without an adequate party political infrastructure, representative democracy at the local level could not function. As such, analysis of party membership and activism forms a crucial element of our audit of local democracy in Burnley and Harrogate.

Table 7.1 provides estimates for aggregated party membership and activism in the two towns. We estimate there to be twice as many party members in the Harrogate and Knaresborough parliamentary constituency than in the Burnley parliamentary constituency, despite the fact that the two areas have very similar populations. It is likely that much of this difference can be explained by the stronger competition between the two main parties in Harrogate. However, we estimate that levels of activism are higher in Burnley, representing around 20 per cent of party members overall, compared to approximately 10 per cent of party members in Harrogate. Our definition of 'activists' assumes that members regularly attend meetings and play a role in campaigning. On the basis of these figures, the 'density' of party membership is estimated to be just 0.6 per cent of Burnley residents, and 1.4 per cent of Harrogate residents. Party activists appear to constitute no more than 0.1 per cent of the population in both towns. While robust statistical data are not available, interviews with party leaders and party secretaries indicate that the number of local party activists has fallen in both towns, in line with the national trend. The only party that appeared to buck this trend in both towns was the Liberal Democrats.

Although the data presented above indicates very high levels of contestation of local council seats among political parties in both towns, interviews with party leaders and party secretaries suggest that such statistics are highly misleading. Consequently, there is a general difficulty experienced by parties, across the board, in recruiting candidates for local elections and several sitting councillors indicated that they had stood as a result of 'having their arms twisted'. In the case of Harrogate, in particular, one party leader explained the tendency for several borough councillors to 'double up' as county councillors with direct reference to the shortage of available candidates. With the exception of the largest parties, there is an admitted need to stand 'paper candidates' in some wards. Furthermore, even among parties putting up candidates for all, or most, local council seats election resources and campaigning may often be targeted on a relatively small number of wards. For the third largest parties in the two towns, full campaigns, involving leafleting and canvassing of households, may be run in as few as two wards.

Table 7.1: Estimated party membership and party activism in the Burnley and Harrogate and Knaresborough parliamentary constituency, 2005

	Burnley	Harrogate
Number of political parties	5	4
Total members of political parties	540	1220
Total party activists	89	118

Source: Interviews with party secretaries, plus authors' estimates.

Running a local election campaign across a town with 50,000 households is a major undertaking. Research consistently shows that genuine party competition, often premised upon door to door campaigning, involving canvassing and leafleting, has a strongly positive impact on local election turnouts. Yet, the figures we have obtained suggest that local election campaigns in each town effectively depend upon around 100 individuals that can be typically be called upon by all political parties. Moreover, in virtually all cases, party activists were also described as 'ageing', with very little recruitment of younger member or activists taking place. The resulting burden for active members, particularly those serving as local councillors, can be considerable. As we illustrated in chapter 6, a very large proportion of party activists are already local councillors and most campaigning is carried out by sitting councillors and candidates with little or no additional support. Surprisingly, door to door campaigning remains remarkably strong in some wards and among the larger political parties. However, there is a growing tendency to favour telephone canvassing and other techniques – a development that some councillors saw as effective in mobilising the 'core vote', although many more spoke of the possible risk of alienating other, 'floating' voters.

With political parties finding it increasingly difficult to mount extensive local campaigns, there is a clear danger that relationships between the electorate and local politicians will weaken further. In this context, the possibility that parties such as the BNP have been able to secure growing local support, in part because of their effective use of 'traditional' campaigning techniques increasingly abandoned by other parties, cannot be overlooked. Certainly, the account of BNP election campaigns in Burnley provided by Smith (2004) underlines the significance that BNP activists have placed upon public meetings, leafleting, displaying high-profile banners, and trailing a 'Vote BNP' A-Board around the town by Land Rover during election campaigns. It is also evident that only very modest financial resources are available to political parties to run campaigns. One leader of a major party reported that election leaflets were produced on an old ink-duplicator kept in his own kitchen, while another indicated a constant need to use his own money to pay for paper and photocopying costs. Despite the enormous work put in by party activists writing, designing and even printing their own election leaflets, it is also evident that such materials compare poorly to the glossy information and publicity materials produced by councils and other public bodies (see chapter 9). Unless such resource imbalances can be addressed, and without a significant increase in the personnel that local parties can call upon, it is difficult to see how effective local election campaigns can be sustained in the short to medium term.

Participatory democracy: Political and civic engagement

As we have already noted, Putnam (2000) argues that there is a symbiotic relationship between 'political' participation and civic engagement. In keeping with this perspective, we sought to produce as comprehensive an assessment as possible of the extent of wider political and civic engagement in Burnley and Harrogate using three principal methods (see appendix 1 for more detailed discussion). First, we obtained estimates of the size of the voluntary and community sector in the two towns from recent large-scale surveys conducted locally (WM Enterprise, 2003; Dowson et al., 2000). Second, we conducted brief telephone interviews with a cross-section of 40 national and local groups present in the two boroughs. Third, we put a series of questions regarding political and civic engagement to the citizens' panels operating in the two towns. It should, of course, be noted that members of citizens' panels are more likely than average to be engaged in local affairs. This proposition is underlined by the fact that 82 per cent of Harrogate respondents and 79 per cent of Burnley respondents reported that they had voted in the most recent district council elections.

There are important methodological issues involved in any attempt to measure the scale of voluntary and community sector activity, and there is enormous variety in the approaches that have been used (see appendix 1). Consequently, making comparisons between the voluntary and community sector in different localities is highly problematic. Recent studies aimed at estimating the size of the sector in Burnley and Harrogate did not use comparable methodologies. Thus, while Table 7.2 presents estimates of the number of voluntary and community organisations in the two towns, as well as an estimated number of employees and volunteers, the figures cannot be assumed to represent a valid basis for comparison.

Table 7.2: The estimated scale of the voluntary and community sector in Burnley and Harrogate

	Burnley: total	Burnley: per 1000 of population	Harrogate: total	Harrogate: per 1000 of population
Estimated number of VCOs	354	4	605	4
Estimated total employees in VCF sector	2460	27	2419	16
Estimated number of volunteers	8,500 (volunteer places)	95	10,080	67
Estimated number of volunteer hours (annual)	1.35 million	15 hours per head	201,600	1.3 hours per head

Source: Derived from WM Enterprise, 2003; Lewis, 2001; Dowson et al., 2000.

However, there are strong grounds for assuming that the estimates provided for the total number of VCOs in Burnley and Harrogate – a density of about four organisations per 1000 of population – are reasonably accurate. Lewis (2001) notes that the 'rule of thumb' among researchers is that the density of voluntary and community organisations (VCOs) in an area will typically be in the region of 3–5 per 1000 of population, although some studies produce estimates of up to 15 per 1000. Other data presented in this table appear to be more problematic, particularly when the Burnley and Harrogate estimates are placed alongside one another. We would not expect volunteering to be more common in Burnley than it is in Harrogate, and the estimated 1.35 million volunteer hours worked in Burnley per annum, equating to 15 hours per Burnley resident, would be almost four times the national average. Likewise, the Harrogate figure is surprisingly low in comparison to the national average of four hours per annum. Our doubts are confirmed by the results of the citizens' panel surveys, which found that 19.7 per cent of Burnley respondents had volunteered formally in the previous 12 months, compared to 26.9 per cent of Harrogate panel members.

Despite our very real reservations that the figures for Burnley represent a serious over-estimation of volunteering, the WM Enterprise study nevertheless provides a useful starting point for local membership organisations in Burnley. It identifies 97 clubs and societies in the town, of which 14 have memberships in excess of 250 and a further 35 have between 100–249 members. While no equivalent figures are available for Harrogate, the results from the citizens' panels confirmed that there is a very broad spread of membership of groups and organisations among local residents in both towns. Overall, membership was proportionately higher among Harrogate respondents in two-thirds of the 30 categories of groups and organisations listed in our questionnaire. Survey respondents from Harrogate belonged to an average of 2.2 groups and organisations, while Burnley respondents had an average of 1.8 memberships per head. This pattern was confirmed by our survey of local groups which suggested that fewer national organisations (e.g. the RSPB, the Royal British Legion, and Amnesty International) have branches or offices in Burnley than in Harrogate.

The citizens' panel results suggest two significant common features of group membership across the two towns. First, membership is generally highest among those groups and organisations that have a direct local role and/or some form of identifiable local infrastructure. Thus, faith groups, trade unions, local voluntary groups, residents' and tenants groups, sports and athletics clubs, social clubs and, to a lesser extent, political parties collectively form the core membership organisations in both towns. Second, while membership of political parties is very similar in both surveys – 6 per cent in Burnley and 6.9 per cent in Harrogate – and in both cases significantly higher than we would expect based on party membership data, it is evident that they are far from being the most significant category of local membership organisation. Not only faith groups and trade unions, but also categories such as residents' and tenants' groups and local voluntary groups all appear to be able to boast higher membership levels than political parties.

Given the well documented decline of both church attendance and trade unionism, the evidence relating to faith groups and trade unions is particularly striking. Membership of faith groups is around 20 per cent in both surveys, ranking as the second most common form of membership in Burnley and third in Harrogate. Indeed, the role of faith groups to wider forms of civic and political engagement locally may well be highly significant, as illustrated by Case Study 7.1. In addition, some 26.4 per cent of Burnley respondents report that they are members of trade unions, indicating this to be easily the largest type of membership held locally. Even in Harrogate, an area that has experienced very little industrialisation, almost 16 per cent of respondents report than they are union members, suggesting this to be the fifth largest 'membership type' held within the district.

Case Study 7.1: Faith groups and local activism

Carmen Sawers, a resident of Harrogate, is a local activist whose contribution captures both the diversification of local political and civic engagement, and the substantial contribution that faith groups make to local activism.

Carmen is principally involved in two campaigns – Make Poverty History and the promotion of fair trade. She is the member of the Harrogate steering group affiliated to the Fair Trade Towns campaign, and known unofficially as 'Make Harrogate a Fair Trade Borough'. This steering group has 20 members and brings together a diverse set of activists, including local councillors, environmentalists and members of local churches. Carmen also runs a Fair Trade Shop, based at a church in central Harrogate and in June 2005 she spoke on the issue of fair trade at a meeting of the Harrogate District Action Group for the Environment, hosted by Harrogate Borough Council. Harrogate Borough Council has since endorsed the Fair Trade campaign. Currently, there are approximately 30 people involved in Fair Trade shops in Harrogate, who also all get involved in regular activities such as signing petitions, letter-writing and organising meetings.

Carmen has been active in issues connected with third world development and trade justice for some 30 years, having first become

(Continued)

Case Study 7.1: Faith groups and local activism (continued)

actively involved as a university student in the 1970s. Since that time her activism has been sustained largely by her Christian faith rather than association with any political party or movement. She draws her inspiration directly from Jesus' teachings about tackling inequality and helping 'the poor', as well as from her direct contact with Third World producers. Her activism has also led on to work with Christian Aid, such as lobbying, and she is in frequent – and friendly – contact with her local MP. Carmen estimates that around 180 members of her local church are involved in some form of local activism – which we estimate to be more than the combined number of political party activists in the town. Given that there are 40 churches in Harrogate, all of which support Fair Trade and many of which are engaged in other campaigns, for instance around environmental issues, the contribution of faith groups to local affairs can be seen to be substantial.

With few exceptions, all the groups we contacted reported dwindling numbers of *active* members and the citizens' panel responses confirmed that there is often an enormous difference between levels of membership and levels of different types of activism: making donations; office holding and committee membership; helping and taking part in events; and campaigning and fund-raising. In the main, the proportion of local residents playing an active role in each category of organisation is in single digits, or even fractions. In several cases, the gulf between membership levels and the five types of activism is enormous. For instance, while 26.4 per cent of Burnley respondents report trade union membership, only 0.4 per cent of respondents describe themselves as union campaigners and only 0.2 per cent as fund raisers. Likewise, those reporting that they help out at or participate in events held by residents and tenants groups constitute only one seventh of those that are members of these groups in both towns. Indeed, across Burnley and Harrogate, group membership only translates into significant local activism in two of the categories of groups listed: faith groups and local voluntary groups. In the case of faith groups, around half of members report that they also regularly donate money to these groups and help out at or participate in events.

There are, however, a number of important differences in membership and activism apparent from the survey data that can be assumed to relate to the contrasting economic and social profiles of the two towns. In addition to having a significantly higher level of trade union membership, the Burnley results also point to a greater membership of working men's, Labour, Conservative and Liberal clubs. While a relatively minor category of membership, Burnley also appears to have membership levels in credit unions and Local Economy Trading Schemes that are ten times those found in Harrogate. By contrast, the Harrogate survey data found that its residents are more likely to be members of groups and organisations concerned with heritage, environmental, and landscape issues. Indeed, a remarkable 31.3 per cent of Harrogate respondents indicate that they are members of heritage groups concerned with buildings, landscape or transport, nearly four times the level in Burnley, and making it the most common type of membership held in Harrogate. A similar pattern is evident in relation to environmental organisations, with 14.7 per cent of Harrogate respondents reporting membership of this type of organisation, almost three times the level recorded in Burnley. As with membership, levels of activism are, overall, generally higher in Harrogate. It would appear that local groups and organisations, in particular, are generally able to call upon a significantly larger number of regular donors and fund-raising assistants in Harrogate than in Burnley. There is a wider gap between Harrogate and Burnley in relation to making donations and participating in fund-raising than on any of the other criteria.

While overall levels of activism appear to be relatively low, the pattern that emerges from interviews with local groups and organisations is one of considerable fluidity rather than simple decline. Certainly, decreasing levels of membership were reported across the variety of organisations contacted. The exceptions were the Ramblers' Association and the Burnley Credit Union – with the latter reporting the largest membership of all the groups contacted in both towns. Declining membership was most frequently explained with reference to demographic factors, primarily the difficulty of recruiting younger members. The ageing membership profile of many groups has caused some to close down entirely, including the Caledonian Society in Burnley which, twenty years ago, had around 100 members. However, membership and activism have grown around specific local issues. For example, Ramblers' Association membership and activism increased around 'right to roam' events. In addition, while some groups have ceased to operate, others have emerged in their place. For instance, both towns have seen *ad hoc* local pressure groups formed around planning issues such as mobile phone masts and wind farms. There appears to be a particular surge in opposition to major planning proposals in Harrogate, with a number of recent proposed developments sparking well organised, but short-lived, local campaigns. Likewise, various residents groups have mobilised in Burnley around issues connected to regeneration plans and compulsory purchase orders (CPOs). Many of these residents groups in Burnley appear to be highly ephemeral, raising important questions about their capacity to contribute to local affairs. However, the recent formation of the South West Burnley Residents Panel, comprising representation from 11 residents' action groups, suggests that a more stable base for community activism may be emerging, at least in some parts of the town.[12]

Case Study 7.2: The contribution of 'super-activists'

Maggie Archer is director of a farming company and a trustee and vice-chair of Claro Enterprises, a workshop for people with severe mental illness. She has been involved in voluntary and community work for many years. She had previously been worked in catering, but as a result of family illnesses, she became involved with Ripon League of Friends, where she is now a team member. This led her to become a member and then chair of the now disbanded Harrogate Community Health Council, during which she was a member of an independent review panel into ambulance services in the district. Maggie is now a non-executive director on Craven, Harrogate and Rural District PCT, and a stakeholder governor at Harrogate and District NHS Foundation Trust. She has also been an associate manger for mental health appeals for fifteen years.

Wendy Graham is a resident of South West Burnley and became active in local affairs out of concern about the decline of her neighbourhood. She played a lead role in establishing the Prestwich and Athol Street South Residents Association and subsequently became involved as a community

(Continued)

---

12 These 11 groups comprise: Rosegrove Action Group; Trinity Action Group; Caring Accrington Road Residents; Picadilly's Moving Lobby Group; Coal Clough Community Residents' Group; Healey Wood Residents Group; Prestwich and Athol Street South Residents' Association; Aidrie Crescent Residents' Association; Barclay Hill Residents' Action Group; Residents of Stoops Estate; and Residents of Cog Lane.

> **Case Study 7.2: The contribution of 'super-activists' (continued)**
>
> representative on the Elevate (housing market renewal) masterplanning steering group. Wendy also works as a volunteer at the Howard Street Community Health Centre and is a community representative at the monthly Police and Community Together meetings for Trinity ward. She has played a key role in bringing together residents groups in South West Burnley and chairs the South West Burnley Residents Panel. In addition to these various formal roles, Wendy often acts as an informal advocate for local residents facing difficulties but unsure about how to seek support from local public agencies.

A striking finding from our interviews with local councillors, voluntary organisations, active residents and local group contacts was that a number of individuals in both towns are active across a range of groups and organisations (see Case Study 7.2 for two examples). There are also close links between some of the groups locally, often generated by these 'super-activists'. While we have not been able to test the proposition in any scientific way, it is highly likely that in both towns a relatively small network of citizens with high rates of political and/or civic participation play a key role in maintaining a significant proportion of the local political and civic infrastructure. Given the overall decline of many forms of local civic and political participation charted in this chapter, we would argue that many, if not virtually all, such individuals should be seen as a precious resource in any attempt to revive local democracy. Rather than dismissing such people as 'the usual suspects', as is sometimes the case, far greater recognition needs to be given to their crucial role in sustaining local communities.

7.6 Conclusion

This chapter puts forward several caveats to accounts suggesting a crisis of local political participation in the UK: for instance, the apparent willingness to engage in political and social activism remains most apparent at the local level; there is strong public interest in local affairs; and surveys suggest that citizens evaluate the significance of local government highly. Concerns about voter turnout and, in particular falling levels of party membership and activism, are valid. But these must be counter-balanced by reference to the relative vibrancy of other forms of political participation. Our audit of political and civic participation in Burnley and Harrogate underline these conclusions, while also pointing to some clear contrasts between the two towns, most notably the higher overall levels of political and civic engagement in Harrogate.

Nonetheless, our analysis of political and civic participation nationally, and in the two towns also, points to some clear common themes. While overall local engagement is relatively stable, a minority of citizens collectively sustain the bulk of an increasingly diverse local political and civic infrastructure. Although political activism has always been a minority pursuit, there is a particular danger that local democracy is becoming too reliant upon a relatively small number of party activists. Local activists appear to be spreading themselves more thinly across a broader range of activities and the impact is most obvious in political parties, where the erosion of membership, and more importantly activism, is so advanced that meaningful local party competition is increasingly difficult to sustain. This poses a challenge in relation to the 'traditional' politics of elected local government, since elections remain the principal single mechanism through which people engage with the local political process, a point that is further highlighted in chapter 8. There is therefore a pressing need for radical action to revitalise the role and significance of local electoral politics. Finally, participation in local affairs is highly uneven among different social groups. There is a pronounced tendency for the 'activist minority' to be drawn from the educated, white middle-classes and, at any moment in time, significant sections of the population do not seem to be engaging at all with the local political process. As we suggest in chapter 8, multiplying and diversifying the mechanisms for citizen engagement may simply consolidate the disproportionate influence of the professional middle classes in local affairs.

8
Power to the Person?:

From participatory democracy to customer responsiveness

In every other walk of life, the position of the consumer has been revolutionised. As their demands changed and became more individualised, so producers of goods and services were forced to customise, to adapt and be flexible … the danger in unreformed public services is clear.

Tony Blair, 2005

8.1 Introduction

Given the decline in party politics highlighted in the previous chapter, it is important to ask whether there is evidence of increased citizen participation in other elements of what we have defined as the 'local democratic mix'. Consequently, this chapter focuses on three contrasting notions of citizen/consumer engagement beyond the ballot box: (i) direct resident involvement in services; (ii) consultation exercises designed to ascertain residents' views; and (iii) complaints procedures introduced to enable individuals to express dissatisfaction with services and, where relevant, seek individual redress. While such mechanisms reflect the forms of 'user' and 'participatory' democracy that we have identified as part of the local democratic mix, it is important to stress that there are very different sets of assumptions underpinning each of these forms of citizen participation in local governance. In particular, a core shift has taken place in recent decades from earlier attempts to promote collectivist notions of citizen engagement and 'participatory democracy' in local affairs towards a more individualistic notion of 'consumer empowerment' and 'customer responsiveness'. The earlier rallying cry of 'power to the people' has increasingly become replaced by a discourse representing 'power to the person'.

Since our focus is on local democracy, the crucial issue here is the extent to which the emphasis on 'power to the person' has been effective in promoting wider citizen engagement, in strengthening relationships between citizens and public agencies, and in holding public agencies to account. The chapter begins with a brief overview of citizen/consumer participation in the public services, focusing on the three contrasting forms of engagement outlined above. This overview charts how the existing arrangements evolved, summarises the principal procedures in place locally, and considers available evidence on the extent to which they promote engagement with local public bodies. The chapter then outlines the key findings drawn from our in-depth analysis of citizen/consumer engagement in the two case study localities. This analysis is based upon: (i) further data drawn from questions put to citizens' panels in the two towns; (ii) a survey of consultation techniques used by the principal public agencies locally; and (iii) an audit of complaints handling procedures among all public agencies operating in Burnley and Harrogate. The chapter raises three key concerns about a more 'consumerist' vision of local democracy. First, consultation exercises and complaints mechanisms are not an alternative to other forms of engagement. Individuals using such mechanisms are rarely those that have otherwise 'disengaged' from local democracy. Second, there is a failure in many agencies to integrate analysis of complaints and consultation information into strategic decision-making. Third, there is a danger that market-based models of participation can have an atomising effect on citizenship and reduce the relationship between local agencies and local residents to concerns with 'market research' and 'consumer rights'. While enhancing the capacity of the individual to influence local public service providers has an important role to play in local democracy, it is crucial that consultation and complaints procedures are embedded more fully in core principles of democracy.

8.2 The evolution of citizen/consumer engagement with public services

Prior to the 1960s, the opportunities for citizens to express their views about public services were effectively restricted to the traditional mechanisms of representative democracy: 'redress could be sought by individuals through politicians' (Birchall and Simmons, 2004, p.16). Since the late 1960s, however, a complex set of arrangements has emerged that enable citizens to participate in, and even directly challenge, the decisions of public agencies. Introduced during several distinct periods of reform, the diversification of forms of citizen engagement with local public bodies has been influenced variously by public law traditions, concepts of participatory democracy, and pro-market ideas drawn from public choice theory. The latter has become increasingly dominant since the 1980s, shifting the emphasis of reforms from notions of participatory democracy, briefly popular in the 1970s, to more 'consumerist' approaches associated with defined service standards, complaints procedures and, increasingly, choice in public services. As a result, we may broadly summarise the evolution of non-electoral citizen engagement with public bodies as occurring in four phases, as follows:

◆ The institution of the Parliamentary Commissioner was introduced in 1967, based on the Scandinavian Ombudsman institution, to investigate cases of 'maladministration'. The early acclaim for the work of the Parliamentary Commissioner subsequently led to the creation of Health Service Commissioners for England, Scotland and Wales in 1973, and Local Government Ombudsmen for England, Wales and Scotland in 1974;

◆ New forms of participatory democracy in policy areas such as planning, housing, health and education were introduced from the late 1960s. This occurred as a result of growing concerns about imbalances of power between professionals and citizens, with new procedures and structures being introduced to support citizens wishing to express their views on public services and, where appropriate, raise complaints about particular aspects of those services. Examples include the requirement to consult residents on local plans (1968), the creation of community health councils (1974) to represent patients in the NHS, and the introduction of a statutory right for parents to be represented on school boards (1980);

◆ The progressive introduction of 'consumer rights' in public service provision took place from the mid-1980s, such as moves to define the level of service that 'consumers' of public services could expect, and to establish procedures individuals could instigate if dissatisfied. The Citizen's Charter, promising 'better redress for the citizen when things go wrong' (Dunleavy et al., 2005. p.8), introduced in 1991, epitomises this trend. A requirement for local authority social services departments to operate complaints procedures was also introduced in 1991, while local education authorities were required to introduce a curriculum complaints procedure as part of the 1996 Education Act, and a single NHS complaints procedure was also introduced in 1996;

◆ Following the recommendations of The Nolan Committee on Standards in Public Life (1995, 1996, 1997a, 1997b), reforms have been made to a number of systems of citizen redress under New Labour, while additional 'consumerist' mechanisms have been introduced in many policy areas. The most significant changes relate to health, education and policing. These include the replacement of community health councils with public and patient involvement forums, moves towards 'choice' in health and education, and reforms aiming to render local police more directly responsive to communities.

These four 'phases' of reform, together with the enormous emphasis on public bodies 'engaging' with local residents, have unquestionably expanded the range of mechanisms through which citizens can seek to influence public agencies. Forms of engagement now vary enormously, ranging from the direct representation of tenants on the boards of housing associations to patient satisfaction surveys carried out by primary care trusts. Indeed, the range of approaches to involvement and consultation have become almost bewilderingly diverse. Lowndes *et al.* (2001a) identify five distinct categories of consultation technique used by local authorities alone, comprising a total of 19 different forms of consultation. At the same time, the tendency for reforms to be introduced in 'layers' has also produced arrangements that are highly complex and, to some extent, contradictory. For these reasons, it is valuable to briefly consider the relative significance of three distinct forms of citizen engagement with public services nationally, before turning to assess their role in local democracy in Burnley and Harrogate.

Direct involvement in public services

In chapter 7, we demonstrated that, despite relatively high levels of willingness to participate, local political action actually depends upon a very small 'core' of activists. It is therefore important to ask whether the attempts to promote direct citizen involvement and input into the running of public services have provided for more widespread participation. Birchall and Simmons (2004) suggest that where citizens are offered meaningful forms of involvement that go beyond local elections, there is often a significant take-up of such opportunities. They cite research which suggests that there are:

◆ 16,484 members of the public serving as police 'special constables';

◆ 30,000 people acting as lay magistrates;

◆ 10 million people involved in 155,000 neighbourhood watch schemes;

◆ 170,000 people volunteering within the NHS, for instance as Red Cross or Hospital Friends Scheme volunteers;

◆ 350,000 people serving on school boards of governors;

◆ 4,600 volunteer members recruited by the patient and public involvement forums attached to primary care trusts in the NHS.

Birchall and Simmons also suggest that, despite the abolition of community health councils in 2003, new forms of public participation in the NHS reforms may have led to increased public involvement (see Case Study 8.1). Public involvement has also been promoted via membership of foundation trusts. The most recent evidence suggests that the first wave of 20 foundation trusts attracted 256,860 members within six months, representing an average of 12,843 per hospital (Lewis, 2005). It is not inconceivable that, with 31 foundation trusts now in existence, there may be almost as many foundation trust members as there are members of political parties in England.[13]

However, while the absolute numbers taking up opportunities for direct participation in specific public services may run into hundreds of thousands nationally, such activity remains a minority pursuit. With reference to examples such as social housing, Birchall and Simmons (2004) estimate that up to seven per cent of public service users have some form of direct, active involvement in those services. However, there are strong grounds to regard this figure as misleading. With the exception of neighbourhood watch, each of the headline figures for public involvement cited above amounts to a fraction of the adult population

---

13   One caveat here is that foundation trusts were allowed to adopt an 'opt-out' membership scheme, where patient and staff membership is assumed unless individuals actively decide not to join.

as a whole. Or, put another way, the country's combined supply of special constables, lay magistrates, NHS volunteers, school governors and foundation trust hospital members is drawn from just 2 per cent of its adult population.

Case Study 8.1: Local democracy and the NHS

Until 2003 the main forums for patient and public involvement in health were the community health councils (CHCs). Established in 1974 as independent bodies to monitor and review local NHS bodies, they normally consisted of 16 to 30 members, with half appointed by the local authority, one-third elected by the local voluntary sector and the rest appointed by the Department of Health. CHCs were intended to keep under review the operations of the local health service, recommend potential improvements, and advise health authorities on appropriate operational matters. During the 1970s and 1980s, CHCs also initiated many of the public consultation and participation activities currently used by the NHS, including: advocacy schemes; support for self-help groups and community networks; surveys of users' views; research on the needs of disadvantaged groups; patients' charters; and providing information and advice. More controversially, some CHCs took to aiding patients in complaints procedures and even acting as the 'patient's friend' in formal hearings, which was not envisaged in the original statutes. However, CHC powers were relatively limited, and they were often severely under-resourced, making it difficult for them to effectively scrutinise health authorities or represent patients. Criticisms of CHCs also began to centre on their alleged lack of representativeness of, and lack of engagement with, the communities they were expected to serve.

CHCs were abolished in England in 2003, and their functions have been taken on by four main bodies: (i) the Patient Advice and Liaison Service (PALS); (ii) the Independent Complaints Advocacy Service (ICAS); (iii) local authority health overview and scrutiny committees; and (iv) patient and public involvement forums (PPIFs). PALS is primarily concerned with providing advice on accessing hospital services – including complaints advocacy (most trusts also run a separate complaints service) – and is provided by, and located within, the NHS. ICAS has a very limited, although independent, remit centred on providing advocacy services for patients who wish to pursue complaints. Local authority health overview and scrutiny

(Continued)

Case Study 8.1: Local democracy and the NHS (continued)

committees allow local councillors to scrutinise the delivery of health services in their area, and must be consulted when a local NHS body is considering substantial development or variation in the provision of local health services. Where these committees consider a proposal to be against the interests of local health care provision, they are able to refer the decision to the Secretary of State.

The bodies with the clearest remit for citizen involvement in health are the PPIFs. Established in 2002, all NHS trusts are required to have one such forum, with their membership made up from local volunteers, appointed by the Commission for Patient and Public Involvement in Health. The forums were designed to act as 'critical friends' and have similar powers to CHCs, such as the power to inspect NHS premises, monitor and review services, survey the views of service users, produce reports and recommendations for their NHS bodies, and refer matters of concern to other bodies. However, like CHCs, the forums have been subject to similar problems of insufficient funding and administrative support, recruitment problems, and what is seen as a low public profile.

Engagement through consultation

Estimates of the overall scale of regular public involvement in local public agencies do not appear to increase significantly if we broaden the definition to include consultation exercises. Based on the responses to a survey of English local authorities carried out by the ODPM (Birch, 2002), Table 8.1 summarises the estimated proportion of the English electorate that was engaged via various mechanisms used by local authorities in 2001. The responses provided by councils suggest that, among the diverse forms of citizen engagement that local councils now use, responses to consultation exercises represent the principal form of non-electoral engagement. Thus, making the highly questionable assumption that the reported 5.6 million responses to local authority consultations represent 5.6 million different citizens, an estimated 15 per cent of the electorate took part in this way. Similarly, citizens' panels and service satisfaction surveys provide feedback from no more than 6 per cent of local voters. Likewise, based on local authority reporting, complaint/suggestion schemes engaged less than 2 per cent of the electorate in 2001, and public meetings less than 1 per cent. Consequently, despite the decline in local electoral turnout to levels as low as a third of the electorate, it remains the principal single mechanism through which residents express their views about local services – more than double the proportion of the electorate estimated to have been engaged via responses to local authority consultation documents. Even if we consider Birch's (2002) suggestion that, if we aggregate all of the reported citizen involvement across 19 different forms of non-electoral public participation, 14 million people have been 'engaged' by local government, this still amounts to just 37 per cent of the English electorate.[14]

Table 8.1: Local election turnout compared to estimates of percentage of electorate engaged by five most popular consultation and participation mechanisms used by councils in England, 2001

	Total citizen involvement*	% councils using in 2001	% electorate engaged**
Local elections	12,208,513	100	33
Responses to consultation documents	5,607,717	84	15.2
Citizens' panels	2,213,824	71	6.0
Service satisfaction surveys	2,065,954	92	5.6
Complaints/suggestion schemes	649,629	86	1.8
Public meetings	202,930	78	0.6

Notes:
*Other than election turnout, estimates of involvement are based on the responses of 55 per cent of English local authorities to an ODPM survey, which have been 'rounded up' on the assumption that they are representative for all English local authorities. The estimates are based on the average number of people reported to be engaged via each mechanism by the responding local authorities, weighted by the percentage of all local authorities estimated to be using this mechanism. In the case of complaints, a weighting of 100 per cent has been used, on the basis that residents will complain, whether there is a formal procedure for capturing complaints or not.
**To calculate the proportion of the electorate engaged, a total English electorate of 36,995,495 has been assumed.
Source: Calculated from Birch, 2002, p.22.

---

14 Given the very high probability that many, if not most, of those engaged by local councils will have been involved in more than one form of participation, this figure will involve significant double-counting and must be assumed to represent a substantial overestimate of total citizen involvement.

User democracy: Citizens as 'consumers'

Despite the impression perhaps given by the quotation opening this chapter, the extension of user democracy over the past 10–15 years has been enormous. In the main, this has involved the adoption of such procedures from the private sector, and the re-definition of users of public services as 'customers'. Policy areas such as social housing and public transport, which involve a direct payment for services on the part of those using them, evidence this tendency most strongly. However, the notion of public agencies serving 'customers' has also become strongly apparent in areas such as street cleaning and refuse collection. Recent government proposals on policing, which reflect practices already used by a number of local police forces also reflect this trend. Thus, the recent White Paper – *Building Communities, Beating Crime* – recommends that members of the public contacting the local police should be given a specific time slot when police officers will attend, and that individual community beat officers should be contactable at all times by local people via publicly available mobile telephone numbers (Home Office, 2004).

The most prevalent feature of this consumerist conception of user democracy is the almost universal adoption by public bodies of mechanisms to respond to customer complaints. As is highlighted in Table 8.1, the ODPM survey of local authorities includes complaint/ suggestion schemes as a form of public participation in local government. Moreover, together with the similarly 'consumerist' technique of service satisfaction surveys, complaints schemes are the most consistently used method through which local authorities in the UK seek to secure feedback from local residents. Indeed, despite the fact that they are non-statutory, around 90 per cent of local authorities operate complaints procedures relating to all of their service areas (Lowndes *et al.*, 1998; Birch, 2002). There is enormous variation in how councils record and deal with complaints, with only social services and some aspects of education being subject to statutory arrangements. By contrast, local health care trusts and local police forces are required to operate full statutory complaints procedures, meaning that relatively standard, formal procedures are applied nationally. Despite such variation, most public sector complaints procedures follow a three stage process that feed into long established mechanisms for citizen redress. Under these arrangements, most complaints are dealt with in the first stage of 'local resolution'. Where initial local resolution proves impossible, the second stage involves more formal or independent review. For the small number of complaints not resolved at stage two, cases may be reviewed by the relevant ombudsman, or in the case of policing, by appeal to the IPCC.

Datasets relating to public service complaints are sketchy. Nationwide surveys carried out in 1985 and 2003 suggest that around half of the population have ever had the inclination to complain about a public service, but that only a quarter of the population had actually gone ahead and done so (Miller, 1988; MORI, 2003). Among the public services, data relating to police and NHS complaints is the most comprehensive, and only indicative information is available for complaints made to local authorities. While there are a number of caveats in interpreting such data, three key patterns can nonetheless be discerned, which are as follows:

◆ Complaint levels are fairly stable or show a gradual increase over time. For instance, complaints made about NHS hospitals and community health services fluctuated between 86,000 and 96,000 annually from 1996–2001, while complaints about family health services rose modestly from 37,000 to 44,500 per annum;[15]

◆ Complaints to local authorities appear to outnumber those made to other public service providers. While roughly 30,000 complaints per annum are made against the police nationally, Simons (1995) found that local authorities receive 30,000 plus complaints annually about social services alone. Based on local authorities' responses to an ODPM survey (Birch, 2002), we can estimate that approximately 650,000 complaints were registered by councils in 2002. This compares to an average of around 130,000 complaints made about all NHS services annually;

◆ The vast majority of complaints about public services are still settled via local resolution. Around 2 per cent of NHS complainants request

---

15 We would strongly warn against interpreting complaint levels as a measure of the quality of public services. Complaints about public service providers would almost certainly show a tendency to increase regardless of changes in service quality, in part because of the growth of a wider 'complaints culture'. More importantly, however, complaints procedures are increasingly seen to have a crucial role in improving the relationship between public agencies and citizens, and there is now a widespread view that genuine complaints should be supported and facilitated.

independent review, and less than 1 per cent of cases are submitted to the ombudsman. However, a growing number of complaints are reaching the second or third phase, such as independent review or submission to an ombudsman. For instance, from 1994–2004, the number of complaints referred to the local government ombudsman rose from just under 16,000 to around 19,000.

8.3 Does public participation enhance local democracy?

We would argue that there are two principal ways in which the forms of public participation considered in this chapter *could* enhance local democracy. First, given the decline in electoral participation, it is possible that broadening the scope for citizen input will increase overall levels of participation in local democracy. Unfortunately, there is only limited evidence available to assess whether public participation mechanisms extend the pool of those involved in local affairs. What evidence is available appears simply to confirm the pattern highlighted in chapter 7, namely that those voting in local elections are significantly more likely to exhibit other forms of citizen involvement. Thus, in line with our experience in Burnley and Harrogate, recent citizens' panels surveys in Doncaster, Barnsley and Chesterfield have all found reported levels of voting among respondents that are 2–3 times the actual turnout locally. More broadly, the widespread reference to 'hard to reach' and 'under-represented groups' among those undertaking public consultation exercises highlights the general difficulty that public agencies have ascertaining the views of young people, black and ethnic minority communities, and those on low incomes – precisely the social groups amongst which electoral turnout is lowest. There is particularly clear evidence that young people tend not to respond to consultation exercises or submit complaints to public bodies. Bromley *et al.* (2000) found that only three per cent of those attending public meetings held by local authorities were aged 18–24 and that young people were far more likely to suggest that they had not been consulted by their local authority. A survey of complainants to the local government ombudsman carried out in 1999 pointed to an under-representation of complainants aged under 35 and a disproportionate number of complaints from those aged 55 and over.

Second, it is possible that the feedback secured through direct citizen involvement, consultation and complaints processes can serve to enhance the democratic quality of local decision-making. However, this can only be achieved if such processes are embedded in wider notions of local democracy. As was highlighted in the introduction to this book, the relationship between consumerist mechanisms in the public services and core notions of democracy is far from straightforward. Consumerist approaches have been argued to undermine more collectivist notions of democracy and to challenge many of the principles of collectivism upon which public services were founded. Yet, recent public sector reforms have been justified as an attempt to render service providers more responsive to individual users and, therefore, as a means of offering citizens far greater influence over public services than can be achieved through periodic elections. We would suggest that, providing certain conditions are met, public participation can enhance local democracy by:

◆ *Increasing transparency in public service provision*: This can only be achieved if local public agencies provide full details of the feedback received, the issues raised and, where applicable, the actions taken as a result;

◆ *Informing processes of internal review, strategic planning and decision-making*: This will require participation mechanisms to be fully integrated into decision-making processes at all levels of the organisation;

◆ *Strengthening the relationship between service providers and citizens*: This will result in greater mutual trust, but will only occur if the above two conditions have also been met.

8.4 Citizen involvement with public services in Burnley and Harrogate

Given these general patterns of contact with public agencies through direct involvement, consultation procedures and complaints mechanisms, we now turn to assess the relative importance of these forms of engagement in Burnley and Harrogate, and their significance for local democracy in the two towns. This analysis is derived from: (i) information obtained from individual local agencies relating to consultation processes and complaints handlings; (ii) interviews with representatives of a number of local agencies and organisations; and (iii) results from questions put to the Burnley and Harrogate citizens' panel members. The citizens' panel data revealed particularly significant findings on the extent to which residents communicate with different local public agencies. Panel members were asked about direct participation in local public services, attendance at public meetings, responses to consultation exercises, and whether they had made complaints to local public agencies. A key concern throughout this part of the research was to identify those local agencies with which residents have the strongest relationships and the types and forms of contact that are used most frequently. We therefore begin by examining overall patterns of contact with local public agencies.

Resident contact with public agencies

Interviews with local councillors and public officials revealed very clear patterns of citizen behaviour in relation to contacting public agencies. Overwhelmingly, the telephone remains the preferred means of contact, rather than post or e-mail. This pattern is particularly evident in relation to contacts made with local councillors, the vast majority of which are made by telephone and only very rarely by letter or e-mail. Indeed, one long-standing councillor indicated that he had received no more than half a dozen emails from constituents during his whole political career to date. The most detailed evidence available can be drawn from Calico Housing's 'customer contact' system. This system reveals that, from 982 contacts initiated by Calico's tenants in Burnley during 2004, the greatest share came via telephone (32 per cent), followed by email (28 per cent) and then letter (21 per cent). Subsequent surveys undertaken by Calico indicated that 94 per cent of tenants expressed a preference to make contact by telephone and an equally strong dislike of filling in forms. Significantly, where accessible facilities exist, there also appears to be a clear preference among many residents to call at local agencies in person. Many local councillors indicated that they receive more visits to their homes from their constituents than they do letters from them. Likewise, the fourth largest 'customer contact' category for Calico in 2004 comprised 'visits made in person'.

In an era when the promise of 'e-government' has been so enthusiastically embraced, particularly by central government, the ongoing significance of local public buildings and community premises as contact points for local residents was one of the most surprising – and largely accidental – findings of the research project. Although the evidence is essentially anecdotal, it is nonetheless powerful. Visits to organisations in the Burnley district as diverse as Padiham Town Council, the Community Alliance, the Howard Street Community Health Centre, and the Burnley Wood Community Action Group, all revealed a surprisingly consistent tendency: a steady stream of visitors making enquiries about a great range of local issues. Although the typical number of approaches made by local residents in this way– approximately 5–10 per day – may appear relatively insignificant, such figures suggest a far higher volume of contact from local residents than are typically received by any ward councillor. The contrast to the attempts by local councillors to offer 'drop in' surgeries, as described in chapter 6, is especially striking.

Moreover, in each and every case, the enquiries being made at these locations span far beyond the direct function of the office in question. It would be no exaggeration to describe the offices of Padiham Town Council, the Howard Street Community Health Centre, the Burnley Wood Community Action Group office at 112 Branch Road, and many others as unofficial one stop shops and access points for the local community. In several cases, most notably at the Howard Street Community Health Centre, the role extends to making the centre a focal point for community engagement with public bodies in general (see Case Study 8.2). Similarly, discussions with council tenants in Harrogate revealed strong preferences for local housing offices, many of which had since been closed down, as a means of contacting the district council on just about any issue. One tenant (A) described how she had campaigned against the closure of these facilities, which had apparently been justified on grounds of costs. Another (B) expressed the view that localised offices are not only more accessible, particularly for the elderly and disabled, but promote closer relationships between council officers and local residents:

> I used to use it regular when the office was up there, the council office. It was for everything, but it was mainly for paying your rent and if you wanted repairs done, or anything. They closed it down, because they said it wasn't being used. So, I went round trying to get people to sign this petition and I brought it up at every meeting: "Why are you closing it?" Their thing was, they had to save money and we lost it. And the number of people that have

come up to me now and said 'I can't get down to Bilton' [...] *and yet they said they didn't have enough people going in there regular. (A)*

You nicely get used to having a means of getting to and from your local housing office. Some bright spark comes along and says "Oh, we're going to close that. Now you'll have to go to so and so". Nobody takes into account the additional costs of travelling to and from, [or] *the fact that the further away from that office you are, the less the people in the office know about your area and the problems that you might or might not have. (B)*

Case Study 8.2: The Howard Street Community Health Centre

The Howard Street Community Health Centre in South West Burnley is housed in a refurbished nursery school building, now owned and run by the Burnley, Pendle and Rossendale Primary Care Trust (PCT). It provides a range of health care services via a community dentist, a community nurse, health visitors, a counselling service and a men's health group. The facility arose directly from the recommendations made by the South West Burnley Citizens' Jury on Health and Social Care, commissioned by Burnley Primary Care Group in 2000, in which poor access to health and social care in the area was identified as a key issue.

Subsequent financial support provided by the Neighbourhood Renewal Fund not only enabled the centre to be established but facilitated the development of a possible model for neighbourhood management provision, through which public services are integrated at a neighbourhood level. As a result, to define the centre solely in terms of health care would be entirely misleading: the centre is used for a great range of activities, many of which have only an indirect (although by no means insignificant) relationship to health. For instance, the centre is used to host a broad array of events ranging from Police and Communities Together meetings to line dancing classes!

More broadly, the centre plays a crucial role in the local community, especially for local activists, who regularly meet there and are able to use the space available to host public meetings of local residents' groups. Paid staff and volunteers at the centre also frequently provide assistance to

(Continued)

The role of public buildings in shaping the relationships between local residents and local agencies is arguably an overlooked facet of local democracy. The location and style of the building in which a local agency is based can, often unintentionally, express strong symbolic messages about the apparent importance of a local organisation and its accessibility and openness to local people. Certainly, for residents of South West Burnley, the Howard Street Community Health Centre provides them with a more direct relationship to Burnley, Pendle and Rossendale PCT than the organisation's headquarters, which is located in an indistinctive, modern office building at the end of a cul-de-sac on an industrial estate, just off junction 12 of the M65 in Nelson. Conversely, for district councils such as Burnley, the mismatch between the late Victorian grandeur of the Town Hall and what the council actually does today may plausibly be a source of some of the tension between local residents and the council. Built to make a clear statement, the architecture and location of Burnley Town Hall reflects the proud history of municipal reformism locally, during an era in which Burnley County Borough exercised significant power. Today, the significance that local people typically still attach to the building is seriously at odds with the realities of local governance, a point made strongly by one local councillor:

Residents come down Manchester Road, see the Town Hall and they think: "This is the centre of power in Burnley". What they don't realise is that the building directly opposite, Chattersley House, £75 million is spent there and about £16 million is spent here [the Town Hall]. *And what's more, although it's got Lancashire County Council on that building now, that sign has only just been put up in the past few months* [...] *And the people of Burnley, I don't think they knew what was going on in that building. But they do know there's a Town Hall, so Burnley gets the blame for everything.*

Attendance at public meetings

For the active citizen, possessing the time, skills and inclination to keep abreast of local issues and hoping to influence local decision-making, the possibilities are arguably greater than ever before. For instance, the requirement now placed on most public bodies to hold board meetings in public has provided almost limitless opportunities for citizens to monitor, in person, the activities of local public sector organisations. We estimate that, in any given month, a resident of Burnley or Harrogate would be able to attend around 20 formal meetings of their local authorities, health bodies, police authorities and other public bodies. This number would rise further if we were to add parish council meetings, public consultation events, and so on. Indeed, for the local resident keen to observe the operation of local democracy, monitoring the activities of local agencies in this way would constitute an almost full-time commitment.

While such transparency is laudable, public attendance at events such as primary care trust meetings and local authority Cabinet meetings tends to be rare, if not non-existent. With the exception of controversial district council planning/development control committee meetings, public attendance tends to be restricted to local residents using the 'right to speak' provision to lobby representatives on specific issues. Moreover, data made available by Burnley Borough Council suggests that even attendance arising from the right to speak occurs infrequently, and is again strongly biased towards development control. Thus, in 2004–05, a total of 10 local residents spoke at full council meetings, 7 at executive meetings and 95 at the development control committee. This picture is broadly confirmed by the results of the survey of citizens' panel members in the two towns. As Table 8.2 shows, only a small minority of local residents have ever attended any type of public meeting hosted by a local agency. Significantly, however, panel respondents were far more likely to have attended a borough council meeting than a meeting held by the county council or NHS bodies.

Table 8.2: Percentage of local residents that claim to have ever attended public meetings of the following organisations

	Burnley	Harrogate
Borough council	10.4	8.2
NHS bodies	5.4	6.4
County council	4.5	5.3

Note: Given the observation that panel members are more likely than average to participate in local affairs, these and other figures in this chapter almost certainly represent an over-estimate of the level of local engagement.

Direct involvement with local public services

Only a small proportion of local residents are directly involved in local public services as volunteers or as representatives of local residents on public bodies. Table 8.3 indicates that even among citizens' panel members in Burnley and Harrogate – among whom we expect to find higher than average levels of public engagement – only a very modest proportion of respondents serve in roles such as special constables, magistrates and uniformed health volunteers. These figures are in line with the levels of national engagement cited by Birchall and Simmons (2004). The broad category encompassing 'school governor, member of NHS body, local councillor or other public office' indicates a higher level of involvement than would be expected from national figures. Nonetheless, the fact that just 3.7 per cent of respondents in Burnley and 6.7 per cent of respondents in Harrogate claim these forms of involvement underlines the tendency for such roles to be undertaken by a minority of citizens. It is also likely that the significantly higher figure for Harrogate in this category results from the citizens' panel including a disproportionately high number of local foundation hospital trust members. At the same time, the significance accorded to such forms of participation should not be judged simply on the numbers of residents involved in them. As Case Study 8.3 shows, the example of Police and Communities Together in Burnley indicates that the direct participation of a relatively small number of community representatives at a neighbourhood level can be highly effective in promoting accountability to local residents.

Table 8.3: Percentage of Burnley and Harrogate citizens' panel members indicating direct involvement in different aspects of local public services

	Burnley	Harrogate
Special constable, territorial army, royal navy reserve or magistrate	0.7	0.6
Uniformed health volunteer (e.g. Red Cross, St John Ambulance)	0.7	0.3
School governor, member of NHS body, local councillor or other public office	3.7	6.7

Case Study 8.3: Police and Communities Together (PACT)

In recent years, public concerns with issues such as anti-social behaviour and the visibility of police officers have accelerated the longer-run shift in how police forces seek to relate to local communities. As part of the efforts spearheaded by the force as a whole, the Pennine Division of Lancashire Constabulary, based in Burnley, has made a significant investment in developing structures promoting close working relationships between individual police officers and local communities.

A Community Beat Manager (CBM) is attached to each electoral ward in Burnley, often supported by one or more Community Support Officers, with the express aim that CBMs spend 90 per cent of their time dealing specifically with community issues. The underlying principle behind the approach is that each CBM develops long-term working relationships with a range of local people, such as ward councillors or representatives of community groups, in order to keep abreast of key issues in the area. Where community mobilisation is relatively weak, local police have often assisted in the establishment of local groups, such as the Brunshaw Action Group, and the force has been successful in securing financial support from the Rank Foundation to support this work with community groups. At the same time, in order to ensure wider accessibility and responsiveness to local people, the CBM's mobile telephone number is widely publicised throughout the ward in which they are working. CBMs also run regular, 'drop in' surgeries in premises such as local post offices, community centres and Sure Start centres, at which members of the public can raise issues about crime and policing in the area.

(Continued)

Case Study 8.3: Police and Communities Together (PACT) (continued)

At the core of this model of community policing in Burnley is the ward-level Police and Community Together (PACT) meeting. Reflecting a concern 'to get real people to come along and influence policing', community beat managers hold meetings in each local ward in the first week of every month. The meetings enable the CBM to bring together a mix of community representatives, ward councillors and representatives of other local agencies to discuss the priorities for policing the area over the next four weeks. Arising from the CBM's analysis of current issues in the area, and the subsequent discussion among the PACT participants, the meeting is used to agree three key policing and community safety priorities for the following months. In many instances, these priorities may have implications for other agencies and, at the following meetings, both the CBM and representatives of those agencies are held to account in relation to the actions agreed a month previously. As such, PACT effectively represents a system of holding the local police accountable to the local community, via a process of deliberative democracy at the ward level. As a senior police officer argued: 'It's a massive thought change for us, because what I'm saying to my Community Beat Managers now is: "The organisation pay you, but effectively the community task you now. You are there for the local community and they set your priorities"'.

In areas such as South West Burnley, where community mobilisation is strong, PACT has forged a demonstrable sense of mutual respect between community representatives and the local police. Significantly, local residents involved with PACT in South West Burnley suggest that it has had a significant impact, resulting in a marked reduction in anti-social behaviour and crime in the past few years.

Engagement through consultation exercises

The explosion of consultation activity among local public agencies over the past decade is such that it is virtually impossible to capture the extent of consultation taking place, even in districts the size of Burnley or Harrogate. In addition to statutory requirements to consult, particularly in local government and the NHS, consultation has increasingly become the norm in relation to most major local policy decisions across the public sector. However, the forms that consultations take, and the influence that consultation findings are accorded within the policy process vary enormously. In general, there has been a shift away from using events such as public meetings towards the use of market research style surveys, citizens' panels, on-line questionnaires, and similar mechanisms (Dolton, 2005). The use of citizens' or users' panels, whereby a demographically representative group of residents regularly receive questionnaires on specific issues, was one of the most commonly identified forms of consultation, used particularly by the respective local authorities and police authorities. However, extensive use is also made of web-based questionnaires, market research surveys and, to a lesser extent, focus groups. One local authority, Lancashire County Council, undertakes some consultation via mobile phones, a possibility that Burnley Borough Council has also considered as a means of boosting response rates among young people.

The proportion of residents responding to consultation would appear to be remarkably consistent across the two towns. In both the Burnley and Harrogate surveys, 28 per cent of residents indicated that they had participated in some form of consultation carried out by one of the public agencies listed (involvement in the citizens' panel was excluded). Similarly, the proportion of respondents indicating that they had been involved in local government consultations is also strikingly similar in both instances. In Harrogate, 13.1 per cent indicated that they had participated in a borough council consultation exercise, only marginally less that the 14.3 per cent of Burnley residents that said they had done so. Conversely, 6.7 per cent of Harrogate respondents claimed to have taken part in a county council consultation process, almost identical to the 6.5 per cent of Burnley panel members that had done so. The higher level of engagement with district councils, compared to county councils and other local public bodies, again appears striking.

Table 8.4: Percentage of local residents that claim to have attended a consultation event or responded to a consultation exercise undertaken by the following organisations (excludes borough council panel surveys)

	Burnley	Harrogate
Borough Council	14.3	13.1
NHS Bodies	6.1	11.1
County Council	6.5	6.7
Police	n/a	4.8
Any public body	28	28

These figures clearly indicate that consultation exercises elicit significantly greater public involvement than direct participation in public services or attendance at formal meetings of public bodies. Moreover, it was suggested by many interviewees that newer consultation techniques are able to overcome many of the shortcomings of traditional attempts at community engagement. In particular, well-designed consultation exercises were felt to have the potential to overcome the tendency for participatory democracy to create a new class of 'super-tenants' or 'super-residents'. As such, a consistent message arising from the interviews with representatives of public agencies was the concern to get beyond the often 'self-appointed' community representatives they encounter and to reach 'real people'. While we expressed some concerns about these assumptions in chapter 7, the diversity of mechanisms used by local authorities and public bodies to engage local residents reflects this ambition. Indeed, where social survey and market research methods are used, such exercises can often claim a higher degree of demographic, and to a lesser extent, social, representativeness than is achieved in local elections.[16] It is also possible to identify some examples of innovative consultation practices that have succeeded in promoting engagement among social groups in which rates of participation are generally very low. For instance, Lancashire Police Authority has made striking, and seemingly highly successful, efforts to engage young people and members of black and ethnic minorities in consultations on crime and policing, adopting a range of interactive and deliberative methods.

However, while the rationale for such forms of community and citizen engagement is widely understood, a persistent concern was also expressed in interviews. It was frequently suggested that, in some cases, consulting local residents can actually undermine attempts to promote better relationships between service providers and users. Particularly where the scope for local policy choice is limited – which we suggest is increasingly the case – or timetables are tight, residents may feel that they are being presented with a *fait accompli*. There is a particular danger

---

16 Unless built into the sampling technique, consultation mechanisms rarely overcome the tendency for greater levels of participation to be found among social classes AB. Analysis of citizens' panel responses in Burnley indicates a 40 per cent over-representation of respondents from social classes AB and a 40 per cent under-representation of social classes DE, compared to the borough average. There is a similar under-representation of ethnic minority groups.

that consultations carried out with specific 'hard to reach' groups, such as young people, may backfire if there is little scope to respond to what is suggested. As one interviewee in Burnley commented on the process of consulting young people on the facilities to be included in the town's proposed new leisure centre:

> They've had a lot of complaints from young people about the council, who've been consulting on the sports facility, and someone from the Youth Council said, "What is the point in consulting? Everything we've asked for, they've said that they can't afford. So why are they consulting, because we can't have what we want? We wanted a climbing wall, and we wanted a diving board, but we can't have 'em because they can't afford 'em, [so] they've asked us what we want, we've told them […] so what is the point in asking us?"

Engagement through complaints mechanisms

As we have already suggested, complaints mechanisms may be taken as a surrogate measure of the significance of wider forms of user democracy, and the data we have been able to obtain suggest that resident complaints are at least as common as responses to consultation exercises. Citizens' panel data suggests that Burnley residents appear to be significantly more likely to complain to local public agencies than their counterparts in Harrogate. Some 40 per cent of Burnley residents claimed to have made a complaint to a public body, compared to around 29 per cent in Harrogate. Indeed, a higher proportion of Burnley than Harrogate respondents indicated making complaints to all but one of the seven principal categories of public body listed in the questionnaire. At the same time, the overall pattern of citizen contact through complaints is remarkably similar to that for other forms of engagement with local public bodies. Local residents indicated that they had most commonly made formal complaints to their district council, while complaints were more likely to have been made to both local police forces and NHS bodies than to county councils. The tiny number of complaints made to local strategic partnerships underlines their disconnection from local residents.

Table 8.5: Percentage of local residents that claim to have ever made a formal complaint to the following organisations

	Burnley	Harrogate
Borough council	20.7	16.0
NHS bodies	6.3	4.0
County council	3.1	3.5
Police	9.0	4.2
Housing association	4.6	0.9
Local strategic partnership	0.2	0.1
Any public body	40	28.6

A second means of measuring the significance of complaints as a form of contact with local public bodies is to ascertain the extent of local agencies' own records of complaints. Tables 8.6 and 8.7 summarise complaints data provided by eight local agencies operating in Harrogate and ten with a service remit in Burnley. Taking the view that the relative volumes of complaints recorded are an indicator of the extent of interaction between local residents and service providers, it is possible to rank complainant contact for public agencies operating in Burnley and Harrogate. Clearly, there are many caveats that must be inserted. As we have already indicated, the complaints systems operated by different public sector bodies are by no means comparable. There are significant questions about the reliability of some of the data, particularly where complaints systems are non-statutory. Moreover, the figures provided by agencies themselves suggest a far lower volume of complaints than is apparently indicated by the results of the survey of citizens' panel members. Again, we would also reiterate that complaint levels should not be taken as an indicator of the quality of public services.

These caveats notwithstanding, a consistent pattern of contact with public bodies is again evident from this dataset. Moreover, the rankings presented in Tables 8.6 and 8.7 conform closely to all of the evidence provided by the citizens' panel findings. There would appear to be a relatively clear hierarchy of levels of contact between citizens and local and regional bodies providing public services. In both towns, the district councils reported the second highest proportional level of complaints received, with local police forces and primary care trusts also ranking relatively highly in both cases. The information provided by county councils was largely inadequate, but suggested significantly lower levels of formal complaints registered in comparison to district councils. Organisations that generally serve specific groups within society, such as probation or Connexion services, receive a fraction of the complaints made to universal services, such as NHS bodies and the police. Finally, the virtual absence of contact between regional bodies and the general public is strongly reinforced by this data, which suggests that staff at regional development agencies and government offices in the regions – serving populations of up to 7 million – will generally be able to count on a single hand the complaints made to them each year.

As we have highlighted above, mechanisms intended to provide for individual citizen redress will only contribute to local democracy in so far as they are integrated into wider processes of debate, decision-making, and strategic review. However, there is limited evidence that public agencies in the two towns welcome complaints as part of broader attempts to secure ongoing feedback from service users. By far and away the most innovative and effective complaints procedure we identified was operated by Calico Housing in Burnley (see Case Study 8.4). With the exception of Calico, however, there was otherwise limited evidence of procedures being put into place to monitor and analyse complaints and to feed this analysis into the decision-making process. A number of organisations including Burnley Borough Council, Lancashire County Council, the North Yorkshire Police Authority, and the Burnley, Pendle and Rossendale Primary Care Trust, do have specific committees in place that regularly review complaints information and any strategic issues arising, or consider complaints data as a regular agenda item at meetings of the governing board. However, it was notable that the four elected local councils had greatest difficulty responding to our request for information on complaints. Only two of the four local authorities, Burnley Borough Council and Lancashire County Council, were able to provide information from a centralised database of complaints and, even in these two cases, there appeared to be limited provision for overall strategic organisational and policy review in response to patterns of complaints.

Table 8.6: Complainant contact with public service providers operating in Harrogate 1999/00–2004/05, ranked by average number of complaints received per 10,000 residents

Organisation	No. years of data available	Ave. annual no. of complaints (total)	Complaints per 10,000 residents per annum	Rank
Harrogate Foundation Hospital Trust	4	186	10.9	1
Harrogate Borough Council	1	151	10	2
North Yorkshire Police	5	381	5.1	3
Craven, Harrogate and Rural District Primary Care Trust	1	42	2.1	4
Harrogate Connexions	3	4	0.2	5
North Yorkshire Probation Service	2	11	0.1	6
Yorkshire Forward	3	6	0	7
Government Office for Yorkshire and the Humber	4	2	0	8
North Yorkshire County Council	0	N/a	N/a	N/a
Tees, East and North Yorkshire Ambulance Service	0	N/a	N/a	N/a

Table 8.7: Complainant contact with public service providers operating in Burnley 1999/00–2004/05, ranked by average number of complaints received per 10,000 residents

Organisation	No. years of data available	Ave. annual no. of complaints (total)	Complaints per 10,000 residents per annum	Rank
Calico Housing	1	469	52.4	1
Burnley Borough Council	1	143	16	2
Burnley, Pendle and Rossendale Primary Care Trust	3	278	11.4	3
Lancashire Police	6	796	5.5	4
East Lancashire Hospital Trust	6	276	5.3	5
Lancashire Ambulance Service	4	125	0.9	6
Lancashire County Council	6	44	0.4	7
Lancashire Probation	1	40	0.2	8
North West Development Agency	6	2	0	9
Government Office for the North West	4	1	0	10

Case Study 8.4: Calico Housing's customer contact system

During 2003 Calico Housing, Burnley's stock transfer housing company, made the decision to invest in a new system for recording customer complaints and wider forms of customer contact. Directly influenced by private sector models that view complaints as an opportunity to improve customer service and secure 'free' customer feedback, the development of the system was conceived as a central part of a fundamental 'shift of mentality' towards social housing management in Burnley. The intention has been, quite deliberately, to encourage tenants to make contact and, where appropriate, to make complaints.

In preference to the standard software packages available, the system was devised internally as a bespoke package for Calico by two members of staff. The system minimises the use of paperwork, starting from the 'customer's' first point of contact. Having established that most of its customers saw forms as a deterrent to making a complaint, a free telephone number was established and publicised to all tenants. Once a customer has made contact, their issue is logged on the system directly and assigned a reference number and placed in one of six categories, for instance 'complaint', 'request for service' or 'compliment'. Any previous contacts from the customer are also viewable on screen.

While the database is available on every PC in the company's offices, a core feature of the system is that complaints and other contacts are logged by a separate staff group from those that will subsequently deal with them. Once logged, the contact is forwarded to the relevant area of the company via email, and a letter to the customer is automatically generated thanking them for getting in touch and detailing what action is being taken. At this point, the area of the organisation that has received the complaint or contact information becomes responsible for it, with the central customer contact team monitoring responses and, where necessary, 'acting as a kind of independent Ombudsman' within the organisation.

In its first eighteen months (it becoming operational on January 1, 2004), the system recorded over 2,000 individual 'customer contacts'. Within two years, the annual volume of complaints recorded has risen almost tenfold, from 63 in 2003 to almost 600 in 2005. From a total of around 4,500 Calico properties, a total of 803 (18 per cent) had made some form of contact with the company within the 18 months of the system being introduced.

(Continued)

Case Study 8.4: Calico Housing's customer contact system (continued)

The staff members responsible for designing the system indicated that they had previously worked in manufacturing enterprises that would have 'bent over backwards' to secure this sort of feedback from their customers.

Detailed consideration has also been given to ensuring that the data collected via the customer contact system influences internal management procedures and strategic decision-making, including input from tenant participants. A weekly management report based on customer contacts is produced, and every second month a full report – outlining key trends and issues – is provided to the senior management team, who comment and respond. This information is subsequently taken to the company executive and then to the full board, which includes tenant representatives. In addition, regular feedback sessions are organised at which complainants are invited to discuss how their complaint was handled, and whether they are satisfied with the action taken as a result. As such, the system is seen to offer genuine scope to empower the company's customers, many of whom are typically among the borough's less affluent residents and thus lack significant 'consumer power' in the private market.

8.6 Conclusion

This chapter has demonstrated substantial contrasts in the levels of contact that local residents have with local public agencies. Based on the evidence presented in this chapter, local residents' relationships with the respective borough councils are far stronger than with any other public agency in both towns. In comparison to other public bodies, local residents are far more likely to have attended a borough council meeting, to have responded to a borough council consultation exercise and to have made a formal complaint to the borough council. Given the 'draining away' of functions and powers from borough councils over the past three decades, this continuing significance of lower-tier councils to local residents seems remarkable. The difference in the levels of citizen contact with the borough councils, compared to the county councils, is striking, particularly given the remarkably consistency of the findings for Burnley and Harrogate. Indeed, based on these two districts, it would appear that, in a two-tier local government structure, local residents are:

◆ Twice as likely to have attended a borough council meeting, compared to a county council meeting;

◆ Twice as likely to have taken part in a borough council consultation exercise, compared to a county council consultation;

◆ Five times as likely to have made a formal complaint to the borough council than to the county council.

Significantly, these patterns strongly confirm both the patterns of constituent contact with politicians highlighted in chapter 7, as well as the overwhelming focus of local press attention on borough – rather than county – councils, which we identify in chapter 9. Similarly, the rankings of different forms of citizen contact with local public agencies presented in this chapter are remarkably similar to those put forward in chapter 2, measuring the closeness of local agencies to local people based on the number of representatives per head. We have also shown that there is evidence to support the view that, where physical provision is made for facilities at a neighbourhood scale that have a multi-functional public use, direct contact between local people and public officials is likely to increase dramatically. Public involvement initiatives located at the neighbourhood level also demonstrate considerable scope to promote citizen participation, render local services more accountable to local communities, and even show potential to address inequalities in social capital locally; Lancashire Constabulary PACT meetings are a particularly good example of how this can be achieved in practice.

At the same time, while public involvement procedures have acquired increased importance in local democracy, there is enormous variation in the extent to which public bodies are geared up to deal with the information gathered from them and how effectively such 'intelligence' is used to review service delivery or in policy development. Our analysis of complaints data and complaints procedures among public bodies operating in Burnley and Harrogate raises particularly significant issues about the limitations of the philosophy of 'power to the person'. While virtually all local public bodies were found to have a complaints procedure, there was great variation in the availability of basic complaints data and in the existence of mechanisms to review the more strategic implications of complaints. While there are some notable exceptions, there is scant evidence overall of the three conditions we specified as necessary (for public participation to be able to enhance local democracy) being met by consultation processes and complaints procedures. Indeed, the citizens' panel surveys revealed that only 24 per cent of Harrogate respondents, and a mere 16 per cent of Burnley respondents, 'feel able to influence local decisions'. In short, there seems to be little evidence that local people feel 'personally empowered' via new forms of engagement with public agencies.

Despite our concerns, various forms of 'participatory' and 'user' democracy do constitute important elements of the local democratic mix. Interviewees in public agencies in Burnley and Harrogate pointed to 'customer feedback' mechanisms having significant impact on service provision and, in particular, in maintaining the quality and responsiveness of local public services. However, the limitations of the more consumerist approaches to participation must also be underlined. Substantial investment in market research, focus groups, consultation events, survey questionnaires, and so on, has clearly not prompted participation on a scale that overcomes the concerns about levels of participation in electoral politics highlighted in chapter 7. Indeed, there is little reason to suppose that 'individualised' approaches help enhance more collective forms of democratic participation or serve to reinvent, or even sustain, notions of democratic citizenship. As Wright (1994, p.91) notes: 'We have a citizen's charter, but not a citizens' charter; and the apostrophe matters'. Indeed, by reducing the relationship between providers and users of public services to the consumption of a service by individuals, such approaches arguably contribute further to the atomisation of social relations. As one interviewee put it: 'The "no such thing as society" argument worked for a lot of people, who withdrew from civic society and went to B&Q instead'.

9
Information's What We Need?

We've just had a crime audit for Harrogate. It runs to 450 pages.
That's 150 pages longer than the Old Testament. And that covers
5000 years. This just covers one.

Cllr Geoffrey Webber, during interview, 2005

9.1 Introduction

Government and public services in the UK have a long tradition of secrecy and aversion to publishing information about their workings. There has also been an unwillingness to provide members of the public with the right to access information kept on them by public bodies. Recent decades have seen a series of reforms aimed at reversing this culture of secrecy and improving the way public bodies communicate with the public. This process has accelerated under the current Labour government, which views the increasing openness of public bodies and the concomitant provision of information to the public as a means of both improving accountability and transparency in public sector governance and of providing more effective public services. In the government's words, 'Unnecessary secrecy in government leads to arrogance in governance and defective decision-making' (Chancellor of the Duchy of Lancaster, 1997). This move to increased openness, combined with the increased use of information technologies, has resulted in a vast amount of information held by public bodies now being available to the public both in print and electronically.

This chapter explores some of the issues connected to the increased provision of information to the public resulting from recent reforms. It begins by summarising recent reforms and, particularly, the Freedom of Information Act 2000. Although continuing problems of access remain (such as a lack of clarity in the various Acts covering information access, broadly defined exemptions, and delays in responding to FOI requests) most public bodies examined for this research appear to be attempting to fulfil the spirit of the Act by providing a general right of access to information they hold. The next section briefly outlines the increasing levels of investment in communications, marketing and 'branding' within public bodies, which is part of the increasing openness of the sector, but also derives from a need to be seen to be meeting central government performance targets. We then turn to a more traditional means through which citizens acquire information about local affairs – the local press. The discussion highlights the central role played by the press in local democracy and once again underlines the tendency for attention to focus on district councils. The chapter concludes by asking whether the increased provision of information is creating a condition of 'information overload', with implications for local democracy. It also remains questionable as to whether this wealth of information is useful to the majority of the population without some form of guidance, assistance or explanation. As such, the increased availability of information may be much more useful to those insiders to the system of local governance.

9.2 Opening up public bodies

Since the early 1980s a series of reforms have progressively challenged the tradition of secrecy within government and public bodies. These include the:

◆ *Data Protection Acts 1984 and 1988*, which, applying to both public and private bodies, provide for individual protection against unauthorised use or disclosure of personal information held about an individual and establish the rights of individuals to obtain information held about them;

◆ *Local Government (Access to Information) Act 1985*, which amended Part VA of the Local Government Act 1972 to provide the public with a right of access – subject to certain exemptions – to local authority meetings and documents, including committees and subcommittees;

◆ *Code of Practice on Access to Government Information 1994*, a non-statutory code regulated by the Parliamentary Ombudsman, and subsequent 1995 code applying to the NHS;

◆ *Environmental Information Regulations 1992 and 2004*, which allow people to request environmental information from public authorities and those bodies carrying out a public function, such as privatised utility companies;

◆ *Local Government Act 2000*, which incorporated a requirement for local authorities to publish 'key decisions,' 'forward plans' and records of executive decisions;

◆ *Freedom of Information Act 2000*, the central purpose of which was to provide a general right of access to all 'recorded' information held by public bodies.[17]

While the Labour government's (1997) White Paper, *Your Right to Know*, proposed a strong freedom of information regime, the subsequent Freedom of Information Act 2000 is regarded by critics as substantially weaker (Frankel, 2002, 2004). However, the provisions of the 2000 Act covered around 100,000 public bodies, including central and local government, all NHS bodies, the police, maintained schools and other educational institutions, and a vast array of other public bodies and offices, such as the full range of quangos. Under the FOI Act, all public bodies have to publish and maintain a 'publication scheme' which has been approved by the Information Commissioner. These schemes specify which information the particular public body publishes or intends to publish, the manner in which the information is or will be published, and whether the information is free or incurs payment.[18] All public bodies covered by the Act had to publish a scheme by June 2004, with full rights of access to information for individuals introduced in January 2005. The Act allows public bodies to withhold information for two main reasons. First, a number of exemptions are specified in the Act; for instance, where information is accessible by other means, is intended for future publication, is personal, or would prejudice commercial interests, including those of the body itself. Second, public bodies can refuse to supply the requested information if the costs of complying exceed the "appropriate limit" – which for non-central government bodies is £450.

There are also specific problems which affect the provision of information. There is a degree of confusion in some areas, partially as a result of earlier legislation not having been amended to bring them in line with the FOI Act 2000. One example, in the case of local authorities,

---

17 Compiled from Cook (2003) and *Issue Briefs: Freedom of information* (n.d.).
18 The Information Commissioner also recommends publication schemes should clearly state which information held by a public authority is exempt under the terms of the FOI Act, although this is not a requirement of the Act itself.

is that decisions to hold meetings in public and the rights of public access to various associated papers are still covered by Part VA of the Local Government Act 1972. However, the FOI Act provides additional rights of access, including to papers relating to business discussed in the absence of press and public. Thus, whilst a report may be exempt under the 1972 Act, it can often be obtained under the FOI Act.[19]

Another issue has been that of substantial delays in dealing with FOI requests (DCA, 2005). As part of our own research, we sent out letters to 27 principal public bodies operating in Burnley and Harrogate, requesting information on complaints data (see chapter 8). Under the FOI Act, these bodies had 20 working days to respond to our requests, with either the requested information, an explanation of why the request would not be fulfilled, or a 'fees notice.'[20] Only 48 per cent of the organisations we contacted responded to our requests within the 20 day statutory limit (see Table 9.1). This suggests a clear failure among a majority of the public agencies contacted to introduce internal procedures capable of responding to freedom of information requests. In follow up contacts, the organisational problems that public agencies were experiencing in fulfilling our request became evident. Around a third of the letters had been mislaid, 'slipped down the pile', lost in an office move or apparently never arrived. In one case the request had not been acted upon because the contact officer was on long-term sick leave and in another because of a failure to enter the request on the organisation's 'FOI tracker system'. In at least two cases the information was not provided on time due to time pressures on the relevant contact officer. In one instance, we received a reply some 40 working days after the original request was made, indicating that the organization wished to invoke the fees regulations contained in the legislation, as the request would cost an estimated £3,450 to fulfil. This pattern of responses conforms closely to figures for response rates among central government departments. Between January and March 2005, the first three months of full implementation of the Act, 43 per cent of requests to the Department of Health and 60 per cent of requests to the Home Office took longer than the 20 day deadline (DCA, 2005, p.10).

---

19 This explanation was provided in a personal communication by Maurice Frankel of the Campaign for Freedom of Information, who also mentioned that the ODPM has proposed amending the 1972 Act to bring the exemptions more into line with those of the FOI Act and make them subject to a public interest test.

20 The issuing of a 'fees notice', detailing the cost of fulfilling the request, allows the public body to suspend the 20 day deadline until after the requester meets the costs.

Table 9.1: Record of responses to request for complaints data, made under the terms of the Freedom of Information Act

	No. of organisations	% of organisations
Total organisations to which request was made	27	100
Total replies received within 20 working days	13	48
Total replies received within 40 working days	16	59
Total replies received within 50 working days	19	70
No or very limited data available: e.g. organisation has negligible contact with the general public	4	15
Written indication of willingness to supply information but information not received	1	4
Organisations seeking to charge for the information	1	4
Organisations providing no written response within 50 days	8	30

Despite such problems, there has clearly been an expansion in provision of information to the public, which can be seen as an important means of improving the democratic accountability of public bodies. Notwithstanding the weaknesses pointed to by critics of the Act, the majority of public bodies examined during this research now provide public access to a wide range of information that was previously withheld as a matter of course. The reforms have coincided with the rapid expansion of information technologies, such as the World Wide Web, which have helped to enable greater provision of information to the public. The websites of the majority of public bodies we examined provided detailed information concerning their structure, statutory duties, management board or elected members, as well as such documents as annual reports and statements of accounts, newsletters, notices, agendas and minutes of meetings, media briefings/press releases, consultation documents, and a range of strategic and policy documents. Despite the provision for exemptions in the Act, the majority of public bodies we approached appear to be striving to fulfil the spirit of freedom of information, and are attempting to provide a general right of access to information. This has resulted in a wealth of information being available to members of the public, either directly through the websites of public bodies or through requests made under the Act. As we indicate below, the Act also enhances the capacity of local journalists to acquire information from public bodies.

In addition to fulfilling the terms of the Act, some public bodies we examined have developed innovative means of broadening access to information. For example:

◆ Lancashire County Council provides webcasts of key public meetings, generally live and through an archive of the previous few months, accessible to anyone with an internet connection;

◆ Harrogate Borough Council's website offers a public access portal to users of the planning service, allowing citizens to view current and historic planning applications, monitor the progress of an application, submit comments on a current application, search a constantly updated list of applications received and decided each week, and view decision notices;

◆ North Yorkshire County Council provides "Trading Standards Newsflash", an email service alerting local businesses to known 'scams' targeting companies and providing updates on legislation relevant to their sector – over 750 local companies have signed up to the service.

In addition, many public service providers are increasingly using their websites as a means of gathering information from the public through a variety of web-based consultation mechanisms (see chapter 8).

9.3 Communications strategies, marketing and 'branding'

In addition to the increased openness resulting from legislative reforms, many public bodies – particularly local authorities, NHS bodies and the emergency services – are developing more sophisticated communications and marketing strategies. In part, these reflect the general trend towards more open governance across all public bodies. However, they also suggest increasing pressure to demonstrate how each service provider is meeting central government targets and particularly notions of 'Best Value'. Most public bodies now have comprehensive communications strategy documents, often publicly available through their website, which usually detail the reasons for having a strategy, break the strategy down for different audiences (staff, customers, stakeholders, media, etc.) and often discuss ways corporate communications can be improved. Some also have separate strategy documents for media relations and for marketing.

The increasing importance of communications came out clearly in telephone interviews with communications managers from eight public bodies operating in Burnley and Harrogate. In part, the interviews aimed to check what publications their organisations were publishing and delivering directly to households (see Figure 9.1). Once again, this exercise underlines the distance of the regional and sub-regional bodies from local residents, as none of these bodies provide direct mailings concerning any of their activities. Most of the communications managers from these bodies mentioned that their organisation had no fixed audience for publications – it may be partner organisations or the general public. If the audience was the latter, then these bodies rely on press releases to disseminate information. All the communications managers contacted said they logged media entries or had a cuttings service to check how their organisation was reported. The regional bodies, on this basis, appear in the media regularly: the North West RDA figured in 5,500 articles in the local, regional and national media in 2004. This averages almost 106 per week, a remarkably high figure although it remains unclear whether this helps to improve public awareness of the role of the RDA.

Many organisations that directly mail publications to households do so on a statutory basis. For example, all PCTs have to produce an annual guide to local health services, which may be a pamphlet briefly describing local health spending and providing relevant contact information, or a more detailed brochure with detailed information about local health services. Interestingly, the communications manager at one PCT mentioned that, although their guide elicits positive responses from people contacting services, it also results in phone calls from members of the public complaining about 'the waste of taxpayers' money'. Local authorities, and the police authorities, have a statutory duty to publish and deliver to households a council tax leaflet providing details of the breakdown of council tax in the coming year. The majority of elected local authorities also produce some type of magazine or newsletter, which is also the case for those authorities covering Burnley and Harrogate.

Figure 9.1: Local service providers' publications delivered directly to households

Burnley

Organisation	Publication(s) (frequency)
Burnley Borough Council	Council tax leaflet (annually) *Burnley Now!* (quarterly)
Burnley, Pendle & Rossendale PCT	*Living Health* (annually)
Lancashire Police Authority	Council tax leaflet (annually) *Newsbeat* (bi-annually)
Lancashire County Council	*Vision* (monthly)
East Lancashire Hospitals NHS Trust	None
Cumbria and Lancashire Strategic Health Authority	None
North West Regional Development Agency	None (7,000 names on mailing list who receive NWDA *Business Plan* and similar)
Government Office for the North West	None
North West Regional Assembly	None

Harrogate

Organisation	Publication(s) (frequency)
Harrogate Borough Council	Council tax leaflet (annually) Best Value summary (annually) *Harrogate District News* (quarterly) – discontinued 2002
Craven, Harrogate and Rural District PCT	*Patient Prospectus* (annually)
North Yorkshire Police Authority	Council tax leaflet (annually)
North Yorkshire County Council	*The Reporter* (bi-annually)
Yorkshire Forward (RDA)	None
Government Office for Yorkshire and Humber	None
Yorkshire and Humber Regional Assembly	None
North & East Yorkshire and North East Lincolnshire Strategic Health Authority	None
Harrogate and NHS District Foundation Trust	None

Reaching local residents via free 'in-house' publications is strongly encouraged by national government. The *Connecting with Communities* project, established by the ODPM in partnership with the Local Government Association (LGA), the Improvement and Development Agency (IDeA) and the Audit Commission sees good communications as central to local authorities acting as community leaders and delivering a high standard of services (ODPM 2002b: 3). Yet, surveys suggest that less than half of local residents feel their councils keep them 'well informed' and only one in ten can name their local councillor or have heard of 'best value' in relation to local government (2002a: 2). Whether a resident actually needs to know the name of their local councillor in order to deal with the council is debatable, as is the value of residents' awareness of a centrally-driven performance monitoring system. However, the research did capture a potentially more significant reason for improving communications:

> [I]*n those councils rated as relatively poor communicators, residents' satisfaction with the council was consistently lower than might be expected, given their overall satisfaction with the area as a place to live. And in many cases, good performance on service delivery wasn't matched by satisfaction ratings. In other words, many councils have a better story than the one they are telling. We're not talking about 'spin', but open and honest two-way communications with residents.*

ODPM 2002a: 3

Yet, there is mixed evidence about the usefulness of this growing investment in external communications being made by local authorities and other local bodies. A MORI survey of residents in a district in the south of England, showed that after local newspapers, council magazines were their second main source of information about the council (ODPM 2002b: 29). Similarly, citizens' panel data from Burnley showed that 71.5 per cent of respondents said local newspapers were their first or second preferred method of receiving communications from the council. Almost three quarters of respondents said they had recently received a copy of the district council publication, *Burnley Now*, but while almost half found it informative and easy to read, only 31 per cent described it as 'interesting'. Harrogate District Council does not publish a regular magazine, having discontinued publication of their *Harrogate District News* in 2003. However, with local authority communications coming under particular scrutiny as part of Labour's modernisation agenda, Harrogate Council is currently considering publishing a new magazine, particularly in light of the recommendations arising from the *Connecting with Communities* project.

9.4 The role of the local press

Apart from being an invaluable guide to local life, your local newspaper is very important in many other ways – not least in holding to account local politicians, be they Members of Parliament or local councillors. It is an essential part of local democracy.

Michael Howard, 2004

The outgoing Leader of the Opposition's views about the role of local newspapers in holding politicians to account and acting as the 'champions' of local communities is seemingly shared by both the Prime Minister (Blair, 2003) and by the general public. Regular MORI surveys find that three-quarters of people cite local newspapers as their principal sources of information about local councils (ODPM, 2002b). Moreover, recent evidence suggests that local newspapers are enjoying something of a renaissance, despite the rise of other media, with circulation levels generally rising across the country. At the same time, however, the survival of local newspapers has become dependent upon a growing concentration of local press ownership. Between 1992 and 2002, the number of local and regional newspaper companies in the UK fell from over 200 to less than 100, and the proportion of titles owned by the five largest company groups rose from 43 to 73 per cent (Competition Commission, 2002). This increasing concentration carries the risk that business decisions made by a single company can have significant repercussions for local democracy across the country. Thus, proposed job cuts at Trinity Mirror Newspapers (the largest local media group in the UK, owning 240 regional and local titles) recently prompted an early day motion, tabled by Labour MP John McDonnell, arguing that 'such moves will lead to poorer coverage of local politics and community issues, thereby damaging local democracy and accountability ... '[21]

---

21 Available at http://www.publications.parliament.uk/pa/cm/cmedm/51111e01.htm

Table 9.2: Local and regional newspapers serving Burnley and Harrogate

Title	Frequency	Catchment/ Coverage	Circulation	Established	Ownership
Harrogate Advertiser	Weekly	Harrogate town and surrounding areas	17,691*	1836	Johnston Press PLC
Yorkshire Post	Daily	Yorkshire	50,541	1755	Johnston Press PLC
Yorkshire Evening Post	Daily	Leeds and surrounding district	68,767	1890	Johnston Press PLC
Burnley Express	Bi-weekly	Burnley and surrounding areas	16,376**	1877	Johnston Press PLC
Lancashire Evening Telegraph	Daily	East Lancashire	35,246	1886 (as *Northern Daily Telegraph*)	Newsquest Media Group
Lancashire Evening Post	Daily	Preston and surrounding districts	38,237	1844 (as *The Preston Guardian*)	Johnston Press PLC

* The circulation of the Ackrill Group, which covers the whole of the Harrogate district, is 36,557.
** The Burnley Express appears on Tuesday and Friday. The figure cited here is the average circulation across these two days. The combined weekly sales are 32,751.
Sources: Holdthefrontpage.co.uk (accessed 15 November 2005).

Table 9.2 summarises information about the main local and regional papers available in Burnley and Harrogate and highlights a number of key issues in relation to local democracy. First, the local and regional press operates at a number of different geographical scales, with catchments for local newspapers often having a relatively poor degree of fit with local government boundaries. The significance of this pattern in relation to Burnley and Harrogate is explored in more detail below. Second, there is a particularly strong demand for the 'most local' newspapers. Both Burnley and Harrogate are served by local papers boasting high circulation rates. The *Burnley Express* is bought by approximately half of households locally, while the *Harrogate Advertiser* can claim to reach as many as three-quarters of households within its catchment area. In both cases, the newspaper serving the town is read more widely, in proportional terms, than papers with regional or sub-regional catchments. For instance, while the *Burnley Express* sells close to 20,000 copies on its principal circulation day (Friday), the daily sales of the *Lancashire Evening Telegraph* within Burnley peak at around 5,000. Third, despite numerous changes of ownership and, in several cases, changes of name, local newspapers serving Burnley and Harrogate are one of the most historically-rooted features of local democracy in both towns. All six of the local papers listed were established between 1755 and 1890, with five being founded during the Victorian era, at a time when local government arrangement were first being formalised. Fourth, the concentration of ownership among these titles is highly evident. Five of the six newspapers are owned by Johnston Press PLC, which controls more than 200 titles nationally and is the fourth largest local newspapers group in the UK. The remaining title, the *Lancashire Evening Telegraph*, is owned by the Newsquest Media Group, the second largest local newspaper group in the UK, with over 300 titles.

The relationship between local government boundaries, the content of local press coverage and newspaper catchment areas is of particular significance in relation to the two-tier local government structure. Senior journalists at both the *Burnley Express* and the *Harrogate Advertiser* indicated that their coverage of local public agencies overwhelmingly relates to the respective district councils. Moreover, in both cases, policing and local health services were defined as higher priorities for coverage than county council issues. This prioritisation of coverage, particularly the attention given to district council issues, further underlines the significantly greater 'closeness' of district councils to local residents and the remoteness of county councils. As the editor of the *Burnley Express* suggested, from among all public agencies locally, 'I'd guess by far and away Burnley Borough Council to have the biggest contact with the public voice'. This is also reflected in the separately branded 'sister' papers, available in those parts of the local authority district that are recognised as having a distinct 'identity'. Thus the *Padiham Express*, a sister paper to the *Burnley Express*, is produced from the same office and shares a great deal of the same content. Likewise, the Ripon Gazette, the *Wetherby News*, the *Knaresborough Post*, and the *Pateley Bridge and Nidderdale Herald* are all produced from linked editorial offices with modest variation in content, essentially reflecting local attachments in areas that, according to one local journalist, 'consider themselves to be a different world and, until 1974, were a different world'.

This tendency is further exacerbated by the fact that there are no equivalent newspapers focusing on county council issues. In Burnley, residents will struggle to find any press coverage of Lancashire County Council affairs in any local newspaper. The *Lancashire Evening Post* is dominated by coverage of Preston issues and its main focus among local public bodies is Preston Borough Council. While the *Lancashire Evening Telegraph* has a broader remit, focusing on East Lancashire and beyond, stories concerned with local politics again tend to be dominated by the affairs of individual East Lancashire districts. Similarly, the Yorkshire Post covers at least ten unitary, seven district and two county councils, while its sister paper the *Yorkshire Evening Post* has a much smaller remit focused around the Leeds area. The communications manager at North Yorkshire County Council reported that the local press do attend the relevant area committees, but there is limited attendance at council meetings by the regional press[22] or other media outlets. It seems clear, therefore, that there are no local newspapers that regard the task of holding the respective county councils to account as a central part of their remit. Significantly, a (2003) North Yorkshire County Council 'public awareness survey' found that the council's own communications were the primary source of information for local residents. Just 37 per cent of residents surveyed named local newspapers as their principal source of information about the authority – almost half the level that appears to be typical for district councils.

These tendencies are exacerbated by the limited scope for local newspapers (and other media outlets) to hold the full range of local service providers to account. As we noted elsewhere, attending the meetings of governing (and other relevant) boards of the range of local service providers operating in either town would be a full-time job, particularly with a number of agencies operating at a regional scale. All the communications managers interviewed for this research indicated that they invite local reporters to their meetings and supply press packs to them. However, time and resource constraints reinforce the tendency for local journalists to focus on key district councils meetings, particularly full-council, executive, and some scrutiny and planning meetings. Meetings of local hospital trusts, and sometimes the PCT may be attended if they were aware that particularly 'newsworthy' items were

---

22 While a quantitative analysis of content has not been undertaken, it is likely that *The North Yorkshire Advertiser* (circulation 26,746), a free sister paper of the *Northern Echo*, based in Darlington, provides more coverage of North Yorkshire County Council than the Leeds-based Yorkshire Post Group.

on the agenda. Attendance at county-level meetings, such as for county councils, police authorities, and fire authorities, was reported to be very rare. One consequence of these patterns of press reporting is that they are seriously out of line with the distribution of public spending locally. As we saw in chapter 3, the county councils out-spend district councils by a ratio of 10:1. Given that the vast majority of residents indicate that they obtain information about local councils via the local press, it would seem reasonable to assume that these patterns of media coverage offer at least part of the explanation for local people tending to overestimate the powers and resources at the disposal of district councils.

The role of local newspapers as the key source of information for local residents raises important issues in relation to possible political bias and the extent to which the local press appeals to a broad cross-section of local people. Overt political bias can be discounted. While local councillors sometimes took the view that local papers exhibit subtle political preferences, we found no evidence of such implicit bias in our reading of either the *Burnley Express* or the *Harrogate Advertiser*. Indeed, from among the cross-section of local councillors we interviewed, no consensus was evident as to whether any individual publication was Conservative, Liberal or Labour. This pattern thus underlined what one interviewee described as 'a golden rule in local papers […] that if you get accused by the Liberals of being a Conservative paper and you get accused by the Conservatives of being a Liberal paper, then you know you're doing something right'. As such, senior journalists were adamant that political bias in the local press would undermine not only their *raison d'être*, but also the commercial viability of a local newspaper. As the editor of the *Burnley Express* argued 'a local paper can't afford to disenfranchise anybody in the town, because you're a paper for the whole town […] that's in the ethical, professional and business sense as well'. Given their very large circulation rates, both the *Burnley Express* and the *Harrogate Advertiser* can claim to appeal to a significant proportion of their respective towns. However, circulation is inevitably lower among some social groups locally. In particular, estimates suggest that circulation rates for the *Burnley Express* are as low as 10 per cent in the predominately Asian wards of the town.

Given the generally strong claims to popular appeal, there is frequently a strong tendency for local newspapers to develop a campaigning style, particularly where there is an evident swell of local opinion around a particular issue. Senior journalists in both towns indicated that their papers regularly play a role in supporting or even generating campaigns on specific local issues. Where an issue appears to have widespread local support and is not associated specifically with an individual political party or lobby group, both the *Burnley Express* and the *Harrogate Advertiser* have encouraged local residents to sign petitions and, in some instances, have become the key vehicle through which large-scale petitions have been organised. As one senior local journalist indicated:

> *... campaigning, we tend to do. We tend to sort of jump on the back of things [...] I mean we printed petitions in the paper for people to sign and lobby cards for people to send to their MP. I think that's important in some ways to a newspaper.*

The growth of local community action groups and residents' associations was noted by journalists in both towns and seen as a form of local mobilisation that local papers would generally want to provide a voice for. In some cases, papers have given relatively high-profile coverage to specific local groups and campaigns, not only because it 'makes good copy' but also because providing such groups with access to the local press is seen as a basic cornerstone of the democratic process in a pluralist society. As one journalist noted with reference to a particular local campaign group:

> [It's a case of] *people with a common problem coming together and working* [it] *out, and using the local media as a way to get their voice heard. Not in, I think, a disproportionate way: we don't exaggerate their voice, we give them a voice. It only seems like exaggeration when, to people who think that the local media shouldn't be controversial and should be completely down-the-middle-of-the-road, totally straight, exact same number of words for every single political party and every single point of view. People don't read newspapers like that; newspapers like that go bust very, very quickly! If someone is shouting, then we should give them a voice. That's the only way that you're going to get any kind of democratic discussion going. You know, you may disagree with what they say, you may disagree with the amount of influence they have, but it's because they're shouting the loudest. If you disagree with them, shout louder!*

A perhaps surprisingly important space for debate in local democracy is the letters page of the local newspaper. Senior local journalists were strongly of the view that a well written letter to the local press was likely to be significantly more effective than writing directly to a council leader or chief executive about the same issue. While there is a known tendency in some areas for letters pages to be targeted by members of local political parties for narrowly partisan ends, no such pattern appears to be observable in Burnley or Harrogate. As such, a vibrant letters page is seen as a healthy indicator of people caring about local issues and having the motivation to engage in sometimes passionate debate about them. In this regard, the editor of the *Burnley Express* suggested that the letters page was arguably more important and more valid an indicator of local opinion on key issues than any market research or public consultation mechanism:

> *Letters pages are very powerful mediums. It's perhaps the best barometer of local fears as well [...] If you said to most people in Burnley 'what's the citizen's panel?', they wouldn't have a clue what you mean; [if] you say to them 'what's the* Burnley Express?', *well 'it's a newspaper' [...] I think people want, people like, the tried and tested ways of getting things done [...] And as I say, the letters page is a very, very powerful way of doing things, very powerful.*

Such responses reflect a wider tendency for local journalists to express a high degree of scepticism about recent attempts to modernise local councils, promote local democratic renewal and promote citizen engagement in public services. Recent national reforms tended to receive a mixed reaction from journalists in Burnley and Harrogate and specific concerns were expressed, for instance, about the abolition of community health councils eroding the limited extent of 'patient power' in the NHS. In the face of such changes, local journalists generally defend the traditional role of an independent local press holding local politicians and local agencies to account, promoting public debate and giving voice to a range of local groups. In this sense, the most significant national reform was seen to be the new Freedom of Information Act. In contrast to initial expectations, FOI is increasingly being seen as having significant relevance to local democracy:

> *The Freedom of Information Act was much trumpeted in the national media, but it is actually useless at the national level*

because of the government veto [...] But at a local level, we are now fantastically empowered [...] I think it is fantastic and it is changing local journalism as we speak because all of a sudden, all the things that we weren't allowed to know, we know now!

The work of public relations teams and press officers in the two boroughs was generally evaluated positively by local journalists. While a growing trend was noted for local councils to use press officers as 'gatekeepers', preventing journalists from gaining access to individual officers, no such tendency was alluded to in Burnley or Harrogate. Although one of the county councils was felt to operate in this manner, it was suggested that such tight media management generally occurs 'in areas where either the media has lost the trust of the council, or the council has lost the trust of the media – it's bad, it really is very bad for local democracy'. In Burnley, moreover, the recent emphasis placed by the borough council on improving public relations was seen as a significant improvement upon previous practice. However, there was a degree of scepticism about the extent to which the proliferation of 'free sheets' distributed by public agencies genuinely helps improve communications between local agencies and the general public. Inevitably, publications issued directly by public agencies tend to be written from the perspective of that agency. Aside from invitations for local residents to respond to consultation exercises or to write in with their views, such publications are clearly not a mechanism for holding those bodies to account or for generating public debate about their work. It is in this sense that the local press provides a unique and crucial role in relation to local democracy, as the editor of the *Burnley Express* argued:

I think it's a vehicle for members of the public to air their gripes, to feel that they can get something achieved, and I'd like to think that it's on the people's side [...] That's how I'd probably sum it up: The Express is on ordinary people's side.

9.5 Conclusion

Legislative reforms and greater emphasis on communications have substantially improved the quantity and (probably) quality of information supplied to the public by governmental bodies. However, our research also suggests that there are more problematic issues relating to the management, filtering and utilisation of such information. First, for local councillors and others involved as board members of unelected local public bodies, there is increasingly a sense of what Toffler (1970) termed 'information overload': a state in which people have too much information to make a decision or remain effectively informed about a topic. During interviews, many local councillors, at district and county levels, expressed frustration with this growing sense of information overload, and the associated difficulty of identifying useful and relevant information. At the same time, a paradox became evident in that a number of councillors also felt that, under the new political arrangements, they had to make significantly greater effort to keep informed about issues and decisions. As backbenchers are no longer members of decision-making committees, their principal source of information is increasingly written documentation rather than direct contact with council officers. It is the copious nature of this paperwork that creates not just a sense of overload, but also a simultaneous concern about overlooking crucial information. As one county councillor explained:

> *Everyday I get something through the post.* […] *But there is so much stuff. The scrutiny committees that you're on, you get a wedge of paper and it's awfully tempting to just sort of nod it through. I'm on the audit and corporate affairs committee* […] *We had reports from internal audit last week. We had a procurement strategy, a risk management strategy and we had reports from internal audit, plus a report on the new property management system. And that was all in two hours. And okay, I read it all and I tried to register the key issues, but it wasn't really put under proper consideration.*

Second, if elected members struggle to make sense of the information available to them, the problem is, without doubt, multiplied many times over in the case of most, 'non-expert' local residents. The majority of information made available by local public bodies will be of little direct interest or use to most members of the public. Rather, the publication of annual reports, statements of accounts, newsletters, notices, agendas and minutes of meetings, plus associated papers, media briefings/press releases, consultation documents, and various strategic and policy documents is probably only of direct interest to activists, journalists and researchers. In the main, this underlines that the significance of freedom of information lies not in relation to promoting greater participation in local democracy, but in its role in underpinning wider mechanisms of accountability and democratic scrutiny. Nonetheless, there is an important issue about whether greater access to information will further increase the local influence of those local residents that are most skilled in making use of it. Moreover, at particular moments in time, citizens will require guidance through the information jungle with which they are suddenly faced. In this regard, the introduction of the PALS service in the NHS (see chapter 8) may come to provide a useful example of mechanisms that can harness the knowledge, experience and skills of 'expert' citizens to potentially enhance local democracy.

10
Strengthening Local Democracy: Lessons and limitations

Schumacher's phrase 'Small is Beautiful', may not point the way for every area of economic activity, but it is valid for important aspects of local administration and politics.
David Blunkett and Keith Jackson, 1987

10.1 Introduction

We introduced this book by noting the widely held view that the re-configuration of local governance during the 1980s and 1990s, particularly the growing influence of unelected bodies in local affairs, represents a fundamental challenge to local democracy. Against this backdrop, this study has found that notable steps have been made in recent years in opening up the local quango state to many democratic principles. As has been documented, these include: greater transparency in appointments to unelected bodies; boards of many unelected bodies now meet in public; greater citizen access information via the Freedom of Information Act; an increase in the extent of user participation in local services; the enhanced opportunities for elected councils to scrutinise the activities of unelected bodies; the reform of mechanisms for individual citizen redress; and new forms of participatory and representative democracy, such as elections of board members to foundation hospital trusts. However, this volume also highlights a number of serious concerns about the state of local democracy in England. Chief among the concerns identified are the following issues:

◆ 50–60 per cent of local public spending is in the hands of unelected public agencies;

◆ The proliferation of partnership arrangements directly counters the attempts to render the local public agencies more transparent and accountable to local people;

◆ Local election turnout remains low and large sections of the population rarely vote in local elections;

◆ The widespread use of participatory mechanisms, such as consultation exercises, is deeply problematic in a context where local public agencies have very limited scope to respond to the issues raised by local people;

◆ Local democracy, particularly local party politics, is sustained by a small and diminishing proportion of the population, and large sections of the population have virtually no engagement with the local policy process;

◆ Far from broadening participation in local democracy, many recent reforms may have served only to increase the influence of those that were previously engaged with local affairs.

This concluding chapter seeks to place our research findings in a broader context and considers a range of proposals for reviving local democracy. We approach this task in two stages. The first section of the chapter places English local democracy in comparative perspective. It draws on wider international evidence, and particularly the experience of other European countries, to assess the relative quality of local democracy in England. This analysis includes an assessment of how local government in England shapes up in relation to the European Charter of Local Self-Government. The second section turns to examine how local democracy could be revived. We begin by considering the extent to which the competing proposals for reform offered by the main political parties in England would be likely to address the concerns identified in the book as a whole. We also ask, on the basis of all the available evidence, whether there is a strong enough case for major reform. This question is posed in light of the tendency towards 'reform overload' in local governance in recent decades. In such circumstances, it is possible that democratic consolidation might be best fostered by a period of relative stability. While there is possibly surprising merit to the 'no change' argument, it is suggested that there is a need to distinguish between centrally- and locally-driven reforms. It is argued that the greatest threat facing local democracy is the spectre of 'continuous reform' from the centre. To this end, the book concludes with a series of recommendations that are felt to maximise the potential for individual localities themselves to foster a process of local democratic renewal.

10.2 English local democracy in comparative perspective

The European Charter of Local Self-Government, originally ratified by the members of the Council of Europe in 1985, declares in its preamble that 'local authorities are one of the main foundations of any democratic regime'. The preamble of the charter also notes that securing local self-government, as a cornerstone of democracy in Europe, 'entails the existence of local authorities endowed with democratically constituted decision-making bodies and possessing a wide degree of autonomy'. Part 1 of the charter, comprising articles 2–11, outlines a series of clear principles that will enable local self-government in practice. These include legal or constitutional recognition of local government, provision for the general competence for local authorities, and powers to vary local taxes. Under the Conservatives, British governments initially refused to sign the Charter.

After the 1997 general election, the incoming Labour government quickly reversed this decision, and the UK became a signatory to the Charter. However, despite the reforms subsequently enacted under Labour, it has been suggested on a number of occasions that the UK is actually in breach of the Charter (Commission on Local Governance, 2002; Beetham *et al.*, 2002). The chair of the independent Commission on Local Governance (CLG), Guardian journalist Peter Hetherington, subsequently submitted a memorandum to the Select Committee on Transport, Local Government and the Regions in June 2002, stating 'there are currently some serious breaches of the provisions of the Charter, which need to be addressed by the government as a matter of urgency'. Similar conclusions were reached by the Democratic Audit team, who suggested that the UK failed to meet the European standards of local government independence contained in the charter (Beetham *et al.*, 2002). Common to both the CLG and the Democratic Audit reviews was the conclusion that the UK is likely to be in breach of at least four 4 Articles contained in the Charter, specifically:

◆ *Article 2* – Constitutional and legal foundation of local self-government;

◆ *Article 3* – Concept of local self-government;

◆ *Article 8* – Administrative supervision of local authorities' activities;

◆ *Article 9* – Financial resource of local authorities.

We would echo this assessment. Article 2 specifies that 'the principle of local self-government shall be recognised in domestic law and, where practicable, in the constitution'. No such provision has yet been made. Article 3 establishes that 'Local self-government denotes the right and the ability of local authorities, within the limits of the law, to regulate and manage a substantial share of public affairs under their own responsibility and in the interests of the local population'. As we have shown in chapter 2 of this book, local authorities work alongside a myriad of unelected bodies and, as is shown in chapter 3, they can claim to be responsible for only half of spending among local public agencies.

Under Article 8 it is stated that 'any administrative supervision of the activities of the local authorities shall normally aim only at ensuring compliance with the law and with constitutional principles'. Moreover, Article 8 also establishes that 'administrative supervision of local authorities shall be exercised in such a way as to ensure that the intervention of the controlling authority is kept in proportion to the importance of the interests which it is intended to protect'. Based on our analysis in chapter 4, we would concur with the conclusions of the CLG that neither the Best Value regime nor the Comprehensive Performance Assessment is consistent with the spirit of this Article. We would also agree with Beetham *et al.* that the UK breaches a number of principles laid out in Article 9, particularly that local authorities should have entitlement to 'adequate financial resources of their own, of which they may dispose freely within the framework of their powers'. We would also question whether local authorities 'have the power to determine the rate' of local taxes, and whether the financial basis of local authorities is 'of a sufficiently diversified and buoyant nature to enable them to keep pace as far as practically possible with the real evolution of the cost of carrying out their tasks'.

That the UK fails to meet widely recognised European criteria for local self-government is not entirely surprising. It has frequently been suggested that the centralised character of the British state left it 'out of step' with the rest of Western Europe and most other liberal democracies (Crouch and Marquand, 1989). It has also regularly been noted that, as measured by population, the UK has the largest units of local government in Europe, and possibly in the OECD, and that the ratio of citizens to elected local politicians is higher in the UK than in any other European country (Wilson and Game, 1994; Beetham *et al.* 2002; Swianiewicz, 2002). Beetham *et al.* (2002) calculate the average population per local authority in the UK as 118,400, by far the largest figure for the 10 West European countries they consider. These figures suggest the average UK council to be 4 times as large as its Swedish counterparts, 24 times the size of the average Germany local authority and a full 74 times larger than the average French municipality. This pattern is further demonstrated by a comprehensive survey of 24 European countries carried out by Swianiewicz (2002), who also establishes that UK local authorities serve much larger populations than the European norm. Citing an average population figure for local authorities in England and Wales of 123,000, Swianiewicz finds that only local government units in Lithuania and Yugoslavia (with average populations of 66,000 and 45,000 respectively) are more than a quarter of the size of English and Welsh local authorities.[23]

Table 10.1: People per elected councillor and average population per council, Western Europe

	People per elected councillor	Average population per council
France	116	1,580
Germany	250	4,925
Italy	397	7,130
Norway	515	9,000
Spain	597	4,930
Sweden	667	30,040
Belgium	783	16,960
Denmark	1,084	18,760
Portugal	1,125	32,300
UK	**2,605**	**118,400**
Mean	814	24,403

Source: Beetham et al., 2002, p.267.

23 The figures for the UK presented in Table 10.1 exclude parish and town councils. If the UK's 80,000 parish councillors are included then the UK has roughly 650 people per councillor. However, including parish councillors in this way raises two serious problems. First, most parish councillors are elected unopposed. Second, the geographical coverage of parishes is highly uneven and the most densely populated area of the UK – the major cities – have virtually no parish councils at all.

At the same time, it is also well known that the UK has by far the lowest rates of turnout in local elections of all EU countries. As Table 10.2 shows, even accounting for a general decline in turnout across the EU, the proportion of citizens voting in sub-national elections in Britain remains a full 30 percentage points below the European average. Even if we discount turnout in countries where some form of compulsory voting is in place (Austria, Belgium and Luxembourg) or where strong negative sanctions apply for non-voters (Italy), turnout in British sub-national elections is around 40 percentage points adrift of the Scandinavian countries.

The stark contrasts between the UK and other European countries presented in Tables 10.1 and 10.2 prompt us to return to the debate about the relationship between size and democracy. What significance, if any, should be attached to these 'rankings' and the possible relationship between them? Can lower electoral turnout in the UK be explained, at least in part, by the tendency for local councils to be larger and by the comparably lower number of local politicians per elector in the UK? As we noted in chapter 1, considerable attention has been paid internationally to the question of whether there is any direct relationship between the size of local authorities and the quality of local

Table 10.2: Average turnout at sub-national elections within the EU

	Before 1995: mean	After 1995: mean	Change
Belgium	93	n/a	n/a
Luxembourg	93	92	−1
Italy	85	80	−5
Austria	82	79	−3
Sweden	85	79	−6
Denmark	80	72	−8
Spain	65	72	+7
Germany	72	70	−2
Portugal	60	62	+2
France	68	59	−9
Ireland	60	50	−10
Netherlands	54	47	−7
Great Britain	**40**	**35**	**−5**
Mean	72.1	66.3	−4

Source: ODPM, 2002c, p.122.

democracy. While the relationship has been approached from a number of perspectives, with the variables used to 'measure' local democracy varying enormously, the results are remarkably consistent. Most commonly, researchers have examined whether there is a relationship between the size of local authorities and turnout in local elections (Morlan, 1984; Rallings and Thrasher, 1997; Frandsen, 2002). While these studies show that a wide range of factors influence turnout in local elections, Frandsen (2002, p.866) suggests that the findings consistently point in the same direction when it comes to the influence of size: 'nearly all studies of turnout at local elections have demonstrated that turnout is higher in small municipalities than in large'. Frandsen's own analysis of the influence of the size of local authorities on turnout in Denmark, the Netherlands, Norway, Switzerland and the UK from 1971–1999 adds credence to this conclusion. While there are significant variations between the five countries, in each case a negative relationship between size and turnout is observed. In addition, once the impact of compulsory voting is discounted, it is found that turnout in local elections tends to be higher where some form of proportional representation is used (Frandsen, 2002).

Given the centrality of local elections to local democracy, the evidence relating to size and turnout would be compelling on its own. However, there is further evidence to suggest a strongly negative relationship between size and most forms of participation in local democracy. Rose (2002) finds that, in Denmark, the Netherlands and Norway, there is a consistently negative relationship between the size of a municipality and the frequency with which citizens contact either local politicians or local council officers. Moreover, this 'size impact' occurs largely independently of other socio-economic variables known to influence political participation, such as social class and levels of education. In Denmark, where reviews assessing the case for merging units of local government have been carried out with similar frequency to the UK, researchers have consistently found that democracy suffers where larger municipalities are created (Larsen, 2002). Larsen (2002) analyses the relationship between the size of Danish municipalities and three forms of participation in local democracy (electoral turnout, citizen contact with local government, and involvement in organised groups). As he notes (p.323), the findings are absolutely unambiguous: 'the results are so convincing that there is no doubt that voter turnout, direct contact and broad organisational participation are greater in small municipalities'.

The findings of the north European studies cited above also relate closely to the results of similar studies carried out in the USA (Verba and Nie, 1972; Oliver, 2000). Using similar categories of civic involvement to Rose's (2002) study of three north European countries, Oliver (2000) demonstrates that the size of units of local government in the USA has a clear impact upon levels of civic involvement. Again, as with Rose (2002), this impact remained evident even after socio-economic factors had been taken into account. Specifically, Oliver argues that civic involvement is greatest in smaller municipalities and that there is 'negative relationship between civic participation and city size' (p.366).

Our own research findings, particularly those on levels of citizen contact with local public agencies, presented in chapter 8, are fully consistent with this body of international evidence. Yet, as we noted in chapter 1, the case for the amalgamation of local authorities in the UK and elsewhere has largely been made on the grounds that larger units of local government will result in economies of scale. A recent unpublished study commissioned by the Number 10 Policy Unit under Geoff Mulgan found very limited evidence of the existence of economies of scale in local government across ten service areas examined in detail. Moreover, international experience suggests that such economies of scale are rarely achieved. Summarising a wide range of international quantitative and qualitative research evidence on local government consolidation, Fox and Richards (2003) suggest that the diversity of factors influencing efficiency in local government is such that the achievement of scale economies is far from certain. Similarly, reviewing 34 major international studies, mainly from the USA and Canada, Byrnes and Dollery (2002, p.393) concluded that only 8 per cent of studies found evidence of economies of scale. By contrast, 39 per cent of the studies found no relation between per capita expenditure and size, while 24 per cent suggested that diseconomies of scale were in operation. Indeed, there is even evidence to suggest that economies may be greater in small units of local government. Examining US empirical evidence, Boyne (1998, p.252) concludes that 'the broad pattern of evidence suggests that lower spending is a feature of fragmented and deconcentrated local government systems'. By contrast, consolidated and concentrated local government structures 'tend to be associated with higher spending' (ibid.). Given such inconsistent evidence, Fox and Richards (2003) argue that no general case can be made for larger local authorities on the grounds of economies of scale and advocate thorough case-by-case evaluation wherever amalgamation of existing units are proposed.

The experience of local government reorganisation in the UK is far from unique. As Chandler (2000) notes, British governments since 1945 have given priority to securing the supposed efficiencies to be gained from co-ordinated large scale administration in virtually all service areas. Current proposals to merge police forces in England and Wales reflect this long-run pattern. Between 1962 and 1974, the number of police forces in England and Wales was reduced from 162 to the current figure of 43. Although there has been ongoing debate about the case for further reducing the number of forces, the Home Office's (2001) White Paper on policing suggested that 'at present there is no sound evidence to determine the optimum force sizes for different circumstances, nor is there firm evidence which suggests that the smaller forces are failing in efficiency or effectiveness.' Despite this conclusion, the Home Office has recently announced its intention to consider reducing the number of forces to as few as 9, including a single national force for Wales. The proposals have been justified largely on the grounds of a recent HMIC report, which suggests that forces with fewer than 4000 officers are poorly equipped to deal with organised crime and, in particular, terrorism (O'Connor, 2005).

Direct parallels can be observed in relation to local health care. The creation of primary care groups (PCGs) in 1999, which subsequently became primary care trusts during 2000–01, was specifically intended to 'shift the balance of power' in the NHS, by enabling the lion's share of health care expenditure to be determined at a local level and by promoting patient involvement in the service. Primary care groups, as the forerunners of PCTs, had numbered 481, reflecting the assumption made in the (1997) White Paper that the average population size would ideally be around 100,000. As such, the PCGs/PCTs initially reflected an attempt to create 'a more devolved, clinically driven and locally responsive NHS' (Walshe et al., 2004, p.871). Thereafter, opinion shifted and it was increasingly assumed that the optimal size would be closer to 200,000. Thus, following the creation of primary care trusts, the number of units was reduced to 315. The number of PCTs was further reduced by a period of 'merger mania' that is in many ways typical of local health care organisation in the UK (Bojke et al., 2001). Current proposals suggest that the Department of Health is looking to reduce the number of PCTs to between 100 and 150, thereby increasing the size of the average population served to around 0.5 million. The principal justification for these proposed mergers has been that performance will be improved while enabling significant economies of scale to be achieved.

Despite the force of the argument behind the 'bigger is better' perspective, it is notable, particularly in the case of primary care, that the position of central government appears to have shifted significantly within the past few years. Yet, many of the arguments that have been made in the face of local government reorganisation apply equally to the cases of health care and policing and other public services. Indeed, it is possible to identify six key themes arising from research in the UK and elsewhere on scale economies in the public services that suggest an overwhelming case for being sceptical about the benefits of 'scaling up':

◆ The range of factors that are seen to influence the performance of PCTs are strikingly similar to those highlighted in relation to local government. Variations in governance structures, management arrangements, budgetary mechanisms, the effectiveness of partnership working and collaboration, and the socio-economic profile of the local population all play a role in accounting for contrasting performance levels (Bojke *et al.*, 2001; Wilkin *et al.*, 2003);

◆ There is no clear evidence of economies of scale arising from the merger of PCTs (Prestwood, 2003, Wilkin *et al.*, 2003). More generally, experience suggests that reorganisation of health care services rarely delivers the benefits forecast (Walshe *et al.*, 2004). Reviewing 5 US and 15 UK studies of the size of primary care bodies, Bojke *et al.* (2001) find no evidence that primary care groups and trusts serving more than 100,000 patients will generate substantial improvements in overall performance or economies of scale. The transition costs involved in mergers and reorganisation are substantial and, where reorganisation takes place frequently (in the case of the NHS every 3–6 years), the costs of reorganisation are incurred without any realistic possibility of benefits ever being realised (Walshe *et al.*, 2004);

◆ The possibility of diseconomies of scale must also be recognised. While the HMIC have suggested an optimal level of staffing for police forces of 6,000 (O'Connor, 2005), other evidence suggests that operating at this scale may bring about diseconomies of scale. Drake and Simper (2002) suggest that there are substantial scale inefficiencies operating in both the largest and smallest police forces and that diseconomies of scale tend to occur in police forces with staff groups over 4,500. With reference to international research on hospital provision, Posnett (1999) finds that evidence consistently suggests that the scope to achieve economies of scale is limited. In the main, economies of scale are evident only for small hospitals, i.e. those with fewer than 200 beds, while hospitals with more than 400–600 beds tend to give rise to diseconomies of scale. Posnett thus suggests that the optimal size for acute hospitals ranges from 200 to 400 beds, noting that in the UK only 26 per cent of hospitals are this size;

◆ Even where economies of scale are achieved, these may come at the expense of problematic 'externalities'. In the case of education, Ferris and West (2004) suggest that, while there is some evidence of economies of scale being achieved through the creation of larger schools, there is a tendency towards a number of problematic externalities as schools increase in size – most notably an increase in bullying and violence;

◆ If we view economies of scale simply as a measure of the unit cost of providing services, then democracy and community engagement may be regarded as an example of an externality, albeit one that is difficult to quantify. Research suggests that moving to larger units does raise problems in relation to community engagement; there is evidence that police forces operating at larger geographical scales are remoter (Home Office, 2001). In health care, there is also a marked tendency towards larger trusts losing touch with the local communities they are intended to serve (Prestwood, 2003). As Wilkin et al. (2003, p.16) note: 'in the rapid move to merge among PCG/Ts there is a risk of … losing the local ownership and participation, which are fundamental to the original vision';

◆ Given the range of factors that influence effectiveness, the advantages of 'scaling up' will generally vary according to policy area or function. Evidence consistently suggests that while bigger may be better for some functions, it will be worse for others. To suggest that there is an optimal size for a police force or health care trust as an organisation is therefore deeply problematic. However, there are a variety of ways of overcoming the 'problem of scale' where it is an issue, including partnership working and collaboration (Wilkin *et al.*, 2003). It may well be that promoting joint-working and organisational alliances is the most effective way to achieve the flexibility required to work at different scales for different functions.

Evidence to support the view that economies of scale can be achieved in the public services is therefore sketchy, at best. It may well be that the logic of amalgamation across local governance is driven by cost constraints imposed by central government and by an almost innate preference among managers to run organisations conferring greater status and power (Wilkin *et al.*, 2003). At the same time, one of the clearest messages is that larger units of provision will militate against democratic and/or community engagement. In this regard, it is significant that there is simultaneous evidence that citizens living in areas with smaller units of local government tend to express higher levels of satisfaction with the services they provide. In the Danish case, smaller municipalities are evaluated more positively than larger ones (Nielsen, 1981), while trust in local government tends to be lowest in big cities (Mouritzen, 1989). Similarly, the work carried out by Denters (2002) shows that, overall, residents of small municipalities in the Netherlands, Denmark, Norway and the UK tend to be more satisfied with the services they receive, and have greater trust in local politicians and officials, than residents of larger municipalities. Likewise, survey research commissioned by the (then) DETR on public perceptions of local government in England found that the proportion of residents expressing satisfaction with how local councils are run was on average highest for district councils (63 per cent), compared to an average of 57 per cent. Levels of satisfaction were notably lower for county councils (56 per cent) and fell to just 48 per cent among those living in areas with unitary authorities (DETR, 2000).

10.3 Reviving local democracy

As we noted in the foreword to this book, the current positions taken by the three main political parties in the UK suggest a basic degree of consensus about local democracy. Indeed, analysis of the content of the Labour, Conservative and Liberal Democrat manifestos for the 2005 General Election reveals a remarkable degree of agreement on two issues. First, all three parties advocate greater freedom for local authorities, a reduction in the number of centrally-defined targets, and streamlined inspection and performance monitoring. Unsurprisingly, this commitment to dismantling the 'target culture' is most apparent among the opposition parties, with the Conservatives promising to 'liberate local government' and both the Conservatives and the Liberal Democrats proposing to scrap targets in local NHS services. Second, there is also an emphasis across the board on the promotion of community- or neighbourhood-based mechanisms to bolster the capacity of people to exercise control locally. In the main, such 'community empowerment' is defined with principal reference to issues such as crime and anti-social behaviour, with all three parties also making clear commitments to increase the number and presence of local police officers.

Indeed, the connections that all three parties make between local control and community involvement on the one hand, and policing, crime and anti-social behaviour on the other, indicate that such issues are likely to be a focal point for debates surrounding local democracy for some time to come. The centrality of such issues to Labour's approach to local communities and local democracy is particularly evident and has since been strongly re-affirmed in government. There is a far greater emphasis in the Labour manifesto on 'neighbourhood policing' than there is on any other 'local' issue; and in chapter 9, which outlines the party's proposals relating to democracy, citizen empowerment and decentralisation, crime and anti-social behaviour constitute the core concern:

> *People want a sense of control over their own neighbourhood. Not a new tier of neighbourhood government, but new powers over the problems that confront them when they step outside their front door – issues like litter, graffiti and anti-social behaviour*
>
> Labour Party, 2005, p.103

Consequently, the Labour manifesto indicates commitments to provide parishes with greater powers to tackle anti-social behaviour, and improved provision for people to be able to report and secure effective responses to crime and anti-social behaviour, as well as greater funding for community-based organisations and provision for local communities to run certain local facilities and services. Such emphasis is paralleled in the Conservative and Liberal Democrat manifestos, although with important differences. A central element of the Conservative approach is the creation of elected police commissioners, allied to greater 'community control' over planning decisions that will enable more direct action to be taken against, for instance 'illegal traveller encampments'. The Liberal Democrats place greater stress on community-based measures, proposing community justice panels through which 'local people will have more say in the punishment offenders carry out in the community' (2005, p.12).

Moreover, closer analysis reveals that much of the sense of emerging consensus on local democracy is, at most, superficial and, in many ways, illusory. None of the three main parties pay considerable attention to issues of local democracy in their 2005 General Election manifestos and there are many issues that are simply not addressed at all. For instance, only the Liberal Democrats proposed any clear response to the growing recognition of the inadequacies of the council tax as a means of funding local government – namely its replacement with local income tax. Likewise, there is no discussion of possible local government reorganisation and only very limited attention paid to local elections and local election turnout. Again, with the exception of Labour advocating a move to local elections every four years, only the Liberal Democrats suggest any major change, through the extension of the use of proportion representation in local elections from Scotland to the rest of the UK. Most significantly, in the case of the Labour Party, it is evident that the most significant policy decisions relating to local democracy currently being considered in government have not been derived from manifesto commitments. The current discussions surrounding the merger of PCTs and police forces have no direct foundation at all in Labour's 2005 General Election manifesto and therefore did not figure in the (anyway relatively marginal) debate on local democracy and local services during the election campaign.

Nonetheless, it is evident that local democracy is becoming an issue of growing concern for all three main parties. To a large extent, the key debates are currently being played out within the parties rather than between them. For instance, a group of Conservative politicians, working under the title 'Direct Democracy', have argued that greater local autonomy is the key to reversing declining local election turnouts, and advocated a vision of local democracy in which 'towns and counties run their own budgets and run their own affairs' (cited in *The Guardian*, 15 June 2005). Given the concerns that have been highlighted in this book, the emergence of such proposals is not surprising. To a large extent, it is a matter of self-preservation. The decline of local party bases in some areas of the country is such that is has become a significant factor influencing the fortunes of the each of the main parties nationally. As Tony Travers recently argued on BBC Radio 4:

> ... *political parties cannot survive without a local activist base* [...] *I don't think a political party can survive* [without it]. *And I give as evidence for that the fact that the Conservative Party has significantly died out in urban England, particularly in the Midlands and the North, and now finds it virtually impossible to win parliamentary seats there or indeed in Scotland*
>
> Travers, 2005

Given this basic need for all the parties to secure their own survival, we would hope that a long-term, cross-party commitment can be secured to act to ensure the UK's compliance with the European Charter of Local Self-Government. This would start with a joint statement from the principal parties clearly establishing the constitutional position of local government. At the same time, however, we are deeply concerned that major reforms are being considered to reorganise key elements of local democracy beyond the ballot box. One of the strongest messages to emerge from this research is the hugely disruptive impact of constant central reform on local public services and on the scope to promote democratic engagement locally. The current organisation of any local public service, whether the NHS, police, or local government, is far from ideal in relation to democratic engagement; however, we would strongly suggest that the temptation to engage in 'continuous reform' from the centre must be strongly resisted. This may sound paradoxical given the analysis of the 'state of local democracy' presented in this book. However, we believe that it would be misleading to see local democracy as something that is 'broke' and which therefore needs to be 'fixed'. Given the constraints under which it operates, it is in many ways remarkable how much the basic elements of local democracy can still be observed. Yet, it is clear that the health of local democracy is failing and we would question how much longer the patient can survive without some form of intervention. Above all else, local democracy needs to be given a chance to heal.

To this end, we wish to advocate a vision of local democracy that is not fundamentally premised on centrally-driven reform. Arising from the basic principle that the cure will only emerge following a period of self-healing, we would like to propose the following set of recommendations for the future of local democracy:

1   **A plea:** First and foremost, we wish to make the following plea to all
    political parties: it needs to be recognised that the problems facing
    local *representative* democracy are deep-rooted. These problems
    cannot be addressed via technocratic 'fixes' or by modifications to
    voting methods, such as postal voting. If anything, postal voting
    has so far further undermined public confidence in democracy
    (Electoral Commission, 2003b). Neither is the problem of falling
    democratic engagement among key social groups being addressed
    by promoting citizen engagement in other activities, such as
    consultation exercises, or by steadily increasing the level of
    information made available to local residents. It is possible that local
    public agencies, working to government requirements and guidance,
    have 'over-invested' in communications and consultation, neither
    of which appear to have so far made any significant difference to
    the quality of local democracy. There is much activity, and much
    resource, that might be better directed elsewhere.

2   **Democratic and civic renewal:** The first key role for national
    government must be to promote a longer-term vision of democratic
    renewal, via an inter-departmental initiative directed at promoting
    citizen engagement in local affairs. We endorse the suggestion made
    by the Commission on Local Governance, and subsequently by the
    Local Government Information Unit (LGIU), that councils could
    develop specific 'civic renewal strategies' within the overall context
    of their existing community plan. Given the sheer volume of existing
    local plans, we would warn strongly against making such strategies
    a statutory requirement. Instead, we would suggest that, in order to
    promote such practice locally, centrally allocated 'civic and
    democratic renewal funds' should be made available to finance
    locally-generated initiatives embedded within, and prioritised by,
    such strategies. Given the common interests of a number of central
    government departments and agencies in promoting civic renewal
    – including the ODPM, the Home Office, the Department of Health
    and the Countryside Agency – we would advocate that the fund be
    designed as a high-profile, inter-departmental initiative. Our research
    evidence suggests that such funds would have greatest impact if
    invested at the lowest possible level, particularly individual
    neighbourhoods or parishes. At the same time, we would echo the
    view of the LGIU that the existence of enormous inequalities in the

resources and capacities of individual neighbourhood and parishes must be recognised and tackled by any such investment.

3   **Local councillors:** Another key element of this vision of democratic renewal would be to render the role of representing a local community a more attractive one and perhaps even to 'make local politicians popular'. The 'package' on offer to most local councillors is clearly less attractive than that available to members of the public serving in broadly equivalent roles, such as board members on NHS trusts. Such anomalies need to be addressed, if not through greater cash allowances or even salaries, then through the provision of other forms of reward and support. Suggested measures put forward by the LGIU's 'perilous democracy' campaign include enabling councillors to contribute to the local government pension scheme, providing them with back-up support from paid caseworkers, and establishing clearer rights for councillors to take time off work for public duties. However, such measures will only go part of the way towards addressing the challenges facing local representative democracy. We would argue that both the role and reputation of local councillors effectively need to be 're-imagined', so as to bring about a fundamental shift in how local politicians are perceived by the electorate. It also needs to be recognised that, given the perilous state of local parties, boosting the pool of potential local election candidates will require either a total re-invigoration of the local party system or an acceleration of its demise.

4   **Local parties:** We would argue that, in the first instance, every effort should be made to revive local parties, particularly in relation to their capacity to run local election campaigns. We accept that state funding of political parties may be considered a step too far. However, we would strongly advocate that national funds should be made available to support local political parties in the task of producing, disseminating and delivering election materials. As the New Politics Network has noted: 'if local parties cannot even afford to print campaign leaflets then we cease to have a competitive party system' (Runswick, 2004, p.9). Runswick argues strongly that 'democracy on the cheap' is no longer viable, and advocates a system whereby match funding could be provided for the income that local parties generate through donations and membership fees. Alternatively, diverting funding from costly public relations materials produced by

local public agencies directly into campaign budgets for political parties, for instance, would surely be a more effective means of strengthening local democracy.

5 **Local autonomy:** The second key role for central government must be to undertake a 'staged withdraw' from local democracy. Current proposals such as 'earned autonomy' and 'local area agreements' do not go nearly far enough, particularly if the goal is to ensure compliance with the European Charter of Local Self-Government. There can be no meaningful basis for local democratic renewal, or local political leadership, unless local autonomy is increased. This will be a bold step, as greater local autonomy will almost inevitably prompt public service variations across England. In many ways a radical shift in thinking is required, in which: national political debate will be expected to promote local differences; local variations in public services are seen as the natural consequence of vibrant local democracy; and occasional local failures are tolerated. Such variation can, we would argue, be entirely consistent with notions of choice in the public services.

6 **Inequalities and finance:** Arising from the above, we would argue that there is no necessary tension between local autonomy, on the one hand, and the goal of reducing inter-regional and socio-economic inequalities on the other. Most other Western European nations have found a means of balancing these concerns and we would argue that government efforts to reduce inequalities must be rooted in fiscal policy rather than in the imposition of targets on over-burdened local agencies. Indeed, it must be recognised that local democracy will only be able to flourish if national policy frameworks take some of the pressure off local public agencies to deliver 'more for less'. At the same time, local autonomy will only be meaningful if it includes significant local freedoms in relation to budgets and financial resources. In view of the local disruption and national political controversy it would cause, we would resist calls for the replacement of the council tax with a new form of local government finance. Proposals advanced by the Centre for Council Tax Reform (2003) suggest that it would be possible to advance politically acceptable reforms of the council tax that would also render it a fairer and more progressive form of taxation.

7 **Stay local:** It may sound tautological, but local democracy should be kept local. The greatest grounds for optimism in the study of local democracy stem from the reported willingness of citizens to engage in local affairs and the significance that they attach to local government and other services. Although we can identify no compelling arguments in favour of retaining two-tier local government, we would also argue that there are strong *democratic* arguments against creating larger local authorities.[24] On balance, and if local government is considered in isolation, the evidence arising from this study does support the case for unitary authorities; but it also emphasises the need for any reform of local government structures to find a way of retaining the unique democratic qualities of district councils. At the same time, given the focus in this study on all local public agencies, it must be recognised that current debates surrounding the structure of local government are part of a much wider review of sub-national governance in England. The democratic implications of any proposals to merge district councils into larger unitary authorities must therefore be considered alongside the likely impacts arising from the proposed mergers of police forces and primary care trusts.[25]

8 **Parishes and neighbourhoods:** Our research has found that there is very strong potential for democratic renewal at the 'most local' level. Where they exist, town and parish councils are often remarkably vibrant and can be highly successful in voicing the views of a community. Similarly, impressive results have been achieved where

---

24 This is not to deny that there is an *organisational* case, in relation to specific policy functions such as economic development, for the provision of local government capacity across larger geographical scales. It is in relation to such functions that the 'economies of scope' provided by county councils are evident. It is possible that alternative arrangements, such as joint committees or sub-regional partnerships, could provide for such capacity.

25 Both Burnley Borough Council and Harrogate Borough Council would like to see Burnley and Harrogate, respectively, served by unitary local government, rather than by the current two-tier system of district and county councils. Both councils recognise that, in the event of re-organisation taking place, it is conceivable that this will be on the basis of larger geographical areas than those currently covered by district councils. Both Burnley Borough Council and Harrogate Borough Council are positive about this prospect, which goes with the flow of the co-operative activity and partnership working that have already done much to develop close working relationships with neighbouring councils in East Lancashire and North Yorkshire respectively.

public bodies have successfully found ways of engaging at a neighbourhood or parish level, with community policing standing out in this regard. In this sense, there is much to endorse in the current governmental agenda of promoting citizen engagement via parishes and neighbourhoods; and we would urge that, whatever the outcome of re-organisation debates, a full agenda for devolving powers, resources and functions to parishes and neighbourhoods is developed. However, there are dangers in assuming that a modest increase in parish and neighbourhood functions will offer a 'democratic fix' by compensating for the remoteness of much larger organisational units locally, particularly in health and policing. We would again reiterate that there are enormous variations in the financial resources, organisational capacities, levels of democratic legitimacy and levels of social capital that can be called upon by existing parish and neighbourhood structures.

9 **Neighbourhood champions:** Arising from the above, we would argue that there must be a clearer and more radical approach to neighbourhood action as a means of promoting democratic engagement. One potential role for 'civic and democratic renewal funds' could be to support the work of local groups, community centres and even individual citizens that play a key role in maintaining voluntary and community-based provision within their neighbourhoods. In many cases, the most useful source of information and advice that residents will turn to is not their local councillor, the Internet, or the glossy publications produced by public agencies – it is instead a trusted and knowledgeable neighbour without any 'official' function. Rather than dismissing such active citizens as 'the usual suspects', consideration should be given to finding ways in which their accumulated knowledge and local respect can be harnessed to enable them to act not as 'community leaders' but as recognised 'champions' of individual neighbourhoods.

10 **Little icons:** As part of this neighbourhood focus, we would suggest that buildings can become a powerful statement of a new belief in local democracy. Our research suggests that almost any public building, from a redundant Victorian town hall, to a community health centre, local school or neighbourhood housing office, has the potential to underpin attempts to strengthen local democracy. The government is currently driving the largest building programme the public sector

has witnessed for 50 years, to include the refurbishment or rebuilding of every secondary school in the country and some 3,000 GP surgeries. As John Sorrell, chair of the Commission for Architecture and the Built Environment (CABE) has noted, this inter-departmental building programme represents 'a once in a lifetime opportunity to transform Britain' (Sorrell, 2005, p.6). Comparisons with the late Victorian period, when the blossoming of 'civic pride' prompted the construction of grand town halls, public libraries and swimming baths across the country, are not far-fetched. There are significant opportunities here to reinvigorate and reinvent contemporary notions of citizenship, particularly at the local level. In the face of growing disquiet about the tendency towards 'iconic' buildings, a concept of 'little icons' is emerging. The 'little icon' building is conceived as 'a building or space that becomes a neighbourhood hero, a place local people feel has been designed and built for them' (Sorrell, 2005, p.8). The new Peckham library, designed by Will Alsop, is frequently cited as an example of such a structure. Experience to date suggests that there are few clear principles underlying this massive construction programme, and that coordination and communication between government departments driving the process is poor. Urgent attention should be given to examining the possibilities for new public sector buildings to serve as 'little icons' that will contribute to local civic and democratic renewal.

11 **Local elections:** Finally, we would argue that the most urgent task facing those seeking to revive local democracy is to re-establish local elections as the centrepiece of the 'new localism'. Despite their shortcomings, from among all the mechanisms available to ascertain the views of local residents, local elections remain the most effective way of promoting a greater equality of local political participation. Maximising local election turnouts will, in our view, require action to ensure that elections have a meaningful impact upon local service provision. This implies a need for greater democratic control over the full range of public services and for a significant increase in local political autonomy. Under conditions of significantly greater local autonomy, local elections would make substantially more of a difference to how public services are delivered than they do currently. Put simply, experience suggests that, where voters understand that there are major local issues at stake, and where they can see that their votes 'count', turnout rises sharply.

References

Atkinson, H. and S. Wilks-Heeg (2000) *Local Government from Thatcher to Blair: The politics of creative autonomy*, Cambridge: Polity Press.

Audit Commission (2005) *Governing Partnerships: Bridging the accountability gap*, London: Audit Commission.

Banks, T. (2005) Cited during *In Defence of Politicians*, broadcast on BBC Radio 4, 1 January 2006.

Beetham, D., Byrne, I., Ngan, P. and S. Weir (2002) *Democracy Under Blair: A democratic audit of the United Kingdom*, London: Politicos.

Benn, T. (2001) *Hansard*, 22, March, Column 510. Available at http://www.parliament.the-stationery-office.co.uk/pa/cm200001/cmhansrd/vo010322/debtext/10322-13.htm (Accessed 16 October 2005).

Birch, A. H. (1993) *The Concepts and Theories of Modern Democracy*, London: Routledge.

Birch, D. (2002) *Public Participation in Local Government: A survey of local authorities*, London: Office of the Deputy Prime Minister.

Birchall, J. and R. Simmons (2004) *User Power: The participation of users in public services*, London: National Consumer Council.

Blair, T. (2003) *Message from the Prime Minister for Local Newspaper Week*. Available at http://www.newspapersoc.org.uk/documents/publications/pr2003/blair-message.html (Accessed 10 January 2006).

Blair, T. (2005) 23 July, cited in D. Lipsey (2005) 'Too much choice', *Prospect (26),* December, pp. 26–29.

Bojke, C., Gravelle, H. and D. Wilkin (2001) 'Is bigger better for primary care groups and trusts?', *British Medical Journal*, 322, pp. 599–603.

Boyne, G. A. (1998), *Public Choice Theory and Local Government*, Macmillan, Basingstoke.

Bramley, G, Evans, M. and J. Atkins (1998) *Where Does Public Spending Go? Pilot study to assess the flow of public expenditure into local areas*, London: Department of the Environment, Transport and the Regions.

Bromley, C., Stratford, N. and N. Rao (2000) *Revisiting Public Perceptions of Local Government: A decade of change?*, London: Department of the Environment, Transport and the Regions.

Bromley, C., Curtice, J. and B. Seyd (2001) 'Political engagement, trust and constitutional reform', in A. Park *et al*. (eds) *British Social Attitudes, the 18th Report – Public Policy, Social Ties*, London: Sage.

Brooks, H. (2002) *A Town Betrayed: Burnley in the ten years to the riots*, unpublished manuscript.

Byrnes, J. and B. E. Dollery (2002) 'Do economies of scale exist in Australian local government? A review of the research evidence', *Urban Policy and Research,* 20(4), pp. 391–414.

Centre for Council Tax Reform (2003) *Council Tax: The answer?*, London: Local Government Information Unit.

Chamberlain, J. (1885) Speech made on 28 April 1885, cited in D. Blunkett and K. Jackson (1987) *Democracy in Crisis*: *The town halls respond*, London: Hogarth Press, p.46.

Chancellor of the Duchy of Lancaster (1997) *Your Right To Know: The government's proposals for a Freedom of Information Act.* Available at http://www.archive.official-documents.co.uk/document/caboff/foi/foi.htm (Accessed 29 October 2005).

Chandler, J. A. (2000) *Joined-up Government: I wouldn't start here if I were you.* Paper for the Political Studies Association 50th Annual Conference, London, 10–13 April.

Commission on Local Governance (2002) *Memorandum to Select Committee on Transport, Local Government and the Region*, LGB24. Available at http://www.parliament.the-stationery-office.co.uk/pa/cm200102/cmselect/cmtlgr/981/981m25.htm (Accessed 2 December 2005).

(The) Competition Commission (2002) *Report on Proposed Merger of Trinity and Johnston*, Cm 5495, London: HMSO.

Cook, M. (2003) 'Access to information in local government: The jigsaw puzzle', *Public Management and Policy Review*, 22, August.

Coulthard, M., Walker, A. and A. Morgan (2002) *People's Perceptions of their Neighbourhood and Community Involvement*, National Statistics.

Cowley, P. (2006) *In Defence of Politicians*, BBC Radio 4, 1 January 2006.

Crouch, C. and D. Marquand (eds) (1989) *The New Centralism: Britain out of step in Europe*, Oxford: Blackwell.

Dahl, R. and E. Tufte (1973) *Size and Democracy*, Stanford: Stanford University Press.

Dahlberg, M., Mörk, E. and H. Ågren (2005) 'On the size of political jurisdictions: an examination of local democracy'. Working paper, Department of Economics, University of Uppsala, Sweden.

Dean, M. (2005) 'Time to go local', *The Guardian*, Wednesday 6th July.

Dearlove, J. (1979) *The Reorganisation of British Local Government: Old orthodoxies and a political perspective*, Cambridge: Cambridge University Press

Democratic Audit (n.d.1) *Patronage and Quangos Appointments*. Available at http://www.democraticaudit.com/download/Quango Appointments.doc (Accessed 18 November 2005).

Democratic Audit (n.d.2) The *Assessment Framework*. Available at http://www.democraticaudit.com/auditing_democracy/assessment framework.php (Accessed 12 May 2005).

Denters, B. (2002) 'Size and political trust: Evidence from Denmark, the Netherlands, Norway, and the United Kingdom', *Environment and Planning C*, 20(6), pp. 793–812.

DETR (1998) *Modern Local Government: In touch with the people*, London: HMSO.

DETR (1999) *Local Leadership, Local Choice*, London: HMSO.

DETR (2000) *Revisiting Public Perceptions of Local Government: A decade of change?* Research summary, London: Department for the Environment, Transport and the Regions.

Department for Constitutional Affairs (2005) *Freedom of Information Act 2000: Statistics on implementation in central government Q1: January–March 2005*, London: DCA.

Direct Democracy (2005) *Agenda for a New Model Party*, London: Telegraph Books.

Dolton, M. (2005) *Best Value and the Requirement to Consult: An evaluation of best value as a framework for citizen participation in local governance*, PhD Thesis, University of London.

Dowson, L., Burden, T., Hamm, T. and A. Petrie (2000) *Valuing the Voluntary and Community Sector in North Yorkshire and York*, Thirsk: North Yorkshire Forum for Voluntary Organisations.

Drake, L. and R. Simper (2002) 'X-efficiency and scale economies in policing: A comparative study using the distribution free approach and DEA', *Applied Economics*, 34, pp. 1859–1870.

Dunleavy, P. (1991) *Democracy, Bureaucracy and Public Choice: Economic explanations in political science*, Hemel Hempstead: Harvester Wheatsheaf.

Dunleavy. P., Loughlin, M., Margetts, H., Bastow, S., Tinkler, J., Pearce, O. and P. Bartholomeou (2005) *Citizens Redress: What citizens can do if things go wrong with public services*, London: National Audit Office.

Edwards, B., Woods, M., Anderson, J., Fahmy, E. and G. Gardner (2002) *Participation, Power and Rural Community Governance in England and Wales*, Aberystwyth: University of Wales.

Electoral Commission (2002) *Voter Engagement Among Black and Minority Ethnic Communities*, London: The Electoral Commission.

Electoral Commission (2003a) *Attitudes Towards Voting and the Political Process in 2003*, London: The Electoral Commission.

Electoral Commission (2003b) *Voting for Change – An Electoral Law Modernisation Programme*, London: The Electoral Commission.

Fanshawe, S. (2005) 'The itch to get involved', *The Guardian (Society)*, 1 June 2005, p.4.

Ferris, J. S. and E. G. West (2004) 'Economies of scale, school violence and the optimal size of schools', *Applied Economics*, 36(15), pp. 1677–1684.

Fox, W. F. and T. Richards (2003) 'Will consolidation improve sub-national governments?' Working paper, University of Tennessee. Available at http://www1.worldbank.org/wbiep/decentralization/library1/amalgamation.pdf (Accessed 12 October 2005).

Frandsen, A. G. (2002) 'Size and electoral participation in local elections', in *Environment and Planning C – Government and Policy*, 20(6), pp. 853–69.

Frankel, M. (2002) 'Full Disclosure' *Progress* Sept/Oct 2002. Available at http://www.progressives.org.uk/magazine/default.asp?articleid=366 (Accessed 3 November 2005).

Frankel, M. (2004) 'Freedom of Information', *Progress* Jan/Feb 2004. Available at http://www.progressives.org.uk/magazine/default.asp?articleid=548 (Accessed 3 November 2005).

Gains, F., Greasley. S, and G. Stoker (2004) *A Summary of Research Evidence on New Council Constitutions in Local Government*, London: Office of the Deputy Prime Minister.

Gay, O. (1999) *Local Elections – Proposals for Reform*, Research Paper 99/46, 28 April, London: House of Commons.

Gould, M. (2004) 'Worth the wait?' *The Guardian* Wednesday, April 21st. Available at http://society.guardian.co.uk/societyguardian/story/0,7843,1195840,00.html (Accessed 21 December 2005).

Gould, M. (2005) 'Health Forums "Ailing"' *The Guardian* Wednesday, May 11th. Available at http://society.guardian.co.uk/societyguardian/story/0,,1480534,00.html (Accessed on 21 December 2005).

Grant Riches Communication Consultants (2003) 'The new political structures – the verdict from communications professionals'. Available at http://www.lgcomms.org.uk/news/moderncouncils_survey.doc (Accessed 20 November 2005).

The Guardian (2005) 'Give power to the people say Tories in call for local autonomy', 15 June.

Harrogate Borough Council (2003) *Housing Revenue Account Summary Statement*, Harrogate: Harrogate Borough Council.

Haus M. and D. Sweeting (2003) *Political Leadership and Notions of Local Democracy.* Paper at European Consortium for Political Research Conference, Marburg, Germany, 18–21 September.

HM Treasury (2002a) *The Role of the Voluntary and Community Sector in Service Delivery: A cross cutting review*, London: HMSO.

HM Treasury (2002b) *Spending Review 2002: Public Service Agreements*, London: HM Treasury.

HM Treasury (2004) *Exploring the Role of the Third Sector in Public Service Delivery and Reform: A discussion document*. Available at http://www.hm-treasury.gov.uk./spending_review/spend_ccr/spend_ccr_voluntary/ccr_voluntary_2004.cfm (Accessed 12 October 2005).

Home Office (2001) *Policing a New Century: A blueprint for reform*, White Paper, cm5326, London: HMSO.

Home Office (2004) *Building Communities, Beating Crime,* White Paper, London: HMSO.

Howard, M. (2004) 'Freedom to report is vital', article for Local Newspaper Week. Available at http://www.holdthefrontpage.co.uk/behind/analysis/040504how.shtml (Accessed 10 January 2006).

Issue Briefs: Freedom of Information (n.d.) Available at http://www.politics.co.uk/issues/freedom-information-$3268047.htm (Accessed 29 October 2005).

IVR (1997) *National Survey of Volunteering in the UK*, London: Institute for Volunteering Research.

Jenkins, S. (2005) *Mad as Hell – Part Two*. Broadcast on BBC Radio 4, 26th June. Transcript. Available at http://news.bbc.co.uk/1/hi/programmes/the_westminster_hour/4120134.stm (Accessed 18 November 2005).

Labour Party (2005) *Britain Forward Not Back. The Labour Party Manifesto 2005*, London: The Labour Party.

Lancashire Probation Service (2004) *Annual Report*, Preston: Lancashire Probation Service.

Larsen, C. A. (2002) 'Municipal size and democracy: a critical analysis of the argument of proximity based on the case of Denmark', *Scandinavian Political Studies*, 25(4), pp. 317–32.

Lewis, G. (2001) *Mapping the Contribution of the Voluntary and Community Sector in Yorkshire and Humberside*, Leeds: Yorkshire and Humber Regional Forum.

Lewis, R. (2005) *Governing Foundation Trusts*, London: Kings Fund.

Liverpool Daily Post (2004) 'Baffling targets costing city £2 million', *Liverpool Daily Post*, 22 September 2004, p.1.

Lowndes, V., Pratchett, L. and G. Stoker (2001a) 'Trends in public participation: local government perspectives', *Public Administration*, 79 (1), pp. 205–222.

Lowndes, V., Stoker, G., Pratchett, L., Wilson, D., Leach, S. and M. Wingfield (1998) *Enhancing Public Participation in Local Government*, London: Department for the Environment, Transport and the Regions.

MacDonald, S. (2005) Introduction to *Talking Politics*, BBC Radio 4, 13 August 2005.

Miller, W. L. (1988) *Irrelevant Elections? The quality of local democracy in Britain*, Oxford: Clarendon Press.

MORI (2003) *Ombudsman Awareness Survey 2003*. Research study conducted for the Parliamentary, Health Service and Local Government Ombudsmen. Available at http://www.lgo.org.uk/pdf/MORI-final-report.pdf (Accessed 8 May 2005).

Morlan, R. L. (1984) 'Municipal vs. national election voter turnout: Europe and United States', in *Political Science Quarterly*, 99, pp. 457–70.

Mouritzen, P.E. (1989) 'City size and citizen's satisfaction: Two competing theories revisited', *European Journal of Political Research*, 17, pp. 661–688.

Naschold, F. (1997) 'Partizipative Demokratie – Erfahrugen mit der Modernisierung kommunaler Verwaltungen', in W. Weidenfield (ed.) *Demokratie am Wendepunkt – Die demokratische Frage als Projekt des 2. Jahrhunderts*, Berlin, pp. 294–307.

Nielsen, H. J. (1981) 'Size and evaluation of government: Danish attitudes towards politics at multiple levels of government', *European Journal of Political Research*, 9, pp. 47–60.

Nolan Committee (1995) *Standards in Public Life: First report of the Committee on Standards in Public Life, Cm 2850-I*, London: HMSO.

Nolan Committee (1996) *Local Public Spending Bodies: Second report of the Committee on Standards in Public Life, Cm 3270*, London: HMSO.

Nolan Committee (1997a) *Standards of Conduct in Local Government in England, Scotland and Wales: Third report of the Committee on Standards in Public Life, Cm 3702*, London: HMSO.

Nolan Committee (1997b) *Review of Standards of Conduct in Executive NDPBs, NHS Trusts and Local Public Spending Bodies: Fourth report of the Committee on Standards in Public Life,* London: HMSO.

O'Connor, D. (2005) *Closing the Gap: A review of the 'Fitness for Purpose' of the current structure of policing in England and Wales*, London: Her Majesty's Inspectorate of Constabulary.

Oliver, J. E. (2000) 'City size and civic involvement in Metropolitan America', in *American Political Science Review*, 94, pp. 361–73.

ODPM (2002a) *The Business Case for Communications: Why investing in communications makes good sense*, London: Office of the Deputy Prime Minister.

ODPM (2002b) *Five Years of Communications: A review of local authority communication*, London: Office of the Deputy Prime Minister.

ODPM (2002c) *Turnout at Local Elections*, London: Office of the Deputy Prime Minister.

ODPM (2005) *Evaluation of Local Strategic Partnerships Interim Report,* Office of the Deputy Prime Minister.

PAC (2001) *Mapping the Quango State,* House of Commons: Public Administration Select Committee.

PAC (2003) *Government By Appointment: Opening up the patronage state*, House of Commons: Public Administration Select Committee.

Parry G. Moyser G. and N. Day (1992) *Political Participation and Democracy in Modern Britain*, Cambridge: Cambridge University Press.

Posnett, J. (1999) 'Is bigger better? Concentration in the provision of secondary care', *British Medical Journal*, 319, pp. 1063–1065.

(The) Power Inquiry (2005) *The Decline of Political Participation and Involvement in Britain: An introduction.* Available at http://www.powerinquiry.org/publications/documents/Intro.pdf (Accessed 18 April 2005).

Pratchett, L. (2004) 'Local autonomy, local democracy and the New Localism', *Political Studies*, 52(2), pp. 358–75.

Prestwood, S. (2003) 'It's not how big your PCT is – it's what you do with it', *Primary Care Report*, vol.5, 19 March, pp. 30–32.

Putnam, R. D. (1993) 'The prosperous community: Social capital and public life', *American Prospect*, 4(13), pp. 35–42.

Putnam, R. D. (1995) 'Bowling alone: America's declining social capital', *Journal of Democracy*, 6(1), pp. 65–78.

Putnam, R. D. (1996) 'The strange disappearance of civic America', *American Prospect*, 7(24), pp. 34–50.

Putnam, R. D. (2000) *Bowling Alone: The collapse and revival of American community*, New York: Touchstone.

Rallings, C. and M. Thrasher (1997) *Local Elections in Britain*, London: Routledge.

Rallings, C. and M. Thrasher (2003) *Local Elections in Britain: A statistical digest*, Plymouth: Local Government Chronicle Elections Centre.

Rose, L. E. (2002) 'Municipal size and local non-electoral participation: findings from Denmark, the Netherlands, and Norway', in *Environment and Planning C – Government and Policy*, 20(6), pp. 829–51.

Runswick, A. (2004) *Life Support for Local Parties: An analysis of the decline of local political parties and the case for state support of local activism*, London: New Politics Network.

Ruston, D. (2003) *Volunteers, Helpers and Socialisers: Social capital and time use*, London: Office for National Statistics.

Select Committee On Public Administration (2002) 'Chapter 1' in *8th Report*. Available at http://www.publications.parliament.uk/pa/cm200102/cmselect/cmpubadm/303/30304.htm (Accessed 6 July 2005).

Seyd P. and P. Whiteley (2004) 'British party members: An overview', *Party Politics*, 10(4), pp. 355–66.

Simons, K. (1995) *Complaints Procedures in Social Services Departments*, York: Joseph Rowntree Foundation.

Smith, S. (2004) *How It Was Done: The rise of Burnley BNP – The inside story*, Burnley: Cliviger Press.

Sorrell, J. (2005) 'Grand Designs', *The Quarter*, Winter, pp. 5–8.

Stoker, G., Gains, F., Greasley, S., John, P., Rao, N. and A. Harding (2004) *Operating the New Council Constitutions in English Local Authorities: A process*, *report*, London: Office of the Deputy Prime Minister.

Stone, C. (2002) *Urban Regimes and the Problem of Local Democracy*, paper presented to European Consortium of Political Research Joint Sessions, Turin, 22–27 March.

Swianiewicz, P. (2002) (ed.) *Consolidation or Fragmentation? The size of local governments in Central and Eastern Europe*, Budapest: LGI Books.

Taylor, D. (2005) Cited during *In Defence of Politicians*, broadcast on BBC Radio 4, 1 January 2006.

Times Online (2005) 'Blair admits that there are too many targets', 29 April. Available at http://www.timesonline.co.uk/article/0,,19809-1590905,00.html (Accessed 18 October 2005).

Toffler, A. (1970) *Future Shock*, New York: Random House.

Travers, T. (2005) Comments made on *Talking Politics*, BBC Radio 4, 13 August 2005.

Verba, S. and N. H. Nie (1972) *Participation in America*, New York: Harper and Row.

Walshe, K., Smith, J., Dixon, J., Edwards, N., Hunter, D. J., Mays, N., Normand, C. and R. Robinson (2004) 'Primary care trusts', *British Medical Journal*, 329, pp. 871–872.

West Midland Study Group (1956) *Local Government and Central Control*, London: Routledge and Kegan Paul.

Wilkin, D., Bojke, C., Coleman, A. and H. Gravelle (2003) 'The relationship between size and performance in primary care organisations in England', *Journal of Health Services Research and Policy*, 8 (1), pp. 11–17.

Williams, R. (1983) *Keywords: A vocabulary of culture and society*, London: Fontana.

Wilson, D. and C. Game (1994) *Local Government in the United Kingdom*, Basingstoke: Macmillan.

WM Enterprise (2003) *Burnley Voluntary, Community and Faith Sector Audit*, Burnley: Burnley Community Network.

Wright, T. (1994) *Citizens and Subjects: An essay on British politics*, London: Routledge.

Appendix 1:
Research Framework

A) Introduction

The central purpose of this study was to undertake a detailed analysis of the current state of local democracy in two northern towns – Burnley and Harrogate – and to assess the implications of these findings for the future of local democracy in the UK. In seeking to achieve these aims, the research was carried out in three principal phases comprising:

◆ A detailed mapping of governance structures in Burnley and Harrogate;

◆ A comprehensive 'audit' of local democracy in the two towns, including public participation in local affairs;

◆ A wider assessment of how local democracy in the UK measures up against established democratic criteria, and in comparison with other European countries.

The research design was built around a mixture of methods including data and documentary analysis, interviews, observation at public meetings, case studies and a set of survey questions put to Burnley and Harrogate residents. The research was carried out over a period of 20 months, from April 2004 to December 2005 and was strongly premised on the view that acquiring an in-depth understanding of local democracy would require the research team to have a strong local presence. In total, the researchers spent more than seven working weeks in each town over the life of the project and, by the end of the study, were able to draw upon:

◆ A wealth of documentary evidence obtained directly from around 40 local public agencies in Burnley and Harrogate;

◆ Around 150 interviews with politicians, policy-makers, community activists, journalists and residents across the two towns;

◆ Extensive notes from observations at a cross-section of 26 public meetings of local councils, health care trusts, police authorities and other public bodies;

◆ Survey data from questionnaires returned by almost 1000 local residents in Harrogate and approximately 500 in Burnley.

B) Institutional mapping

Following initial desk research, comprising a review of existing studies plus analysis of socio-economic conditions in the two towns, an comprehensive institutional mapping exercise was carried out between July and December 2004. This exercise involved an assessment and breakdown of:

◆ Which organisations are responsible for which service areas;

◆ The geographical area that each organisation serves;

◆ Each organisation's total expenditure;

◆ To whom they are accountable and in what ways;

◆ The nature of appointment and election procedures;

◆ Provision made for community consultation and involvement;

◆ Evidence of how community input influences decision-making;

◆ Significance and extent of partnerships and joint-working.

The mapping exercise was based on three primary sources of information. First, basic organisational information, such as details of board membership, appointment procedures and total expenditure, was obtained from organisational websites, annual reports, annual accounts and other published sources. Second, more detailed information on organisational activity and decision-making processes were gleaned from policy and strategy documents, consultancy reports and additional written information provided to the researchers. Third, additional information not readily available in published sources, as well as data providing a more qualitative assessment of local democratic processes, was gathered via an initial round of 50 semi-structured interviews conducted with local policy-makers across Burnley and Harrogate.

C) The local democratic audit

The local democratic audit followed on directly from the institutional mapping exercise and was carried out from January to August 2005. In contrast to the institutional mapping exercise, which approached local democracy 'from the top-down', the overall aim of this phase was to examine local democracy from the citizen's perspective. In particular, it sought to identify the relative significance of four distinct forms of local democracy in each town: representative (voting), user (accountability of services to users), consultative (surveys, focus groups) and participatory (community involvement). The audit also sought to identify key trends in the development of the local democratic mix in both towns, as well as the linkages between the different forms of local democracy. As such, the main elements of the audit were:

◆ A comprehensive analysis of the full range of mechanisms designed to allow local residents to influence local decision-making and service provision;

◆ A 'health check' of the state of local representative democracy in the two towns, including an assessment of the impact of the introduction of the Leader plus Cabinet model and scrutiny arrangements;

◆ An analysis of whether local political participation shows evidence of diversifying, whereby a decline in representative democracy is, in part, counter-balanced by a growth in participatory democracy;

◆ An assessment of the extent to which the local democratic process enables local residents as a whole to shape decision-making, and whether local political participation and political outcomes are biased towards particular social groups.

The local democratic audit comprised the core of the research as a whole and was built up using eight principal sources of information, as follows:

(i) *Collection and analysis of statistical data:* Statistical data providing 'headline indicators' of local democratic participation was collected relating to: trends in local electoral turnouts; membership of local political parties; membership of community, voluntary and faith organisations locally; and the number of complaints received annually by public agencies;

(ii)   *Interviews with local councillors:* Thirteen semi-structured interviews were conducted with district councillors in Burnley and eighteen with district councillors in Harrogate. In both cases this sample consisted of all party leaders and deputy leaders, all executive members, all scrutiny chairs and a cross-section of backbench members, reflecting a balance of the parties and an attempt to provide a balance across wards. The interviews focused on three main issues: (a) how councillors relate and respond to their constituents; (b) their view of the local party political infrastructure; and (c) their perspectives on the introduction of new political arrangement in local government. Interviews were conducted with a cross-section of councillors, including party leaders, executive members, committee chairs and backbenchers. A smaller sample of county councillors and parish councillors were also interviewed, as were local members of parliament;

(iii) *Interviews with public officials:* Approximately 15 interviews were conducted with key staff in the principal public agencies operating in the two towns with responsibility for mechanisms through which local residents express their views about local public services, such as consultation exercises and customer complaints mechanisms. The principal purpose of these interviews was to explore the extent to which there is evidence that such mechanisms provide a means via which local people are able to influence local decision-making;

(iv)   *Interviews with community-based organisations:* A further 15 interviews were carried out with staff and volunteers working in organisations that provide the interface between the community/ voluntary sector and public agencies. These included Citizens Advice Bureaus, community groups and networks, voluntary sector umbrella bodies, and parish councils. Interviews were also carried out with community representatives on regeneration schemes and local consultative bodies;

(v)   *A survey of local residents:* A survey of local residents was carried out via the Harrogate District Panel and the Burnley Citizens' Panel. The survey questions focused on issues concerning membership of organisations and participation in local affairs, ranging from voting to responding to consultation exercises and complaints made to local bodies. Directly equivalent questions were used for both surveys and, in both cases, the questions were put to residents during July–August 2005;

(vi)   *Observation at public meetings:* The researchers sat in on a total of 26 public meetings to which the general public were invited or permitted to attend. These included council meetings, consultation events, and board meetings of unelected public bodies;

(vii) *Case studies:* Drawing upon all of the above, a limited number of case studies were undertaken to illustrate some of the key themes emerging from the research.

D) Assessing local democracy in the UK

This phase of the research, carried out from September to November 2005, sought to place the research findings in a wider context, by:

◆ Assessing the extent to which local democracy remains possible in the UK (e.g. given constitutional and resource constraints);

◆ Analysing how typical trends in the two towns are of local democracy in the UK as a whole;

◆ Examining how well the state of local democracy in the two towns, and the UK more widely, measure up against international benchmarks;

◆ Undertaking brief case studies of initiatives undertaken by local public agencies that appear to offer scope to strengthen local democracy.

This phase of the research involved detailed consideration of: the literature on local democracy; national datasets on electoral turnout; national survey evidence relating to wider forms of political and civic participation; comparative indicators of the health of local democracy in Europe; the UK's record in conforming to the European Charter of Local Self-Government; and a review of the current policy positions of the UK's principal political parties towards local democracy.

E) Methodological issues and limitations

We are confident that the research design provided for a robust and comprehensive set of data. Inevitably, however, there are a number of methodological issues and limitations that must be highlighted. These are as follows:

(i)   While we have endeavoured to be as comprehensive and accurate as possible in our mapping of local democracy (presented principally in chapters 2 and 3), we are aware of several shortcomings in the data sets we have produced, particularly in relation to the distribution of local expenditure. These issues are outlined in full in chapter 3. Given the scale and complexity of the task at hand, it is almost inevitable that there will be some inaccuracies and errors in the data;

(ii)   Although representatives of the three main UK political parties took part in the research, British National Party councillors in Burnley refused to participate. This refusal to participate was explained with reference to the BNP's objections to the financial support for the research study provided by the Joseph Rowntree Charitable Trust;

(iii)   While data for party membership, together with estimates for levels of political party activism, were in most cases obtained directly from party secretaries, there were two instances where levels of membership and activism had to be estimated by extrapolating from national data. In addition, in the case of the BNP in Burnley, information could only be gleaned from the local party organiser's account of the Burnley BNP from 1997–2004 (Smith, 2004). In order to maintain confidentiality about the membership of individual parties, the figures were aggregated to provide overall levels of estimated party membership and activism in each town;

(iv)   As is highlighted in chapters 7 and 8, it is evident that membership of citizens' panels is likely be biased towards local citizens exhibiting above average levels of participation in local political and social affairs. This bias is, furthermore, likely to be greater still among those returning completed questionnaires. Evidence of this bias is seen in the fact that 79 per cent of respondents in Burnley and 78 per cent of respondents in Harrogate indicated that they had voted in the 2004 Borough Council elections. Turnout in these elections was actually 55 per cent and 53 per cent respectively. Similarly, over 90 per cent of respondents in both towns claimed to have voted in the 2005 General Election, compared to the average 61 per cent turnout nationwide. The survey results presented in this study cannot, therefore, be seen as socially representative of local voters as a whole. Rather, they are best interpreted as a demographically weighted profile of the population that exhibits at least a minimal level of participation in local democracy.

F) The Project Advisory Group

The research project was served by an advisory group, which included representatives from the Joseph Rowntree Charitable Trust, senior councillors and officers from the respective borough councils, academic specialists, and other co-opted members. A key feature of the advisory group was that it includes representation from all three of the principal political parties in England. The membership of the advisory group, which met five times over the course of the project, was as follows:

- ◆ Lord David Shutt, Joseph Rowntree Charitable Trust (chair)
- ◆ Mr Stephen Pittam, Joseph Rowntree Charitable Trust (secretary)
- ◆ Professor David Beetham, Democratic Audit
- ◆ Mr Kevin Douglas, Harrogate Borough Council
- ◆ Cllr Dr Mike Gardner, Leader, Harrogate Borough Council
- ◆ Ms Maggie Jones, Chief Executive, NCVCCO
- ◆ Cllr Peter Kenyon, Deputy Leader, Burnley Borough Council
- ◆ Dr Bano Murtuja, Consultant
- ◆ Dr Lawrence Pratchett, De Montfort University
- ◆ Dr Gillian Taylor, Chief Executive, Burnley Borough Council
- ◆ Mr Mike Waite, Burnley Borough Council
- ◆ Mr Mick Walsh, Chief Executive, Harrogate Borough Council

Appendix 2: Interviews Conducted

We would like to extend our gratitude to all of the following people who gave up time to be interviewed for this study, in some cases more than once. The vast majority of interviews were conducted face-to-face, but those marked (*) were carried out over the telephone.

◆ Cllr Heather Adderley, *Harrogate Borough Council*

◆ Scott Amos, *Neighbourhood Action Team Manager, Calico Housing*

◆ Maggie Archer, *Non-Executive Director, Craven, Harrogate and Rural District Primary Care Trust*

◆ Cllr Margaret Atkinson, *Harrogate Borough Council*

◆ Nick Aves, *Monitoring Officer, Burnley Borough Council*

◆ Cllr Colette Bailey, *Burnley Borough Council*

◆ Carol Barber, *Manager, Harrogate Citizens Advice Bureau*

◆ Barbara Barnes, *Harrogate and Knaresborough group of Amnesty International* (*)

◆ Cllr Keith Barnes, *North Yorkshire County Council*

◆ Lynette Barnes, *Director, Ripon CVS*

◆ Helen Barry, *Manager, Burnley Action Partnership*

◆ Cllr Caroline Bayliss, *Harrogate Borough Council*

◆ Cllr Stan Beer, *Harrogate Borough Council*

◆ Michael Birkett, *Director of Housing and Regeneration, Calico Housing*

◆ Cllr Gordon Birtwistle, *Leader Liberal Democrat Group, Burnley Borough Council*

◆ Cllr John Blackie, *North Yorkshire County Council*

◆ Elizabeth Bolton, *Town Clerk, Padiham Town Council*

- Stewart Bone, *Community Activist, Burnley*

- Matt Boulter, *Information Officer, Burnley Borough Council*

- Malcolm Bowker, *Director, Harrogate Families Housing Association*

- Jo Bray, *Head of Corporate Affairs, Harrogate & District NHS Foundation Trust*

- Cllr Christopher Brown, *Harrogate Borough Council & North Yorkshire County Council*

- David Brown, *Director of Environment, Burnley Borough Council*

- Ken Brunner, *Harrogate Lions Club* (*)

- Cllr Jean Butterfield, *Harrogate Borough Council*

- Cllr Stuart Caddy, *Leader, Burnley Borough Council*

- Cllr Frank Cant, *Burnley Borough Council*

- Christine Carter, *Burnley Area Community Credit Union* (*)

- Mick Cartledge, *Director of Leisure Services, Burnley Borough Council*

- Mark Codman, *Scrutiny Officer, Harrogate Borough Council*

- Ian Collins, *Yorkshire Forward*

- Cllr Richard Cooper, *Deputy Leader, Harrogate Borough Council*

- Pat Couch, *Project Officer, PPI Forum Support, East Lancashire Partnership*

- Larry Coulston, *Citizens Advice Bureau, Burnley*

- Cllr Joan Crowther, *Harrogate Borough Council*

- David Curry, *MP for Skipton and Ripon*

- Chris Daggett, *Editor, Burnley Express*

- Kevin Douglas, *Director of Leisure Services, Harrogate Borough Council*

- Cllr Peter Doyle, *Leader of the Conservative Group, Burnley Borough Council*

- Cllr Leslie Ellington, *Harrogate Borough Council*

- Sue Evers, *North Yorkshire Police Authority*

- Jim Fender, *Independent Member, North Yorkshire Police Authority*

- Brian Fenn, *Burnley Wood Community Action Group*

- Jackie Flynn, *Burnley District Partnership Officer, Lancashire County Council*

- Tom Forshaw, *Head of the Chief Executive's Office, Burnley Borough Council*

- Cllr John Fox, *Harrogate Borough Council*

- Chris France, *Lancashire Area Team Leader, Government Office for the North West*

- Cllr Paul Freeman, *Harrogate Borough Council*

- Cllr Roger Frost, *Burnley Borough Council and Briercliffe Parish Council*

- Elaine Furness, *Barden Community Association, Burnley* (*)

- Cllr Carole Galbraith, *Burnley Borough Council*

- Cllr Ian Galloway, *Harrogate Borough Council*

- Cllr Mike Gardner, *Leader, Harrogate Borough Council*

- Cllr Heather Garnett, *North Yorkshire County Council*

- Chris Gay, *Performance Improvement Manager, Burnley Borough Council*

- Judi Goddard, *Director of Strategic Developments and Partnerships, Craven, Harrogate and Rural District PCT*

- Chief Superintendent Jerry Graham, *Divisional Commander, Pennine Division, Lancashire Police*

- Wendy Graham, *Representative, ELEVATE Masterplanning Steering Group, Burnley*

- Cllr Richard Grange, *Harrogate Borough Council*

- David Green, *Piccadilly's Moving, Burnley* (*)

- Jean Greenall, *Member, Piccadilly Area Residents Association, Burnley* (*)

- Cllr David Halsall, *Burnley Borough Council*

- Tony Harrison, *Non-Executive Director, Burnley, Pendle and Rossendale Primary Care Trust*

- Cllr Kevin Hawkins, *Harrogate Borough Council & Knaresborough Town Council*

- Cllr David Heginbotham, *Burnley Borough Council*

- Terry Hephrun, *Chief Officer, Burnley, Pendle and Rossendale CVS*

- Brian Hobbs, *Chair, Burnley Action Partnership*

- Derek Holmes, *Chair, Burnley, Pendle and Rossendale Patient and Public Involvement Forum*

- Cllr Bill Hoult, *Harrogate Borough Council & North Yorkshire County Council*

- Cllr Marcus Johnstone, *Lancashire County Council*

- Cllr Pat Jones, *Harrogate Borough Council*

- Peter Jordan, *Head of Legal and Democratic Services, Harrogate Borough Council*

- Victor Jull, *Society of St George, Burnley* (*)

- Clare Kelley, *caseworker for MP and County Councillor*

- Cllr Peter Kenyon, *Deputy-Leader, Burnley Borough Council*

- Louise Kirkup, *Neighbourhood Action Plan Co-ordinator, Burnley Borough Council*

- Ian Lovell, *Communications Director, Yorkshire and Humberside Regional Assembly*

- Hazel McGrath, *Director, Harrogate CVS*

- Lisa Mansell, *Communications Manager, North and East Yorkshire & Northern Lincolnshire Strategic Health Authority*

- Tim Mansfield, *Head of Multi-Agency Service Development, Burnley Pendle and Rossendale PCT*

◆ Cllr Tony Martin, *Lancashire County Council*

◆ Peter Mearns, *Director of Marketing, North West Regional Development Agency*

◆ Lynne Mee, *Communications Manager, Harrogate Borough Council*

◆ Michael Molsher, *Chief Reporter, Harrogate Advertiser*

◆ Jane Money, *Environmental Strategy & Development Officer, Harrogate Borough Council*

◆ Alison Moore, *Scrutiny Officer, Lancashire County Council*

◆ Gillian Neild, *Communications Manager, Harrogate and District NHS Foundation Trust*

◆ Cllr Denis Otter, *Burnley Borough Council*

◆ Sarah Palmer, *Office of the Chief Executive, Lancashire County Council*

◆ Peter Pike, *former MP for Burnley*

◆ Wendy Ratcliffe, *Burnley Luncheon Club*

◆ Doreen Rawstron, *Chair and Member, Burnley Business and Professional Ladies Group and Burnley Ladies Speaking Club* (*)

◆ Shufkat Razaq, *Vice-Chair, Burnley Action Partnership*

◆ Kath Reade, *Chair, Cumbria and Lancashire Health Authority*

◆ Julie Rickwood-Gann, *Brunshaw Action Group, Burnley* (*)

◆ Susan Riddle, *London Borough of Brent*

◆ Cllr Paula Riley, *Leader of the Independent Group, Burnley Borough Council*

◆ Cllr Keith Rothwell, *Harrogate Borough Council*

◆ Carmen Sawers, *Make Poverty History & Harrogate Fair Trade Town campaign* (*)

◆ Dawn Saxby, *Policy and Private Sector Housing Manager, Harrogate Borough Council*

◆ Miles Scott, *Chief Executive, Harrogate & District NHS Foundation Trust*

◆ Sgt. Martin Selway, *Burnley Neighbourhood Policing Coordinator, Lancashire Police*

◆ Rev. Tony Shepherd, *Non-Executive Director, Harrogate Foundation Hospital Trust*

◆ Cllr David Simister, *Harrogate Borough Council*

◆ Cllr Alan Skidmore, *Harrogate Borough Council*

◆ John Smith, *Principal, Burnley College*

◆ Nina Smith, *Corporate Policy Officer, Burnley Borough Council*

◆ Vanessa Streeton, *Bus Development Coordinator, Harrogate and District Community Transport*

◆ Cllr Janice Swainston, *Burnley Borough Council*

◆ Gillian Taylor, *Chief Executive, Burnley Borough Council*

◆ David d'Arcy Thompson, *Hon. Secretary, The Stray Defence Association, Harrogate*

◆ Cllr Matthew Tomlinson, *Lancashire County Council*

◆ Gordon Townsley, *Royal British Legion, Harrogate*

◆ Kitty Ussher, *MP for Burnley*

◆ Mike Waite, *Community Cohesion Unit, Burnley Borough Council*

◆ Andrew Walker, *Planning Consultant, Planning and Development Network, Clitheroe*

◆ Clare Walker, *Communications Manager, North Yorkshire County Council*

◆ Mike Walker, *Research Manager, Lancashire County Council*

◆ Naomi Walker, *Communications Manager, Lancashire Police Authority*

◆ Cllr Geoffrey Webber, *Harrogate Borough Council*

◆ Lynda Wigley, *Director of Primary Care, Craven, Harrogate & Rural District Primary Care Trust*

◆ Hugh Williamson, *Head of Scrutiny and Corporate Performance, North Yorkshire County Council*

◆ Les Williamson, *Head of Housing, Harrogate Borough Council*

◆ Phil Willis, *MP for Harrogate and Knaresborough*

◆ Cllr Nick Wilson, *Harrogate Borough Council*

◆ Cllr Andy Wright, *former Labour Group leader, Harrogate Borough Council, member Knaresborough Town Council*

◆ Anne Marie Wrigley, *Board Member, Burnley Community Network*

◆ Judy Yacoub, *Chief Executive, Community Alliance, Burnley*

Appendix 3:
Membership Organisations Contacted

◆ Albert Street Residents Group, Burnley

◆ Barden Community Association, Burnley

◆ Bilton Working Men's Club, Harrogate

◆ Brunshaw Action Group, Burnley

◆ Burnley Area Community Credit Union

◆ Burnley Business and Professional Ladies Group

◆ Burnley Ladies Speakers Club

◆ Burnley Lions Club

◆ Burnley Luncheon Club

◆ Caledonian Society, Burnley

◆ Club Vivendi, Harrogate

◆ The Dale Centre, Harrogate

◆ East Lancashire Green Party

◆ East Lancashire LETS (Local Economy Trading Scheme)

◆ Forensic Science Society

◆ Harlow Hill Club, Harrogate

◆ Harrogate & District Environment Centre

◆ Harrogate and Knaresborough group of Amnesty International

◆ Harrogate and Knaresborough Peace Group

◆ Harrogate and Nidderdale Art Club

◆ Harrogate Central Discussion Group

◆ Harrogate Lions Club

◆ Inner Wheel Club of Padiham

◆ The National Trust, North West office

◆ The National Trust, Yorkshire regional office

◆ Ramblers' Association Burnley & Pendle Group

◆ Ramblers' Association, Harrogate Group

◆ The Royal British Legion

◆ RSPB, Harrogate Family Group

◆ RSPB, North West England Regional Office

◆ Piccadilly Area Residents Association, Burnley

◆ Piccadilly's Moving, Burnley

◆ Prestwich and Athol Street South Residents Association, Burnley

◆ Society of St George, Burnley

◆ Soroptimist International of Burnley

◆ The Stray Defence Association, Harrogate

Appendix 4:
Meetings Attended

◆ Harrogate Local Strategic Partnership, Annual Conference, 15th July 2004

◆ Burnley Borough Council, Full Council Meeting, 1st September, 2004

◆ Burnley Borough Council, Full Council Meeting, 27th October 2004

◆ Tenants Advisory Forum Meeting, Harrogate Council Offices, 9th November, 2004

◆ Harrogate Borough Council, Cabinet Meeting, Council Offices, 10th November 2004

◆ Harrogate Borough Council, Environment Overview and Scrutiny Commission Meeting, Council Offices, 11th November 2004

◆ Burnley, Pendle and Rossendale Primary Care Trust Board Meeting, PCT HQ, 24th November 2004

◆ Elevate 2nd Round Area Action Plan Consultation Event, Padiham Town Hall, 28th January 2005

◆ Harrogate Community Safety Partnership, Crime Audit Consultation Meeting, 1st February 2005

◆ Burnley Borough Council, Executive, 22nd February 2005

◆ Harrogate Borough Council, Community Services Overview and Scrutiny Commission, 14th March 2005

◆ Harrogate Borough Council, Council Resources Overview and Scrutiny Commission, 16th March 2005

◆ North Yorkshire County Council, Health Overview & Scrutiny Committee 28th June 2005

◆ Harrogate and District NHS Foundation Trust, Board of Governors, 6th July 2005

◆ Harrogate Tier 1 Police and Community Committee, 11th July 2005

- ◆ Knaresborough Town Council, Full Council, 18th July 2005
- ◆ North Yorkshire Police Authority, Community Engagement Board, 18th July 2005
- ◆ North Yorkshire County Council, Full Council, 20th July 2005
- ◆ Tockwith Parish Council, Full Council, 20th July 2005
- ◆ East Lancashire Hospitals NHS Trust, Board of Directors, 26th July 2005
- ◆ Lancashire Police Authority, 28th July 2005